Parerga and Paratexts

How Things Enter Language

Practices and Forms of Presentation in Goethe's Collections

Volume 2

A book series edited by

Johannes Grave · Wolfgang Holler

Christiane Holm · Cornelia Ortlieb

SPONSORED BY THE

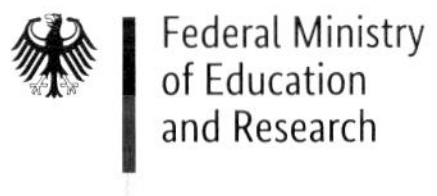

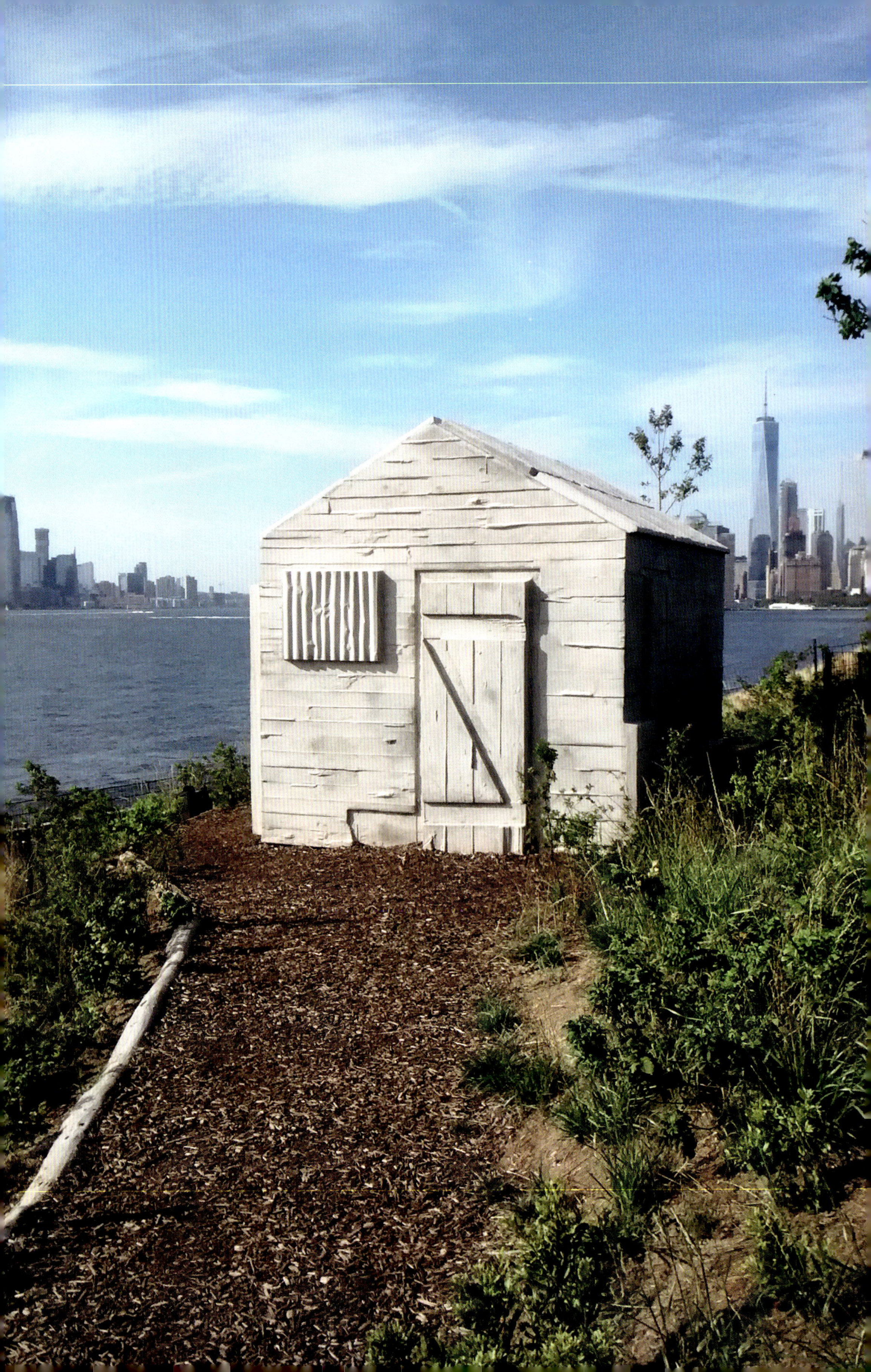

The Agency of Display

Objects, Framings and Parerga

EDITED BY
JOHANNES GRAVE · CHRISTIANE HOLM
VALÉRIE KOBI · CAROLINE VAN ECK

Table of Contents

2. Parergonal Operations

Acknowledgements

This book is the result of the conference *Collections, Displays & the Agency of Objects* organized in September 2017 as part of the research project *Parerga and Paratexts—How Things Enter Language. Practices and Forms of Presentation in Goethe's Collections,* and in collaboration with the Department of History of Art in Cambridge. The event and the publication of its proceedings were made possible by funding from the German Federal Ministry of Education and Research, and the hospitality offered by St John's College, Cambridge. We would like to express our gratitude to both institutions for their very generous support.

We also wish to thank a number of people who put their expertise at the service of this intellectual undertaking and provided invaluable assistance in its realization: Silke Becker, Christina Faraday, Wolfgang Holler, Sylvia Plitt, Katherine Rickett (together with the Cambridge Union Society's staff), Mira Claire Zadrozny and Hannah Uhlen. This volume has also benefited from the kindness of David Ward and Maureen Gallace, who graciously granted us access to their work so that we could illustrate Ivan Gaskell's article. Finally, Rebecca Whiteley read all the texts with great care and efficiency. We are extremely grateful for her valuable contribution.

JOHANNES GRAVE | CHRISTIANE HOLM
VALÉRIE KOBI | CAROLINE VAN ECK

The Agency of Display.
Objects, Framings and Parerga—Introductory Thoughts

I

Decentring 'Agency'

For at least two decades, the humanities and social studies have been fascinated by new conceptualisations of the apparent power of things to speak and act. 'Things that talk,'[1] 'art and agency,'[2] 'the power of images,'[3] and the 'agency of objects'[4]—to quote only the most influential keywords and phrases of these manifold and diverse discussions—more and more have attracted the attention of scholars from various disciplines. It seems that neither structuralist approaches that insist on general preconditions guiding our social life, nor semiotic theories, are able to illuminate and completely explain our complex interactions with tangible things. Current approaches underline the peculiar, sometimes idiosyncratic intrinsic logic of things by referring to multifarious experiences of not being able to fully control them. The stubbornness of the so-called inanimate has become a challenging problem that can no longer be ignored.[5] Scholars of science studies, art history, media studies, sociology, ethnology and anthropology have provided a wealth of evidence that puts the 'power' of things onto the agenda.[6]

Moreover, the most radical thinkers in this field, for example Bruno Latour or Philippe Descola, have taken this evidence as a reason to fundamentally question our familiar ontology and its distinction between subjects and objects.[7] However, Latour's proposal to consider a 'symmetrical anthropology'[8] that—from a methodological point of view—deals with human and 'non-human actors' in the same way has provoked strong criticism; and the same holds true, for example, for Horst Bredekamp's 'theory of image acts.'[9] Both scholars did not

1 Daston (ed.), *Things That Talk*, 2004. **2** Gell, *Art and Agency*, 1998. **3** Freedberg, *The Power of Images*, 1989. **4** Gosden, 'What Do Objects Want?,' 2005. **5** See, e.g.: Brown, 'Thing Theory,' 2001; Ferus and Rübel (eds.), *Die Tücke des Objekts*, 2009; and Frank, Gockel, Hauschild, Kimmich and Mahlke (eds.), 'Fremde Dinge,' 2007. **6** See: van Eck, *Art, Agency and Living Presence*, 2015. **7** See: Latour, *Reassembling the Social*, 2005; and Descola, *Par-delà nature et culture*, 2005. **8** See: Latour, *We Have Never Been Modern*, 1993, especially pp. 91–129; and Latour (interviewed by Miranda), 'A Dialog About a New Meaning of Symmetric Anthropology,' 2016. **9** See: Bredekamp, *Image Acts*, 2018 [2015].

hesitate to indicate the practical consequences of their theories: Latour drew the outlines of a new 'politics of nature' that forces us to rethink political ecology,[10] whereas Bredekamp insisted on the 'right to life' that should also be attributed to images and artefacts.[11] But, above all, such approaches raise the question of what 'agency' means, if it is also assigned to things. As Alfred Gell, in many respects the most rigorous theorist of the agency of objects, has already argued, there can be no attribution of agency to objects without at least considering the question of whether there can be any agency without intentionality and consciousness.[12]

The harsh criticism that such approaches have provoked indicates a fundamental conflict between ontology and phenomenology in our dealings with objects. As language often mirrors ontological presuppositions, the problem might be connected to the limitations of our semantics: applying the phrase 'agency of x' to things or artefacts seems, at first sight, to suggest that these objects ought to be regarded as full equivalents to (human) subjects. Whereas Latour's actor-network theory proposes to question and to overcome the established dichotomy of subjects and objects, the inherent 'logic' of our semantics tends to reinstate such dualisms and thereby persistently shapes our ontologies and epistemologies. This is one of several reasons why theories that try to do justice to the inescapable human need to attribute the power to act to objects, and to interact with them as if they are animate or even sentient, are often criticized. As Latour's and Bredekamp's theories tend to perpetuate the familiar semantics that implicitly attribute agency to *one* single actor, they seemingly assign the same agency that humans are capable of to objects. For that reason they are charged with animism, fetishism or the anthropomorphisation of the inanimate.[13] From such a point of view the actor-network theory or Bredekamp's concept of image-act would simply attribute to things what previously was taken for a unique capacity of human beings. If that were the case, we would still stage the same drama—merely having exchanged the actors that perform the roles.

However, the broad and productive reception that, for example, the actor-network theory has found in anthropology, archaeology, art history, and many other disciplines, points to the fact that it not only enlarges the scope of 'actors' in social life, but changes the way in which actions and interactions have to be conceived of. If the central assumptions of Latour's actor-network theory are taken seriously, we have to break with the tendency to attribute agency exclusively to one person or even one object. Instead we have to understand 'agency' as an effect that is produced in and through the interactions between human actors and artefacts, in networks, art nexuses, collectives and processes. From such a perspective, agency is not exercised by only one actor but decentralised and

10 See: Latour, *Politics of Nature*, 2004. **11** See: Bredekamp, *Das Beispiel Palmyra*, 2016; and Bredekamp, *Image Acts*, 2018 [2015], p. 282: 'It is in the right to life that images may [...] claim for themselves that there arises the command that one care for them, use them, but also address them critically.' **12** See: Gell, *Art and Agency*, 1998, pp. 12–26; and van Eck, 'Alfred Gell,' 2018. **13** See, e.g.: Wiesing, *Sehen lassen*, 2013, pp. 78–105; and Büchsel, 'Das Ende der Bildermythologien,' 2014. **14** Knappett and Malafouris, 'Material and Nonhuman Agency,' 2008, p. XI. **15** Gell, *Art and Agency*, 1998, pp. 12–26 and 28–38. **16** Latour, *Pando-*

distributed 'in relational networks'[14] or 'art nexuses[15] that may constantly change. It 'resides'—as Latour put it himself—'in the blind spot in which society and matter exchange properties.'[16] Action does not merely rely on a single actor who intentionally uses things to act on passive objects. Rather, it implies situations in which humans become entangled with non-human entities. Therefore, Carl Knappett and Lambros Malafouris have emphasized that we should be 'more concerned with understanding agency as a situated process, rather than debating what or who is or is not an agent.'[17]

Current developments in the humanities offer a good basis to do so. Several approaches from different disciplinary contexts share the common objective of overcoming traditional definitions that trace agency back to causal relations between human intentions and events. Developed mostly independently from each other, these new approaches highlight phenomena that effectively codetermine the situations in which agency is produced, but which were hitherto underestimated or dismissed and condemned as idolatry, primitivism or fetishism. They throw light on factors that are different from the involved subjects and objects but nevertheless are indispensable for performing specific actions. The theory of affordances, recent research on 'cultural techniques' as well as practice theories, to mention only a few of the relevant approaches, show a shared interest in leaving behind the subject-object-dichotomy by exploring the relations and networks in which actions are situated. In doing so, these approaches prove to be highly attentive to largely neglected factors and to the potential relevance of contingencies for the production of agency.

By the neologism *affordance* James J. Gibson has conceptualized offerings or action possibilities in the environment of human actors that are not necessarily identical to specific functions of the thing concerned. One of Gibson's key examples is an object that may be used as a seat without being constructed for this purpose: 'If an object that rests on the ground, has a surface that is itself sufficiently rigid, level, flat, and extended, and if this surface is raised approximately at the height of the knees of the human biped, then it affords sitting-on.'[18] Focussing on action *possibilities*, Gibson has not attributed agency to objects that exhibit affordances, nevertheless he has underlined that this perspective cuts across traditional distinctions between subject and object or actor and environment:

'The affordances of the environment are what it offers the animal, what it provides or furnishes, either for good or ill. The verb to afford is found in the dictionary, the noun affordance is not. I have made it up. I mean by it something that refers to both the environment and the animal in a way that no existing term does. It implies the complementarity of the animal and the environment.'[19]

ra's Hope, 1999, p. 190. **17** Knappett and Malafouris, 'Material and Nonhuman Agency,' 2008, p. XII. **18** Gibson, 'The Theory of Affordances,' 1977, p. 68. See also: Hodder, *Entangled*, 2012, especially pp. 48–50. **19** Gibson, *The Ecological Approach to Visual Perception*, 1979, p. 127. See also: McGrenere and Ho, 'Affordances,' 2000 [http://graphicsinterface.org/proceedings/gi2000/gi2000-24/; DOI 10.20380/GI2000.24 (last accessed 3 March 2018)]: 'By cutting across the subjective-objective barrier, Gibson's affordances introduce the idea of actor-environment mutuality, the actor and the environment make an inseparable pair.'

Affordances, therefore, unlike traditional understandings of agency, cannot be traced back to intentional decisions or acts of subjects. They are different from functions, scripts or programmes that were materially incorporated by providing certain things or constructing specific instruments. They are independent of the actor's ability to perceive them, but their potentials only are put into effect if an actor carries out what is afforded.

The concept of *cultural techniques* has been emerging in a completely different context, in the framework of German media studies, though it also turns away from the subject-object-dichotomy and from structuralist and semiotic conceptualizations of culture. Basically, the hardly translatable notion of *Kulturtechnik* (cultural technique) has been 'employed to describe the interactions between humans and media, and, most recently, to account for basic operations and differentiations that give rise to an array of conceptual and ontological entities which are said to constitute culture.'[20] Culture, its basic notions, its conceptual framework as well as its ontological presuppositions are not taken to be something given, but to emerge and to evolve from a network of operations. Therefore cultural techniques—such as counting, writing, reading, producing images, but also corporeal techniques, tacit knowledge and skills—are understood as 'operative chains that precede the media concepts they generate.'[21] Instead of merely relying on given, established structures, cultural techniques produce, maintain, displace or reflect the differences by which culture is characterized and articulates itself. The emphasis on chains of operations and on the networks of actors, artefacts, and techniques bears resemblances to the actor-network theory.[22]

Recent practice theories that have been mainly elaborated by sociologists like Andreas Reckwitz and Frank Hillebrandt point in a similar direction.[23] Building on impulses and intuitions by Pierre Bourdieu, Anthony Giddens, Bruno Latour, Theodore Schatzki and others, practice theories try to avoid the shortcomings of the antagonism between structuralism and theories of action or rational choice. Instead of focussing either on supposedly sovereign actors who decide on their own or on social, economic and technical structures that predetermine individual actions, these approaches understand practices as the basic unit of the social. By 'practice,' however, they do not consider individual actions, but 'a routinized type of behaviour which consists of several elements, interconnected to one other: forms of bodily activities, forms of mental activities, "things" and their use, a background knowledge in the form of understanding, know-how, states of emotion and motivational knowledge. A practice—a way of cooking, of consuming, of working, of investigating, of taking care of oneself or of others, etc.—forms so to speak a "block" whose existence necessarily depends on the existence and specific interconnectedness of these elements, and which cannot be reduced to any one of these single elements.'[24]

20 Winthrop-Young, 'Cultural Techniques,' 2013, p. 3. **21** Siegert, 'Cultural Techniques,' 2015, p. 11. **22** See: Engell and Siegert, 'Editorial,' 2013. **23** See: Reckwitz, 'Grundelemente einer Theorie sozialer Praktiken,' 2003; Hillebrandt, *Soziologische Praxistheorien*, 2014; and Schäfer (ed.), *Praxistheorie*, 2016. **24** Reckwitz,

Practices are dependent on their constant realisation and repetition in individual actions. At the same time, they can be subject to subtle, but important modifications while being carried out repeatedly. Therefore they can contribute to continuing and stabilizing social structures, or may subvert and change them. By emphasizing the situatedness of practices and routines, practice theories leave room to do justice to contingencies and the relevance of things, artefacts and objects that are involved: 'For practice theory, objects are necessary components of many practices—just as indispensable as bodily and mental activities.'[25] Like the other approaches that we briefly introduced, practice theories thus decentre agency from subjects and their minds, intentions and discourses to practical knowledge, bodies and things. Most researchers in this field are probably not particularly interested in things and artefacts; nevertheless the approach opens a door to overcome the traditional concept of mute, passive objects that are used and manipulated by subjects.

It is not our aim to underestimate or to downplay the differences between these approaches. They emerged in different disciplinary fields, pursue diverse agendas and put various phenomena at the centre of their attention. Nevertheless they all share the idea that our interactions with things cannot be reduced to subjective intentions on the one hand and to a given structure or material prerequisites on the other hand. In different ways, the theory of affordance, the concept of cultural techniques and practice theories seem to be involved in the even more comprehensive project to decentre the notion of agency. Sometimes without explicitly raising the question of whether it is adequate to refer to an 'agency of objects,' the briefly presented approaches give an impression of what it would mean to understand agency as a product of networks, relations, processes and situations.

All these approaches prove to be productive when they are put into practice by referring to specific case studies. Therefore, we propose not to discuss these questions only on a general theoretical level, but to turn our attention to objects and to keep the challenging questions and concepts in mind without taking them completely for granted. The questions and approaches outlined here not merely call for restructuring the ontological distinctions and relations but for concentrating on processes, encounters and interactions between various kinds of human and institutional actors and things. Instead of referring to projections of subjects or to cultural conventions on the one hand, and animism or fetishisation on the other hand, it is reasonable to focus on situations, entanglements and networks in which humans and artefacts are involved. Viewed in this light, it becomes clear that there are more factors that should be taken into account. Besides human beings and things, there are routines, conventions, institutions, dispositifs and in particular small seemingly parasitic accessories, the *parerga*, that can have a decisive impact on the question of which agency may be produced in a given situation.

'Toward a Theory of Social Practices,' 2002, p. 249. **25** Reckwitz, 'Toward a Theory of Social Practices,' 2002, p. 252.

Parerga: Framing Operations

Particular problems arise if a specific type of action is taken into account: acts of perception. There can be no doubt that looking at things or contemplating pictures should also be regarded as an action or—to be more precise—as a rather complex type of action. Even if the beholder seems to stand passive and motionless in front of the object she or he perceives, the perception itself is performed in a process that involves the object, its material and aesthetic qualities, the particular situation of the encounter between viewer and thing, the viewer's body and senses, as well as his intentions, thoughts or memories and also more general routines and conventions of viewing.[26] Both features of the object and idiosyncrasies of the subject are able to influence how the process of perception unfolds. The more the object seems to distinguish itself by aesthetic qualities, the stronger the impression that it might exert some 'power' over the viewer. But, generally, any peculiarities, even deficiencies, are able to attract the viewer's attention and to force him to direct his gaze in a certain direction—as long as this is permitted by the situation and its circumstances.

One factor that is decisive in such situations is widely underestimated: the role of framings and displays.[27] It is by *parerga*, by frames, pedestals, showcases and furniture as well as by acts of isolation, arrangement and display, that objects can be perceived as such: as things deserving and attracting attention. Hence, we propose to understand practices of framing as an important basic cultural technique, as the production of affordances and as acts that allow for other practices: namely acts of perception. In our opinion, what is described by the 'power' or 'agency' of things cannot fully be comprehended without taking into account the manifold framing devices that adjust objects, make them usable and secure their identity and integrity.

Referring back to Immanuel Kant's notion of *parergon* (Beiwerk), Jacques Derrida has argued that *parerga* do not belong to the thing itself and yet are indispensable in order to mark differences between the object of perception, the *ergon*, and its context.[28] Only *parerga* reliably clarify what belongs to the thing or to the work. However, as much as *parerga* participate in the constitution and protection of the object, they threaten to become conspicuous and distract attention from the object. Furthermore, they may suggest certain evaluations and semantizations or particular understandings of the object concerned. The accessory, therefore, not only ensures that the object can be clearly addressed, but already brings connotations to it. *Parerga* like pedestals, glass cases, and repositories do not frame an already-available, self-contained object, but rather prepare the environment that constitutes it as an object of perception in a particular context.

26 With a focus on the perception of pictures, see: Grave, 'Der Akt des Bildbetrachtens,' 2014. **27** For an overview of the field of frame studies see: Beyer, *Rahmenbestimmungen*, 2008; Duro (ed.), *The Rhetoric of the Frame*, 1996; Harlizius-Klück, Kacunko and Körner (eds.), *Framings*, 2015; Körner and Möseneder

Against this background, it becomes clear that individual concrete things may not always be understood as given. Rather, those seemingly trivial processes, practices and interventions are of central importance, in which things emerge from the abundance of natural or everyday objects and become identifiable as individual entities.[29] Before focussing on semantizations, symbolizations, or codifications, it is, therefore, important to examine the constitutive processes of isolation, framing and (re-)contextualization of supposedly individual things that potentially might appear as 'eloquent' objects. Which material and performative interventions of isolation, focussing, framing and staging make the object addressable as a single object so that it can be discussed?

Only on the basis of these seemingly marginal procedures can a thing be understood as evidence of facts or as a medium of thoughts and feelings. However, the processes of isolation, framing, and (re-)contextualization not only prepare the thing in a way that allows for attaching semantics and affects to the object. Rather, these processes influence all further interactions between human and thing. They determine what belongs to the thing or is excluded; they suggest a perspective from which to look at the thing, emphasizing certain aspects and forcing others to step back. It would be a shortcoming to merely trace these processes back to intentions and reflections of individual subjects. Many decisions about what is considered to be the object and how it should be regarded are demanded of the curator, conservator, designer, museum pedagogue or anybody else who is involved in making a display, although the choices that are made this way may go unacknowlegded. And many decisions are conditioned by the 'thingness'[30] and stubborn materiality of the object itself, for example, when usual frames cannot technically be fixed or when specific operations are necessary to protect the object or the museum's staff and visitors from dangerous interactions.

The tangible materiality of objects means that the isolating and recontextualizing interventions result in material and sometimes perceptible changes to things. Already here, and not only on the level of representations and modelling, aesthetic questions—insofar as we understand the aesthetic in the sense of *aisthesis* as the sensibly perceptible—are of particular importance. Once these aesthetic interventions have been completed, it can no longer be easily determined what has been changed, and it becomes even more difficult to detect which modifications were deliberately aimed at or merely accepted as a result of arrangement requirements. In at least two ways, these inevitable interventions affect the processes in which things come to the fore: on the one hand, with its selection, isolation, and framing, a thing is constituted as a potential object of discourses. On the other hand, however, the modifications often made without specific intentions, which go hand in hand with the constitution of the thing, also have the potential to encourage

(eds.), *Format und Rahmen*, 2008; Körner and Möseneder (eds.), *Rahmen*, 2010; Platt and Squire, *The Frame in Classical Art*, 2017. **28** See: Derrida, *La vérité en peinture*, 1978, pp. 19–168. **29** See: Grave, 'On the Aesthetics of Scientific Objects,' 2007. **30** Brown, 'Thing Theory,' 2001.

over-determinations. The presentation of the thing can be the starting point of far-reaching conclusions: the thing then—refering to Lorraine Daston's concept—'speaks' in a fundamentally different way by producing a specific and situated agency.

To describe those *parerga* in the field of display practices, the curator and artist Joseph Grigely has suggested the term 'exhibition prosthetics.'[31] Without straining the idea of the artwork as a living organism, Grigely focuses on the relation between the artwork and its framing as prosthesis: 'That is, a prosthesis remediates—it fills, it extends, it supplements. But it does not do this without also becoming a part of, not apart from, the body that it fills, extends and supplements.'[32] So Grigely deals with the same fundamental question that was already raised by Derrida: '[...] to what extent are these various exhibition conventions actually part of the art—and not merely an extension of it?'[33] In the light of these considerations, the investigation of the agency of an artwork or an artefact needs to include its various framings, which participate substantially in producing agency.

The ambivalent status of these interventions can be conceptualized more clearly by characterizing the different operators that serve to focus, isolate, or frame as *parerga*. Thus, the constitution of a thing as an object, as *ergon*, depends on the supplementation by *parerga* (accessories, frames, pedestals, containers, furniture, etc.), which may be subject to change over time. Such a conceptual approach allows for explaining why things sink back into the mass of mute matter and why their eloquence and agency remains fundamentally fragile. However, this parergonal logic is not only based on material interventions, but is also used in presentations and spatial arrangements, as well as in the written and textual frames of things.[34]

Parerga may be characterized as framing operations in a double sense: they do not merely serve as accessories or décor, but always perform a constitutive differentiation between the object and its surrounding. At the same time they frame and thereby deeply influence the act of perceiving. Framing devices are decisive for the processes of viewing and quite often initiate particular performative effects in the course of perception. Therefore, *parerga* may be understood as a hinge or a threshold between object and subject. By definition, they do not directly belong to the thing itself, but, at the same time, they also cannot be fully controlled by the perceiving subject. Hence, they are an important part of the various factors that contribute to the production of 'agency' without being reducible to either the object or the subject.

31 Grigely, *Exhibition Prosthetics*, 2010. Grigely contours his approach refering to the literary critics Gérard Genette's and David Wills' concepts of *paratext* and *prosthesis*. **32** Grigely, *Exhibition Prosthetics*, 2010, p. 8. **33** Grigely, *Exhibition Prosthetics*, 2010, p. 7. **34** For a recent study about written frames, which is the first edited volume of the research project *Parerga and Paratexte*, see: Knebel, Ortlieb and Püschel (eds.), *Steine rahmen, Tiere taxieren, Dinge inszenieren*, 2018 (forthcoming).

3

The Case Studies

The case studies presented in this volume investigate both specific and contingent situations of showing, regarding and handling artworks or objects in their effects to produce or receive agency. The first section of contributions focusses on complex display situations shaped by curatorial decisions. Without privileging an unidirectional constructivist idea of agency, those essays conceive agency as a moderated and calculated phenomenon based on more the doing than the saying of tacit knowledge and institutional conventions. The second section focusses less on a whole spatial ensemble than on specific parergonal operations within displays. This approach takes a closer look at the materiality and formats of *parerga* and leads to the incalculable processes in the relation of the frame and the framed.

By reflecting *Display Displayed* Ivan Gaskell introduces the main issue of the first section. The starting point of his argument is perception capability, which can focus on things, but never isolates those from other things surrounding them. Firstly regarding things as framed things is an inevitable *conditio humana*. Secondly it is difficult to define the zone between art and the greater physical whole. By investigating indoor and outdoor displays mainly of contemporary art, Gaskell shows that 'the distinctions between art and the rest of the world lose coherence and relevance.'

The fact that the performative incorporation and reflection of *parerga* is not confined to conceptual art is shown in the contribution of Elsje van Kessel, who analyses the *Street as Frame* during the feast of Corpus Christi in early modern Lisbon. During the procession, art objects in houses and churches were taken 'off their pedestals' and into the outdoors. The ephemeral and performative display in the street produced a specific mode of presence and impacted the agency of the objects, leveraged and increased by the Eucharistic practice. Because of the not just visible but touchable presence of Corpus Christi in the street, 'there was no outside from which one could look in; rather, the integration of work and frame gave the procession its remarkable agency.'

Hannah Williams also deals with a case of *Staging Belief* and turns the viewpoint to the indoor displays of three churches in eighteenth-century Paris. In her case studies of the Abbey of Saint-Denis, the Jacobin chapel and the church of Saint-Roch, Williams differentiates three spatial techniques of spectator involvement, opening an affective experience of agency. The setting and framing of a picture can establish spatial continuity between the pictorial and the spectator's realm. But, moreover, interactive patterns can be found, when the spectator is led by intentionally orchestrated viewpoints and offered the role of a witness, or when she or he is confronted with alternating spaces in one church, which have to be related to theological reflection.

Studying a collection of highly affective objects, Mechthild Fend stresses the role of the 'display prosthetics' in the dermatological wax moulages at the Hôpital Saint-Louis. The framings in that historical display, which was founded in the late 19th century, take up a central function to balance *Order and Affect*. Fend reflects on the complex curatorial task which is challenged by the semantic implications of the wax: the *parerga,* paratexts and spatial arrangements for the dermatological casts as a new diagnostic tool had to be conceived against a background of traditional forms of religious votive practice, as well as rising shows of waxen celebrities at Madame Tussaud's or the Musée Grevin in Paris.

The next two contributions deal with the much-debated Barnes Collection. In her essay *The Barnes Ensembles, Again* Cindy Kang analyses the theoretical implications of transfering the display from the original building in the suburbs into a new building in downtown Philadelphia. Replicating the *parerga,* the original spatial and material framing, brings the tacit knowledge of display to public attention. So with the opening of the new house in 2012 both positions—the scathing critics and the devoted supporters of the replicated display—exemplified the idea that the agency of all the artworks is not based on themselves but on their framing, which makes them real or fake.

The second essay on the Barnes Collection opens the second group of the anthology. Dario Gamboni investigates a specific parergonal operation focussing on the ironwork as an unique and complex kind of frame in the context of art exhibition, what he describes as a *Ready-Made Eye-Opener.* Both the attraction and the confusion induced by the close neighbourhood of fine art masterpieces with such used iron pieces as a keyhole escutcheon or a ram's horn hinge, is calculated for a 'school of seeing.' Furthermore Barnes did not only aim at formalistic insights, but wanted to appreciate the former handiwork as an expression of its maker's experience equivalent to the fine art items. After relating Barnes's display devices to museums for decorative and applied arts and for ethnography, Gamboni adresses Duchamp's ready-mades to highlight the hidden semantics of affordance. In Barnes's written and displayed idea 'of the heuristic agency of objects, *ergon* became a shifting quality susceptible to scale and exchange positions with that of *parergon.*'

Peter Schade also concentrates on the frame as a well-established *parergon* of displayed artworks. He takes up the perspective of the conservator, who has to handle the challenge of (re-)constructing historical *parerga.* The *reframing of Lazarus,* Sebastino del Piombo's masterpiece and a key work in the foundation of the National Gallery, is related to the history of the institution and the changing conventions of framing. It becomes evident that the conservator's work of reframing is closely linked to purposive investigations and the fortuity of a well observed art market. Both research and sudden fortune allow 'a visual resurrection of *The Raising of Lazarus.*'

As another type of *parerga* that is used to display and/or to store objects, Diana Stört investigates *Goethe's Cabinets as Epistemic Furniture.* She refers to a debate in the scientific community around 1800 concerning the advantages and disadvantages of using glass and drawers, showcases and closed cabinets. By doing so, she not only stresses the visuality and tactility of objects of natural history, but also accentuates how those furniture structure scientific findings. The agency effects discussed in that case not only concern moments of aesthetic experience, rather they are better understood by refering to the concept of affordance: the way the items are stored and presented in the furniture shapes their perception and exploration.

Beside the framing which fixes the object technically, the written label puts it into the scientifc, the institutional and the economic discourse. Angela Matyssek investigates those paratexts in various situations and types of display. The question, if an artwork gets *Death by/Life by Wall Label* does not only concern its discursive framing, but also covers the label's material and spatial interference with its specific agency effects. Matyssek differentiates two positions in the aesthetical and curatorial debate on the relation between the label and the work of art: firstly the antagonistic and secondly the collaborative relation, which is finally linked with an analysis of the recent curatorial practice not to eliminate but to marginalise the wall label.

The fact that framings of objects not just produce aesthetical, institutional and economic, but also social and political effects is discussed in the last essay. Noémie Étienne reflects on the *Materiality and Agency between Conflict and Contact Zones* in ethnographic and anthropological museums. She examines an unpublished report of the National Museum of the American Indian, which recorded the conservation methods that Native Americans requested for the very objects once produced and used but not longer owned by their families. To those the act of framing apears not only as a symbolic demonstration of power but also as a very risky interference concerning the agency of the objects, because the conservator's well intentioned measures could damp it. Étienne shows that this conflict is grounded in 'two different conceptions of what agency can be.'

Bibliography

V. Beyer, *Rahmenbestimmungen. Funktionen von Rahmen bei Goya, Velázquez, van Eyck und Degas* (Fink, 2008).

H. Bredekamp, *Das Beispiel Palmyra* (Verlag der Buchhandlung Walther König, 2016).

H. Bredekamp, *Image Acts. A Systematic Approach to Visual Agency*, trans., ed., and adapted by E. Clegg (De Gruyter, 2018 [2015]).

B. Brown, 'Thing Theory,' *Critical Inquiry*, 28 (2001), pp. 1–17.

M. Büchsel, 'Das Ende der Bildermythologien. Kritische Stimmen zur deutschen Bildwissenschaft,' *Kunstchronik*, 7 (2014), pp. 335–342.

L. Daston (ed.), *Things That Talk. Object Lessons from Art and Science* (Zone Books, 2004).

J. Derrida, *La vérité en peinture* (Flammarion, 1978).

P. Descola, *Par-delà nature et culture* (Gallimard, 2005).

P. Duro (ed.), *The Rhetoric of the Frame. Essays on the Boundaries of the Artwork* (Cambridge University Press, 1996).

L. Engell and B. Siegert, 'Editorial,' *Zeitschrift für Medien- und Kulturforschung*, 13/2 (2013), pp. 5–10.

K. Ferus and D. Rübel (eds.), *Die Tücke des Objekts. Vom Umgang mit Dingen* (Reimer, 2009).

M. C. Frank, B. Gockel, T. Hauschild, D. Kimmich and K. Mahlke (eds.), 'Fremde Dinge,' Special Issue of *Zeitschrift für Kulturwissenschaften*, 1 (2007).

D. Freedberg, *The Power of Images. Studies in the History and Theory of Response* (The University of Chicago Press, 1989).

A. Gell, *Art and Agency. An Anthropological Theory* (Clarendon Press, 1998).

J. J. Gibson, 'The Theory of Affordances' in R. Shaw and J. Bransford (eds.), *Perceiving, Acting, and Knowing. Toward an Ecological Psychology* (Erlbaum, 1977), pp. 67–82.

J. J. Gibson, *The Ecological Approach to Visual Perception* (Mifflin, 1979).

C. Gosden, 'What Do Objects Want?,' *Journal of Archaeological Method and Theory*, 12/3 (2005), pp. 193–211.

J. Grave, 'On the Aesthetics of Scientific Objects. Three Case Studies' in S. Vackimes and K. Weltersbach (eds.), *Wandering Seminar on Scientific Objects* (Max-Planck-Institut für Wissenschaftsgeschichte, 2007), pp. 35–47.

J. Grave, 'Der Akt des Bildbetrachtens. Überlegungen zur rezeptionsästhetischen Temporalität des Bildes' in M. Gamper and H. Hühn (eds.), *Zeit der Darstellung. Ästhetische Eigenzeiten in Kunst, Literatur und Wissenschaft* (Wehrhahn Verlag, 2014), pp. 51–71.

J. Grigely, *Exhibition Prosthetics* (Bedford Press, 2010).

E. Harlizius-Klück, S. Kacunko and H. Körner (eds.), *Framings* (Logos, 2015).

F. Hillebrandt, *Soziologische Praxistheorien. Eine Einführung* (Springer, 2014).

I. Hodder, *Entangled. An Archaeology of the Relationships between Humans and Things* (Wiley-Blackwell, 2012).

C. Knappett and L. Malafouris, 'Material and Nonhuman Agency: An Introduction' in C. Knappett and L. Malafouris (eds.), *Material Agency. Towards a Non-Anthropocentric Approach* (Springer, 2008), pp. IX–XIX.

K. Knebel, C. Ortlieb and G. Püschel (eds.), *Steine rahmen, Tiere taxieren, Dinge inszenieren* (Sandstein, 2018, forthcoming).

H. Körner and K. Möseneder (eds.), *Format und Rahmen. Vom Mittelalter bis zur Neuzeit* (Reimer, 2008).

H. Körner and K. Möseneder (eds.), *Rahmen – zwischen Innen und Außen. Beiträge zur Theorie und Geschichte* (Reimer, 2010).

B. Latour, *We Have Never Been Modern*, trans. by C. Porter (Harvard University Press, 1993).

B. Latour, *Pandora's Hope: Essays on the Reality of Science Studies* (Harvard University Press, 1999).

B. Latour, *Politics of Nature. How to Bring the Sciences into Democracy*, trans. by C. Porter (Harvard University Press, 2004).

B. Latour, *Reassembling the Social. An Introduction to Actor-Network-Theory* (Oxford University Press, 2005).

B. Latour (interviewed by C. Miranda), 'A Dialog About a New Meaning of Symmetric Anthropology' in P. Charbonnier, G. Salmon and P. Skafish (eds.), *Comparative Metaphysics. Ontology After Anthropology* (Rowman & Littlefield International, 2016), pp. 325–341.
J. McGrenere and W. Ho, 'Affordances: Clarifying and Evolving a Concept' in *Proceedings of Graphics Interface 2000: Montréal, Québec, Canada, 15–17 May 2000*, pp. 179–186 [http://graphicsinterface.org/proceedings/gi2000/gi2000-24/; DOI 10.20380/GI2000.24].
V. Platt and M. Squire (eds.), *The Frame in Classical Art. A Cultural History* (Cambridge University Press, 2017).
A. Reckwitz, 'Toward a Theory of Social Practices. A Development in Culturalist Theorizing,' *European Journal of Social Theory*, 5/2 (2002), pp. 243–263.
A. Reckwitz, 'Grundelemente einer Theorie sozialer Praktiken. Eine sozialtheoretische Perspektive,' *Zeitschrift für Soziologie*, 32/4 (2003), pp. 282–301.
H. Schäfer (ed.), *Praxistheorie. Ein soziologisches Forschungsprogramm* (transcript, 2016).
M. Schlosser, 'Agency' in E. N. Zalta (ed.), *The Stanford Encyclopedia of Philosophy* [https://plato.stanford.edu/archives/fall2015/entries/agency].
B. Siegert, *Cultural Techniques: Grids, Filters, Doors, and Other Articulations of the Real*, trans. by G. Winthrop-Young (Fordham University Press, 2015).
C. van Eck, *Art, Agency and Living Presence. From the Animated Image to the Excessive Object* (De Gruyter and Leiden University Press, 2015).
C. van Eck, 'Alfred Gell' in P. Atkinson, S. Delamont, M. Hardy and M. Williams (eds.), *The SAGE Encyclopedia of Research Methods* (Sage, 2018, forthcoming).
L. Wiesing, *Sehen lassen. Die Praxis des Zeigens* (Suhrkamp, 2013).
G. Winthrop-Young, 'Cultural Techniques: Preliminary Remarks,' *Theory, Culture and Society*, 30/6 (2013), pp. 3–19.

I. Display Situations

IVAN GASKELL

Display Displayed[1]

I

Introduction

In discussing display, I wish to make two main points. First, nothing shown to us, nothing humans view, is isolated. Humans never look at single things oblivious to those other things that surround them. Second, in questions of display, art is not everything—the entirety of the world is—though art itself can remind us of this state of affairs. Because this is a volume addressing questions of agency, I also wish to make a third point as a coda, though without going into any detail regarding recent notions derived from the work of Bruno Latour and Alfred Gell (in their different ways), and others.[2] This point is that at least some appeals to agency are hampered by philosophical naiveté.

First, though, let us remind ourselves that display is not an exclusively human phenomenon. Many living creatures engage in display, notably for courtship and conflict. Humans act similarly, and for a wide range of purposes. They enact displays of aggression, as in a Māori *haka*, performed by warriors to intimidate their foes. Humans arrange commercialized displays of sexual competition, as in the annual Miss World contest. They also show off hierarchy and status, as Cambridge University demonstrates each year at its Congregation ceremony to confer honorary degrees. Clad in academic robes, the participants process through the streets, displaying themselves. These are all displays as forms of performance, but display can also be a contrivance to show things off statically. Such

1 I am grateful to Caroline van Eck and her colleagues for the invitation to give the introductory address at the symposium *Collections, Displays, and the Agency of Objects* at the University of Cambridge in September, 2017. My revision of the text preserves aspects of its origin as a lecture, although in published form it cannot be as generously illustrated as when delivered. I was able to undertake research and writing thanks to my permanent fellowship at the Lichtenberg-Kolleg (Advanced Study Institute in the Social Sciences and Humanities) at the Georg-August University, Göttingen. I should like to acknowledge the stimulation provided by the director, Martin van Gelderen, his colleagues, and the other fellows at the Kolleg. Jane Whitehead was my companion in just about all the explorations that inform my thoughts here expressed. She is also my most consistently stringent critic. This essay is for her. **2** For Latour, see, among other publications, his *Reassembling the Social. An Introduction to Actor-Network-*

displays concern many kinds of human activity: from commercial displays of goods; to displays for religious purposes; to assertions of power or vainglory through structures in the built environment; or a determination to perpetuate a social memory by means of conspicuous monuments, often incorporating statuary. Humans engage in displays for more numerous reasons than other animals, and displays, both static and performative, or both, frequently jostle within a few yards of each other. Clearly, not every display contrived by humans concerns art, but it is with some among that relatively small group of things displayed as art—art in the European manner—that I shall begin.[3]

2 Inside

Consider *The Geographer* by the seventeenth-century Dutch painter, Johannes Vermeer. Art historians usually point out that this painting is likely one of a pair, the other work being *The Astronomer*, for they are recorded together a number of times between 1713 and 1797 when they were separated at an auction sale. Their pairing is far easier to accomplish in reproduction than in actuality, for the *Geographer* is in Frankfurt, and the *Astronomer* is in Paris (Fig. 1). These things cannot simply be hung side by side on a whim, although they have been brought together several times, including in an exhibition in Frankfurt in 1997 to mark the 200th anniversary of their separation.[4] Instead of discussing further an art historical arrangement that defies the usual state of affairs in which the *Geographer* exists, I want to attend to that current existence. The *Geographer* is displayed in the Städel Museum, Frankfurt. Standing in front of it, a viewer might like to try to attend to it as a single thing, but she faces insuperable difficulties. She might try to exclude the surroundings from her peripheral vision by approaching the painting as close as possible without provoking the disapproval of a gallery attendant. She might try to focus on details, such as the dividers the geographer holds in his right hand. While it is true that a viewer—especially a practiced viewer—can mentally focus on such a detail (or on an entire single work to the exclusion of others beside it) by exercising a cognitive skill that temporarily excludes adjacent features from mental consideration, it is nonetheless the case that perceptually, however hard a viewer tries, she can never see those dividers unreservedly in isolation.[5] They form part of a greater whole. That whole is the entire painted surface. But neither is

Theory, 2005; for Gell, see: *Art and Agency. An Anthropological Theory*, 1998. **3** I acknowledge that, whereas display is pancultural, all my examples concern art and artefacts in the European manner. Certain strategies of framing for display are culturally specific—including the physical enclosure of a rectangular pictorial field—whereas others—such as the deliberate setting of a thing within a specific environment—need not be. **4** Maek-Gérard (ed.), *Johannes Vermeer*, 1997. **5** I am grateful to Dario Gamboni for pointing out that viewers can concentrate on details with some success in spite of the inevitable presence of other things in the field of vision. Steven Lubar points out the invention of the 'sciascope' in the early twentieth century by Benjamin Ives Gilman, secretary of the Museum of Fine Arts, Boston between 1893 and 1925. This device was designed to narrow the field of vision to enforce attentive looking at individual works or their details: Lubar, *Inside the Lost Museum*, 2017, pp. 171–172.

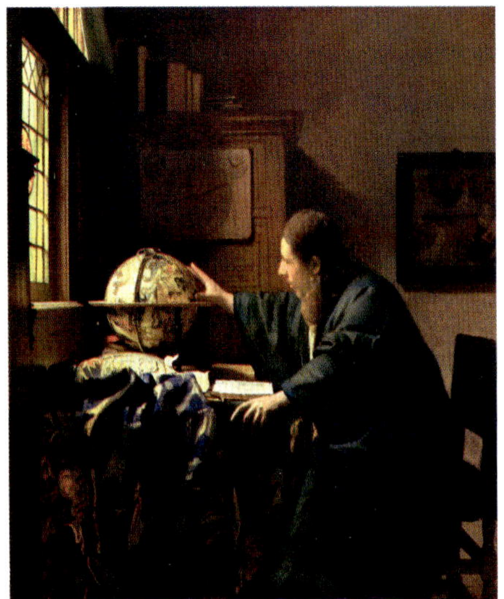

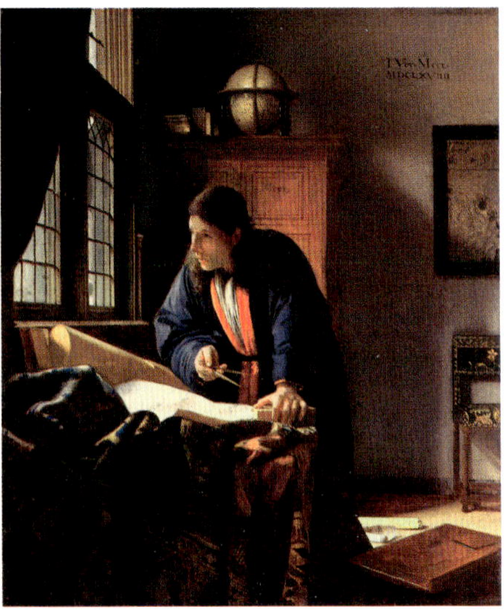

Figure 1:
Johannes Vermeer, *The Astronomer*, 1668, oil on canvas, 50 × 45 cm. Paris, Musée du Louvre;
and *The Geographer*, c. 1668–1669, oil on canvas, 53 × 46.6 cm. Frankfurt, Städel Museum.

the entire painting available to viewers in isolation, for it is in a black wooden frame that itself has an assertive physical presence in spite of its function of demarcating the pictorial world of the painting from the actual world in which it exists.[6] That actual world begins with the blue wall on which the framed painting hangs. Also on the blue wall, immediately next to the framed painting, is its label that the viewer must find impossible to exclude from her field of vision. From a moderate distance, the blue wall seems to threaten to overwhelm the painting. This is inevitable, for no wall on which a painting hangs can dematerialize (although displays of paintings on transparent free-standing panels or by suspension within independent armatures have been contrived). On either side of the *Geographer* are further paintings, placed at a tactful distance, but an unavoidable presence nonetheless (Fig. 2). These paintings—including the *Geographer*—constitute an ensemble whose elements interact with one another. The relative importance of the Vermeer is signalled by the distance between it and the next painting on either side being greater than the distance between those flanking paintings and the other ones immediately adjacent to them. Not only the central placement of the Vermeer emphasizes its precedence, but

6 Jacques Derrida discussed aspects of the effects of framing in *La vérité en peinture*, 1978. I do not see a difference in kind between literal framing (including those artefacts associated with many pictures in the European manner) and the placement of an item so as to be deliberately framed by its surroundings.

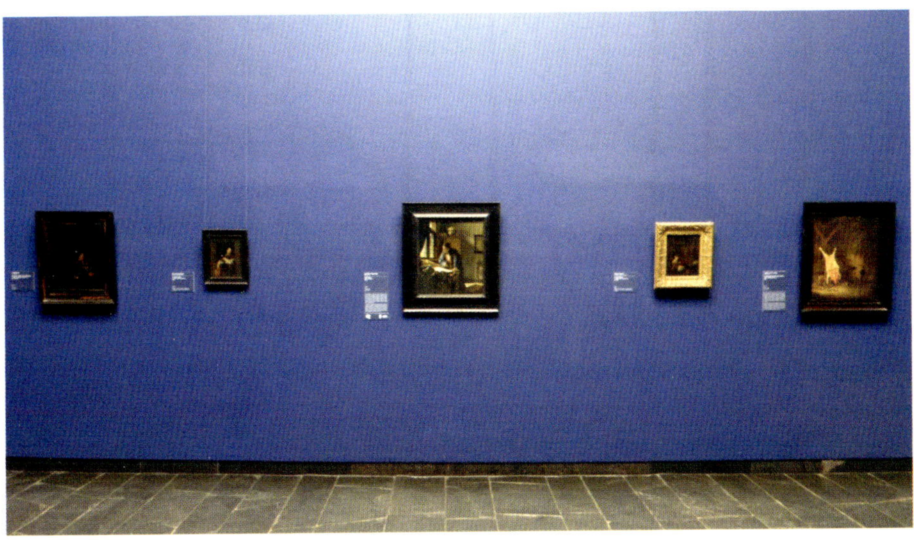

Figure 2:
Installation shot of Johannes Vermeer, *The Geographer* and other paintings.
Frankfurt, Städel Museum.

so too does the subtle differentiation of relative distance. The paintings form a hierarchical ensemble. That those five paintings, centred on the Vermeer, form a coherent group is stressed by their being framed by the doorway into their gallery when viewed from the adjacent gallery. From further back, that doorway frames the Vermeer alone, but on either side of that doorway are further paintings that from this more distant vantage point accompany the Vermeer and set it off. This arrangement doubles the device of flanking the Vermeer with ostensibly less important paintings, reinforcing its position within the display as being at the very top of this local hierarchy. Try as viewers might, they cannot consistently and sustainedly see the Vermeer as an isolated thing. The experienced and scholarly curator, Jochen Sander, has taken this into account. The company the *Geographer* keeps is specially chosen to make points concerning the character of seventeenth-century Dutch painting, and a hierarchy within it. The contrivance of such displays is one responsibility of curatorship. In exhibits, curators deliberately bring out particular aspects of things through positioning, mounting, juxtaposition, lighting, and the choice of wall colour and casework. The display centred on the *Geographer* in Frankfurt is an exposition of art historical ideas about seventeenth-century Dutch painting. But there are other ways of displaying paintings.

One collecting institution that stands out for its unusual mode of display is the Barnes Foundation, founded in 1922 in Lower Merion in suburban Philadelphia, but, since 2012, in a new downtown exhibition facility. Albert Barnes conceived of his collection as an educational tool. He displayed his collection along lines directly inspired by the philosopher John Dewey, disregarding art historical considerations. Dewey dedicated his major aesthetic statement, *Art As Experience* (1934) to Barnes.[7] This means that the dense hang intermingles major European paintings by artists such as Cézanne, Matisse, Renoir, Seurat, and Modigliani with New Mexican devotional paintings of saints (*retablos*), sub-Saharan African carvings, Pennsylvania Dutch painted chests, and European ironwork, such as keys and door hinges. As the Website states: 'The ensembles created by Dr. Barnes combine art and craft, cosmopolitan and provincial styles, and objects from across periods and cultures.'[8] This arrangement has long frustrated many conventional art historians who have longed to 'liberate' the great impressionist and post-impressionist paintings from what they dismiss as their surrounding 'distractions.' Yet such are the terms of Barnes's will that the foundation's new building in Philadelphia replicates the original galleries in Lower Merion almost precisely, and repeats its philosophically inspired hang in accordance with formal principles of line, space, light, and colour to demonstrate the supposed universalism of human expression.[9]

To suggest briefly that display radically affects how people apprehend things, let us focus not on a Seurat or a Cézanne, but on a New Mexican *retablo* of the kind sometimes characterized as 'folk art.' Many are dispersed among the other works in several of the galleries. Two among them are devotional images by Pedro Antonio Fresquís, who died in 1831: *The Virgin as Our Lady of Protection* and *Saint Rita of Cascia*. They flank an ensemble dominated by four paintings by Henri Rousseau, the most prominent being *Woman Walking in an Exotic Forest* (1905). The women in these three paintings may be approximately the same size and similarly oriented towards the viewer, but the two *retablos* have nothing further to do with the works of the self-taught French post-impressionist. We can compare this idiosyncratic use of such paintings with another use, still current, to be found in New Mexico churches, such as Nuestra Señora del Rosario (Our Lady of the Rosary), Las Truchas. Devotional paintings by Pedro Antonio Fresquís dominate its interior.[10] The display of devotional images in this interior is no less contrived and purposeful than that in the Barnes Foundation. It would be a mistake to claim—as is often done—that the church is the proper context, whereas the museum is not. Rather, the museum proposes a recontextualization—in this instance perfectly ethically permissible—though such redeployments of culturally sensitive materials are not invariably legitimate. Certain northwest Pacific coast peoples' masks, for instance, or Russian Orthodox icons, may not be appropriate items for museum collections given their inalienable sacred status.

Let us consider other instances of recontextualization. Some involve the use of reproduction, such as the perfectly legitimate pairing of reproductions of the Vermeer *Geographer*

7 Dewey, *Art As Experience*, 1934. He had earlier collaborated with Barnes to produce Dewey and Barnes et al., *Art and Education*, 1947 [1929]. **8** See: https://www.barnesfoundation.org/whats-on/collection (last accessed 23 October 2017). **9** Gaskell, 'The Museum of Big Ideas,' 2016, pp. 70–71. **10** See: Hayman,

and *Astronomer*. Many art historians create such displays of reproductions, rather than consider the actualities available to them in a variety of settings, including museums, as in the case of the *Geographer*, or in churches such as Nuestra Señora del Rosario. Indeed, some art historians who have never worked in a museum 'believe that the aims and constraints of display lead it almost invariably to be a clog on alert, adaptable, and radical thinking,' as I expressed it on a previous occasion.[11]

Why this hostility to the display of things in the world on the part of so many art historians? They claim to seek to attend to individual works, but since the days of Heinrich Wölffin, have instead contrived their own displays of reproductions with slide projectors, and latterly with PowerPoint, producing fantasy pairings irrespective of the physical character—most obviously the size—of the things reproduced. As a second example, following the Vermeer *Geographer*, we can take one painting isolated in reproduction as a slide: the *Assumption of the Virgin*, begun in Florence by Filippino Lippi, and completed after his death by Pietro Perugino in about 1506. I can project it side-by-side with Titian's painting of the same subject of about ten years later, and make art historical points about differences between Florence and Venice, *disegno* and *colore*, and so on. But—and this seems vital—my wholly artificial display of reproductions can give the viewer no idea of the actual existence of these things in the world. Furthermore, whereas in my earlier example there is plentiful evidence that the two paintings by Vermeer were once treated as a pendant pair in actuality, in the case of the two *Annunciations*, the paintings have nothing to do with each other conceptually—other than theologically—or physically. Any art historical points I make by drawing the comparison concern the differences between these two paintings, not any association between them. The *Assumption* by Lippi and Perugino is in the Chapel of the Assumption of the Basilica della Santissima Annunciata in Florence, a quite different kind of space from that occupied by the Titian, which is over the high altar in the apse of the Basilica di Santa Maria Gloriosa dei Frari in Venice. Furthermore, whereas the Titian retains its physical integrity, the Lippi and Perugino is but one element of a polyptych that was long ago dismembered and dispersed. It is a repurposed fragment. This is not to say that nothing of value can be claimed by making the kind of contrived comparison I have described, but I want to stress that the display of actual things in the world, rather than reproductions, invites different forms of attention: attention to each thing as part of a greater physical whole, a greater physical whole that can change radically over time, but that remains an element of actuality.

Each and every work is sited—is displayed—and has its being in particular circumstances more or less controlled by humans for a period sometimes of minutes, sometimes of decades, centuries or millennia.

'Hidden Gem of the Taos High Road,' *ColonialMexicoInsideandOut* (3 July 2017): http://colonialmexicoinsideandout.blogspot.com/2017/07/new-mexican-gem-of-taos-high-road.html (last accessed 23 October 2017). **11** Gaskell, 'Museums and Philosophy,' 2012, p. 80.

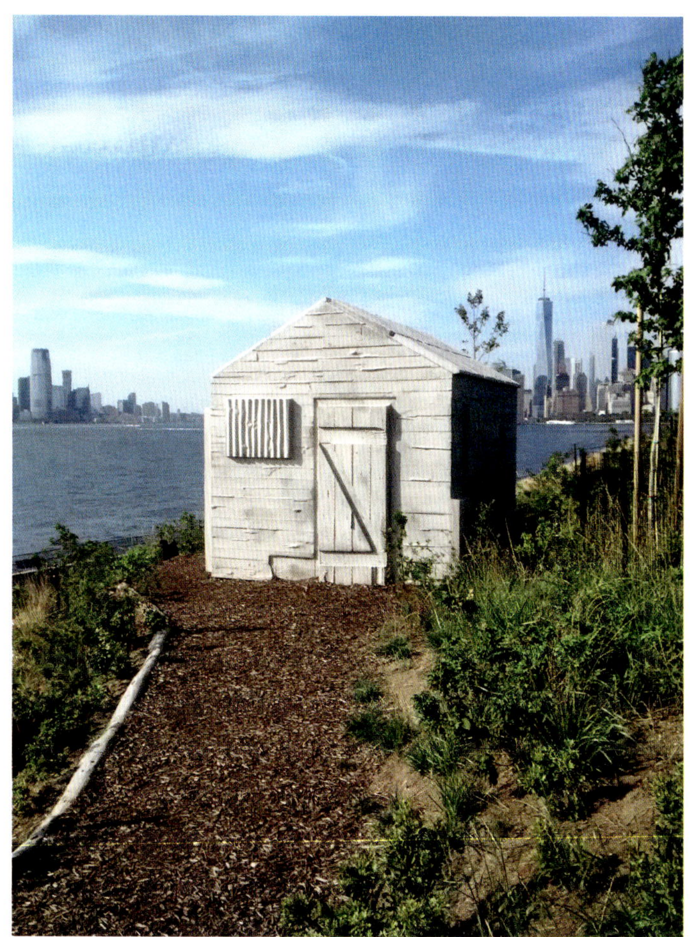

Figure 3:
Rachel Whiteread,
Cabin, 2016,
concrete and bronze.
New York,
Governors Island.

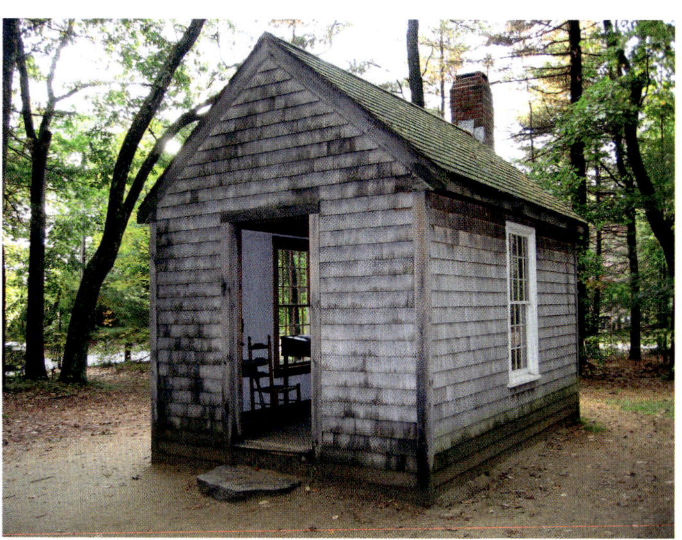

Figure 4:
Replica of Thoreau's
cabin. Walden Pond
Reservation,
Concord,
Massachusetts.

3

Outside

I want now to move beyond the portable art within museum walls, and things that function within interior spaces, such as churches, to things outside them, which are equally items of display. A recent instance is Rachel Whiteread's *Cabin* (2015), a commission executed in cast concrete and bronze for one of the artificial hills on Governors Island, New York, in an area that opened in July, 2016 (Fig. 3). It is a display in a particular, carefully chosen place. Circumstances can be casual or contrived, but display is invariably the latter, so when a work is displayed, circumstances matter. Just as I have argued in the cases of Titian's *Assumption* in the Frari, or Lippi and Perugino's *Assumption* in the Santissima Annunciata, to grasp certain aspects of Whiteread's *Cabin*, we have to perceive it in its circumstances, however inconvenient that may be. I want to stress that I am not seeking to evoke every aspect of any such thing. Some aspects may be apprehensible were *Cabin* to be removed to, say, the Museum of Modern Art, just as some aspects of Titian's *Assumption* were surely apprehensible when it was shown in a museum—the Accademia in Venice—between 1818 and 1919. Some aspects may be apprehensible in reproduction, though viewers can never know what they are missing if they do not see a thing itself but instead rely on reproductions alone. I can confirm that I have seen both Whiteread's *Cabin* and Titian's *Assumption*—and every other item I am discussing—but I nonetheless regret that all those who work with specific things are subject to the tyranny of the unique, both in terms of a thing's own properties, and its circumstances.

Cabin is an artwork, but the same holds true for other, equally—sometimes more—important things, such as the thing that Whiteread's recently created *Cabin* specifically evokes, as its label states: Henry David Thoreau's cabin at Walden Pond. Readers hardly need reminding that Henry David Thoreau, whose most celebrated book is his account of his life alone at Walden Pond in Concord, Massachusetts between July 1845 and September 1847, is one of the most significant original thinkers of the nineteenth century. The one-room cabin, built by Thoreau in 1845, has long since gone. A replica stands near the parking lot (Fig. 4). It is simply furnished, and visitors can enter it before following a trail along the shore to the original cabin site. That site was discovered in 1945, and is now a place of pilgrimage and reflection.[12] In a sense, that site is displayed in a manner as contrived as that of any artwork, though it could scarcely be more matter-of-fact. Rough-hewn stone markers linked by a single chain delineate the outline of the cabin. A wooden sign gives visitors a glimpse of the profundity of Thoreau's thought: 'I went to the woods because I wished to live deliberately, to front only the essential facts of life, and see if I could not learn what it had to teach, and not, when I came to die, discover that I had not lived.'[13] The sign is in the same form—white lettering on a brown ground—that the

12 Robbins, *Discovery at Walden*, 1999 [1947]. **13** Thoreau, *Walden; Or Life in the Woods*, 1854; Atkinson (ed.), *Walden and Other Writings*, 1992, p. 86.

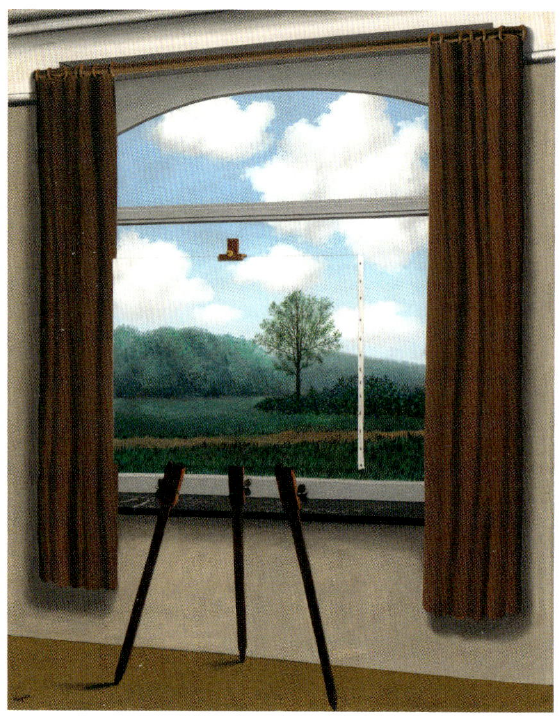

Figure 5:
René Magritte, *The Human Condition*, 1933,
oil on canvas, 100 × 81 cm.
Washington, DC, National Gallery of Art.

Massachusetts Department of Conservation and Recreation uses to tell visitors the cost of parking.[14] If there is such a thing as actuality, the site of Thoreau's cabin is it on display. Yet to try to view the site of Thoreau's cabin purely in isolation is not only impossible—just as we saw in our earlier cases—it would be a failure of the imagination. Just as the significance of the *Geographer* depends on the museum gallery that contains it, and the significance of each *Assumption* depends on the church that enfolds it, the significance of Thoreau's cabin—like that of Whiteread's *Cabin*—depends on its natural surroundings. Allowing for the growth of trees, the pond and its setting demand a form of attention comparable to that given it by Thoreau and his visitors through the open doorway of his cabin.

14 A sign that had been in place for many years, and that had begun to degrade, was replaced in the summer of 2017 by a new sign that employs several initial letters that are slightly more elaborate than those on its predecessor. However, the new sign remains characteristic of Department of Conservation and Recreation signage. **15** Lemire, *Black Walden*, 2009.

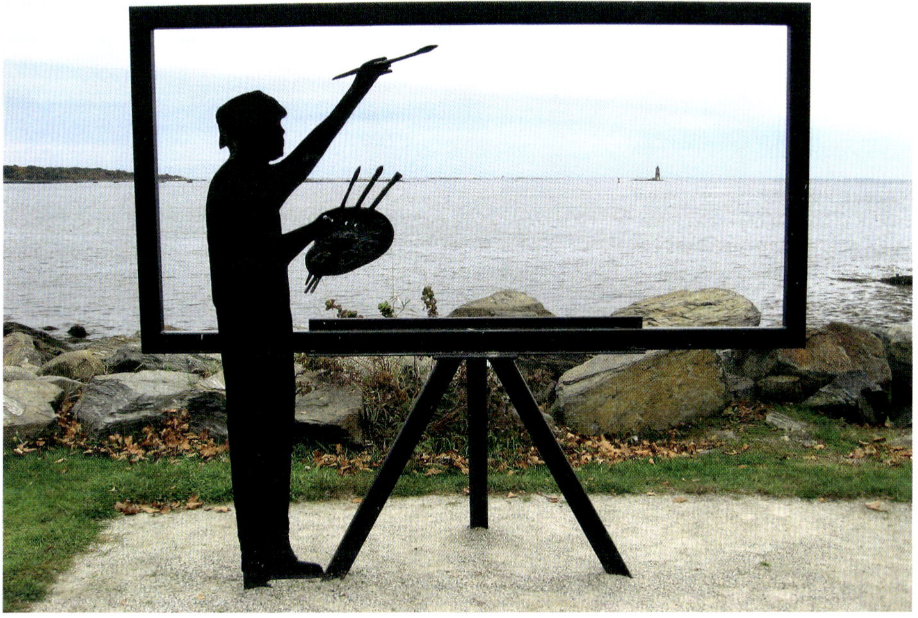

Figure 6:
Painter and frame, New Castle, NH, Great Island Common.

Many are familiar with this form of attention, discussed in European art theory as the picturesque. One form of the picturesque is to frame the landscape with a window or door to create a composition comprising what might appear to be—and in some instances might actually be—an inadvertent array of natural forms. In the case of the view from Thoreau's doorway, the landscape was indeed natural, even if his Concord contemporaries had modified the surroundings. In the 1840s, most of this land comprised individually owned woodlots from which the townsfolk extracted the cordwood they needed to see them through harsh New England winters. Thoreau built his cabin on the woodlot owned by his friend and mentor, Ralph Waldo Emerson. Other pockets of marginal land were formerly the sites of modest cabins that had been inhabited by elderly blacks, former slaves who had gained their freedom during the turmoil of the Revolutionary War fifty years previously.[15] It was—and remains—a landscape shaped by human intervention, from that of nineteenth-century woodcutters to the twenty-first-century Massachusetts Department of Conservation and Recreation, though it is not, and never has been, a landscape deliberately contrived for aesthetic contemplation. That description might rather characterize those parks designed in the allegedly naturalistic manner in the eighteenth and early nineteenth centuries by English garden designers such as Lancelot 'Capability' Brown and Humphry Repton, to be seen not only *in situ*, but in designs that Repton, with the help of his son, John Adey Repton, published in 1816.[16] The character of the calculatedly picturesque display of the landscape as viewed from a building was made explicit in an exhibition on *The Landscape of Lancelot 'Capability' Brown* at Alnwick Castle in Northumberland in 2016.[17] The curators placed frames on a terrace to make explicit the viewing practice of composing the parkland into pictures.

What might seem to be a straightforward cognitive exercise for simple enjoyment of the landscape can readily become a topic for second-order reflection. Belgian artist René Magritte explored the propensity that people have to identify and conflate their own perceptions of an ostensible actuality with contrived representations in a series of works from 1933 onwards, titled *The Human Condition* (Fig. 5).[18] Within a room with a view through a window or a simple archway he depicted a painting on an easel representing precisely that part of the landscape behind the painting so that the painting within the painting appears to be continuous with the scene beyond. Magritte thereby suggests that the equivocal relationship between actuality and representation is an inescapable aspect of being human.

Probably with less intellectual ambition than Magritte, the Select Board of New Castle, New Hampshire sanctioned the construction at Great Island Common, a park on the New England coast, of a metal silhouette of a life-size painter standing at an easel through which visitors can frame the view across the Piscataqua River (Fig. 6). Although evoking the practice of painting, and the picturesque, the Great Island Common structure does not invite consideration of the equivocal relationship between actuality and representation as a part of the human condition, as do Magritte's paintings, so much as serve as an invitation to the visitor to photograph the scene. The photograph rather than the painting has become the ordinary person's portal to the picturesque. What is more, the amateur photograph that reveals the present state of the human condition—at least the human condition of a fair portion of the First World—is not the straightforward landscape, but the selfie, as the officious labelling of a site above the beach at Morningstar Bay, St. Thomas, makes clear—one possible example among many. The label points out to visitors that this a 'selfie spot.' The scene is a display on hold for anyone who comes by who is ready to obey instructions as to where to record themselves. But this land is private, and those who come along that trail, carefully avoiding the basking iguanas, are guests at an expensive hotel that commands this particular borrowed view of the ocean from its proprietary beach. The hotel, Frenchman's Reef and Morning Star Beach Resort, displays the

16 Repton, *Fragments*, 1816. **17** See: http://www.capabilitybrown.org/event/landscape-lancelot-capability-brown-alnwick-castle (last accessed 6 November 2017). **18** *The Human Condition*, 1933, oil on canvas. Washington, DC, National Gallery of Art; *The Human Condition*, 1935, oil on canvas. Geneva, Simon Spierer Collection; and *The Human Condition*, 1945, watercolour, crayon over graphite, ink and gouache

beach as a background for the capture of the self as an image that can only be bought for the price of accommodations: the First World human condition indeed.[19]

If the shores of Walden Pond are an inadvertently altered, though carefully managed, site of natural beauty, and if the Frenchman's Reef and Morning Star Beach Resort on St. Thomas is a giant concrete excrescence of fake luxury overrunning what was once a site of natural beauty, Rachel Whiteread's *Cabin* represents an even greater feat of human contrivance, for, unlike Walden and the site of Frenchman's Reef, the very ground on which it sits is human-made. Whiteread's *Cabin* is perched towards the top of a heap of rubble from recently demolished nearby government buildings, artificially covered with imported top soil, and planted with native grasses and shrubs. And that 70-foot-high artificial hill is itself on the part of the island that had been created as landfill in the early twentieth century. As though to echo the sheer artifice of its setting, *Cabin*, like so many of Whiteread's works—most famously her fugitive 1993 work in London, *House*—is inside out, a negative three-dimensional solid ghost of a structure that must be uninhabitable—indeed, unenterable—so its windows can give no picturesque view. Their embrasures protrude uselessly rather than recede gracefully. *Cabin* is a display as anti-display: you can only see the Statue of Liberty, New York Harbor, and the Manhattan skyline from outside *Cabin*, never framed from within.

4

Jedermann sein eigener Kurator

From Whiteread's eery *Cabin*, I turn to equally unsettling works—small oil paintings on panels—by contemporary New York artist, Maureen Gallace. Gallace deprives many of her deceptively simple beach cabins of any doors or windows. Critic Alex Jovanovich began his preview of her 2017 monographic exhibition at PS1, New York with the words, 'I would like to die inside of a Maureen Gallace painting.'[20] This portentous sentiment obliquely catches the deathlike quality of these chilly scenes, devoid of human presence. In some of her most recent diminutive works, Gallace has introduced a prospect right through each cabin, for instance in *July Beach House, 2013*, and *Beach Shack, Door, August 14, 2015* (Fig. 7). A door on the land side gives a view through what can presumably only be another door facing the ocean, but a one room cabin this size with two doors opposite each another is an absurdity among the beach shacks of the New England coastal dunes. Gallace has invented a means of turning the beach cabin into a variant of the camera obscura in which the rear door serves as a screen capturing the prospect in front of the cabin, continuous with the scene itself. Each is like a camera obscura version of Magritte's

on paper. Cleveland Museum of Art. **19** Frenchman's Reef and Morning Star Beach Resort on St. Thomas was badly damaged by Hurricanes Irma and Maria in 2017 and is currently closed pending extensive repair. **20** Jovanovich, 'Critics' Picks: New York: Maureen Gallace,' *Artforum* (posting undated): https://www.artforum.com/picks/id=68853 (last accessed 24 October 2017).

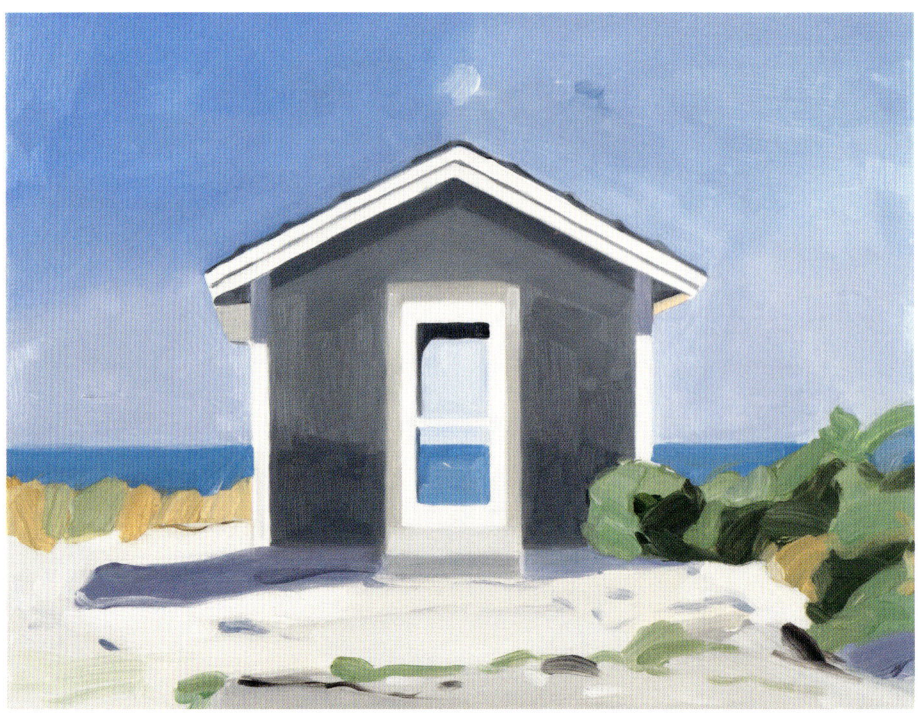

Figure 7:
Maureen Gallace, *Beach Shack, Door, Aug. 14th, 2015*,
oil on panel, 22.9 × 30.5 cm. New York, private collection.

The Human Condition, and reflects on that condition no less thoughtfully. But to pair reproductions of Gallace's *Beach Shack, Door, Aug. 14th, 2015* and Magritte's 1935 *The Human Condition* would be to do just what I described art historians as doing when they make their points about works that could—in practical terms—never be seen together, compounded by the offence of altering their relative sizes: the Gallace is far, far smaller than the Magritte.

Instead of pursuing merely clever comparisons, let us try to get an impression of just how Gallace's paintings were actually to be seen at PS1. Peter Eeley, chief curator at PS1, decided on an arrangement that, like the paintings themselves, would disconcert viewers. These tiny paintings were hung on the line, unframed, widely and evenly spaced, on white walls. The brief labels were consolidated on discreet panels with a plan of each gallery,

21 Harvard University Press Website publicity for Lubar, *Inside the Lost Museum*, 2017: http://www.hup.harvard.edu/catalog.php?isbn=9780674971042 (last accessed 14 December 2017). See also Lubar, *Inside the Lost Museum*, 2017, pp. 176–191, 'Organizations and Juxtapositions.' **22** Masthead of the Berlin Dada magazine, *Jedermann sein eigner Fussball*, 15 February 1919, with a photomontage by J. Heartfield.

and were installed well away from the individual paintings themselves, so that nothing should distract from their presence. Although the row of seventeenth-century Dutch paintings centred on Johannes Vermeer's *Geographer* in the Städel Museum is spaciously hung, it seems dense in comparison with the sparseness of the Gallace installation in PS1. Former museum curator Steven Lubar writes: 'Curators consider visitors' interactions with objects and with one another, how our bodies move through displays, how our eyes grasp objects, how we learn and how we feel.'[21] I have no doubt that Peter Eeley did just this at PS1 when installing *Maureen Gallace: Clear Day*, just as did Jochen Sander at the Städel Museum in respect of Vermeer's *Geographer* and the paintings that accompany it. Their task includes considering just about every aspect of the display of the artworks in their trust. Such senior curators do not work alone. They direct a team of curatorial colleagues, conservators, exhibition and graphic designers, preparators, installers, and lighting designers. Precision is everything. An eighth of an inch to the right or to the left can make the difference between harmonious success and complete disaster, as can the tilt of a lamp or the strength of a dimming filter inserted in it. The differential fall of light in a single gallery can lead to the need for up to four slightly different shades of a single hue on the walls in order to preserve the appearance of evenness throughout. Museum display is a highly technical and precise art that depends on the skills and experience of each member of a team of specialists coordinated by a curator. Yet many people who have never worked in a museum feel they can do it themselves, if not in a museum, then in their own domestic spaces—and—strange as it may seem—within limits they are right.

Today, everything is curated and everyone is a curator, though in much the same sense as John Heartfield in 1919 proclaimed everyone to be his own soccer ball: 'Jedermann sein eigner Fussball.'[22] Today, 'Jedermann sein eigener Kurator.' In 2010, then director of Tate Modern, London, Chris Dercon, discussed the phenomenon of how professions and the skills they represent are being undercut. He wrote: 'Today everyone is his [or her] own curator—and also master in the art of living ('Lebenskünstler'), or even more, artist of surviving ('Überlebenskünstler'). Naturally. Just as everyone blogs, so everyone has become a journalist, and everyone is also a Web designer.'[23]

We can find curated collection displays of many, many kinds in many, many places. A display of coffee pots hanging from hooks on the ceiling at a café near the Kyffhäuser Monument in Thuringia comes randomly to mind. But rather than look at a whole range of amateur collections and displays, I want to return to Maureen Gallace, for her works can lead us to a particularly widespread and poignant mode of everyday display in my own country.

23 'Heute ist jeder sein eigener Kurator—aber auch Lebenskünstler, vielmehr: Überlebenskünstler? Natürlich. So wie jedermann bloggt. Jedermann ist Journalist geworden, jedermann ist auch Webdesigner.' C. Dercon interviewed by H. Liebs, 'Das Künstlerprekariat sitzt in der Falle,' *What's Next?*, 040 (2010): http://whtsnxt.net/040 (last accessed 30 August 2017); translation by the author.

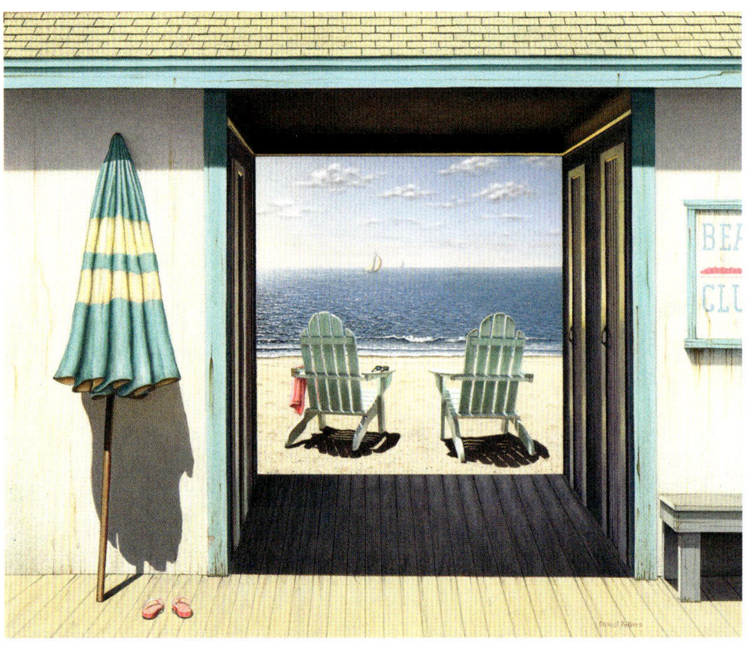

Figure 8:
Daniel Pollera, *The Beach Club*, n.d., art print, two sizes: 28 × 35.5 and 56 × 71 cm.

On seeing Gallace's paintings, few can fail to recognize an affinity with the works of one of the most admired American artists of the twentieth century, Edward Hopper. Hopper spent many summers in a dune house in Truro on the outer part of Cape Cod. But it is not with Hopper's works that I want to make a particular comparison, but rather with the work of an art historically and critically disregarded contemporary painter and print designer named Daniel Pollera (Figs. 8–9). I do so because Pollera's work is far more homey and appealing to members of a middle-brow demographic serving as their own curators, arranging such things in their own living spaces, than Hopper's disconcerting images with their elitist associations. After all, Hopper's *October on Cape Cod* fetched $9.6 million when it was auctioned in 2012. Furthermore, Pollera's works are attractive to many ordinary folks because colour prints such as *The Beach Club* and *Spring House View* focus on a widespread motif of great social significance in America: a pair of chairs arranged so that their occupants can contemplate the landscape—or seascape—before them. The arrangement connotes relaxation, tranquillity, and togetherness. The chairs concerned are not just any chairs, they are Adirondack chairs of the kind patented by Irving Wolpin in 1938, though based on an earlier design first made in 1903 and patented in 1905. Pollera makes explicit that these chairs are items, invested with the greatest imaginable sentimentality, that serve as icons of national cultural values. Even more than that, he shows in *Spring House View* that they are the chairs of patriots by showing the Stars and

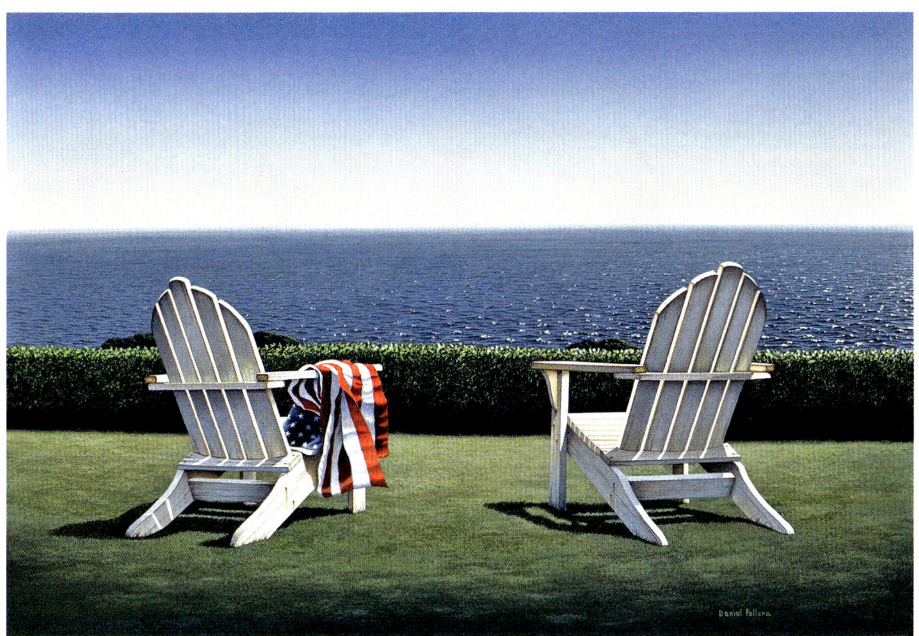

Figure 9:
Daniel Pollera, *Spring House View*, n.d., art print, dimensions vary.

Stripes casually draped over one arm. These chairs signify the American Dream, in which the perfect couple acquires the property on which to place them, and attains the tranquillity inspired by the contemplation of nature displayed just for them.

Although a traditionally conservative motif—at least since the 1940s—in these days of social change, Adirondack chairs have the great advantage of being gender neutral, so miniatures can serve as wedding cake ornaments for a couple of any kind.[24] But Adirondack chairs are markers of class as well as ideology. The rich buy Adirondack chairs made of high-density polyethylene, or sustainably harvested mahogany and eucalyptus, for around $300 each.[25] $19.99, on the other hand, buys you a somewhat flimsy version in garish plastic.[26] Note that the class coding is by colour as well as by material and construction. High end versions are either unpainted, white, or what in New England have long

24 '2 Adirondack Plain Wood Chairs and 2 Fences Cake Decorations': https://www.amazon.com/Adirondack-Plain-Chairs-Fences-Decorations/dp/B00IZIYOSI/ref=sr_1_1?ie=UTF8&qid=1508870905&sr=8-1&keywords=adirondack+chair%2BDarice (last accessed 24 October 2017). **25** For instance, at Pottery Barn, where the regular price of a 'Classic Adirondack Chair' is $312: https://www.potterybarn.com/products/pb-classic-adirondack-painted-chair/ (last accessed 24 October 2017). **26** From Ace Hardware, in ten colours: http://www.acehardware.com/product/index.jsp?productId=81344026&cp=2568443.2568445.2598565.2598660.1971658 (the purple version; last accessed 24 October 2017).

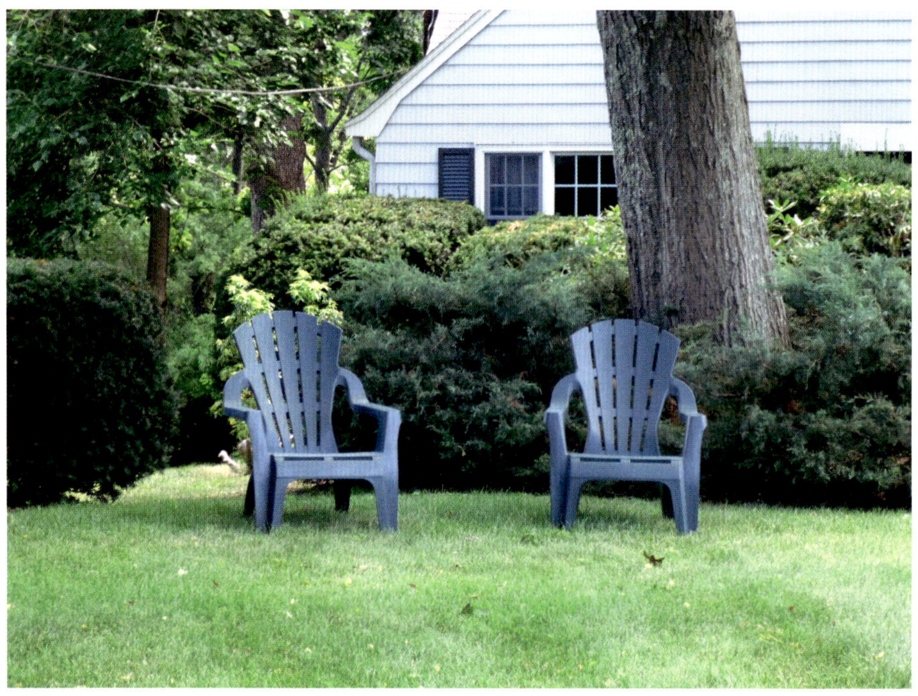

Figure 10:
Front yard with Adirondack chairs, Lexington, Massachusetts.

been called 'sad colours': muted maroon or deep green; whereas low end models are in what some might uncharitably describe as trailer trash hues—bright purple or pink—although deep green is sometimes an option.[27]

If a Pollera print featuring Adirondack chairs might form part of an interior domestic display, a pair of chairs themselves, set out in the front yard, proclaims the inhabitants' all-American values. I did not have to go far to find an example. I found a pair in a front yard about 200 yards down the street from my own house in Lexington, Massachusetts (Fig. 10). Like many other pairs of such chairs, they are arranged so that their occupants' views might converge in every sense, though they are strictly for display only, and are never to be physically occupied. They are visual synechdoches, their occupants present in spirit only. By means of their display, though, their owners proclaim to all who pass by their convergent adherence to sentimental American values until death—or divorce—do them part.

27 On 'sad colours' see Fischer, *Albion's Seed*, 1989, p. 140. **28** Gaskell (ed.), *Canopy/David Ward*, 1997; Gaskell, 'Art, Theory, Poetry,' 2014. **29** Heaney, *Human Chain*, 2010, pp. 44–45. The poem first appeared in a volume I edited—*Canopy*—and was written as a gift to David Ward, Myra Mayman, and myself.

5

Art and Actuality

From an amateur display of signifying chairs in a leafy Lexington yard, I want to turn to displays contrived by a consummate artist: not Rachel Whiteread, in front of whose *Cabin*, down the hill, stand—guess what?—a pair of Adirondack chairs. Rather, I turn in my final set of examples to artworks that directly enhance viewers' apprehension of actuality.

At the culmination of his Harvard University residency in 1994, British artist David Ward created an installation in Harvard Yard that took place between dusk and darkness each evening in mid-May. Ward suspended thirty tape players in the trees of Harvard Yard. Each played a different individual voice recorded by the artist. Each speaker told his or her own story about place—memories, poems, folk tales—or spoke passages from the English translation of Italo Calvino's book, *Le città invisibile* (1972; *Invisible Cities*, 1974). Large theatrical lights high in the neighbouring buildings gently caught the tops of the newly leafed trees, making the canopy glow as daylight faded. Beneath, listeners wandered from pool of sound to pool of sound under the trees, catching the stories told by disembodied voices. When darkness fell, the voices ceased and the lights went off. *Canopy*, as Ward named the work, was, of course, fugitive, and only an illustrated book of the same name, published in 1997, physically records some of its features.[28] *Canopy* was a display apparently of great simplicity, but actually of considerable complexity, interweaving sound, human-made landscape, light both natural and artificial, and people.

For the opening evening, David Ward contrived a further display, a fugitive artwork, *Air Waves*. The artist rented a small airplane of the kind that flies low over sporting events or above beaches, towing advertisements or greetings to loved ones. He had it tow these words into sight just as the voices began their susurrations from the trees: 'WORDS OF AIR OPEN TO THE EAR.' He had fashioned this new translation of a fragment of Sappho's verse for a novel setting: the sky above the canopy of trees in Harvard Yard. Ward and I watched this aerial revelation with our mutual friend, the Irish poet Seamus Heaney. When it appeared, the three of us turned to each other in delight. It was as though the ancient Greek poet herself was circling above, intervening through the most banal yet spectacular of media. Later, Heaney contributed a poem to the book on the project, which he subsequently included in his last collection, *Human Chain* (2010). In his words:

> It was like a recording of
> tree congregations stirring,
> giving thanks for the summer.
> [...] People were cocking their ears,
> gathering, quietening,
> stepping on to the grass,
> stopping and holding hands.
> Earth was replaying its tapes,
> words being given new airs.[29]

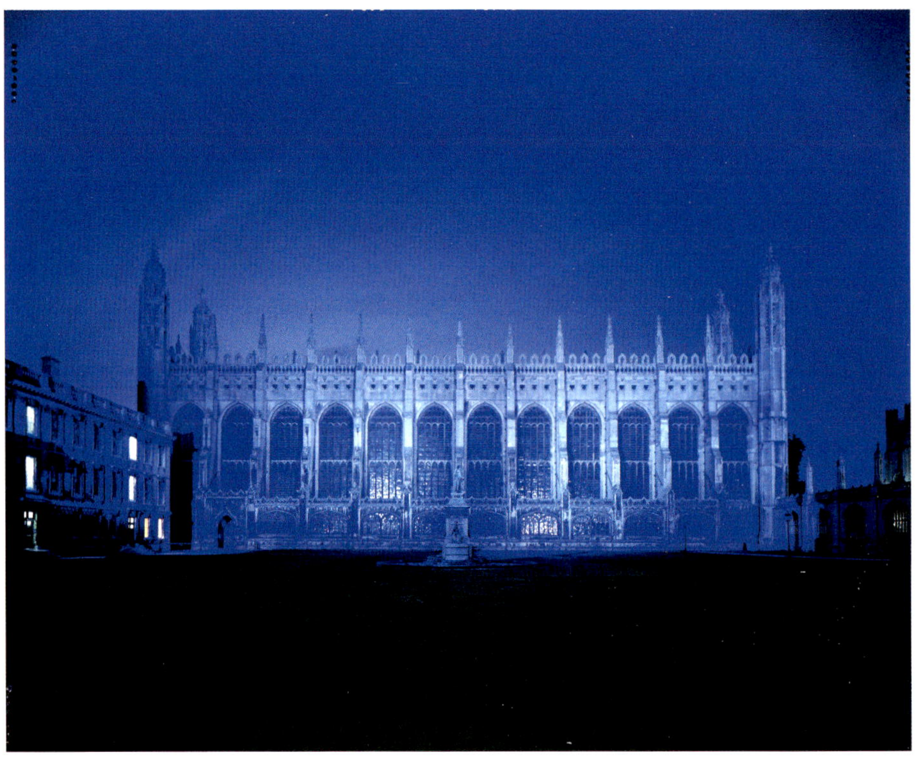

Figure 11:
David Ward, *Cast*, 1991, light projected onto the chapel of King's College, Cambridge.

David Ward's artwork—his display—incorporating poetry and poetic prose, had in turn inspired a great poet to make verse that could otherwise not exist. I doubt that there ever is an end to artworks, however fugitive, whose lives are prolonged through their capacity to prompt new work. Although this can occur as artworks and theory give rise to and shape one another, just as satisfying—if not more so—is the aesthetic charge that flows between artwork and poetry. That charge exceeds what the philosopher Jacques Derrida termed the 'thematics and semantics' of meaning, constituting an aesthetic excess, which, he acknowledged, 'provokes discourse *ad infinitum*.'[30]

Finally, I want to bring things back to Cambridge, England, for David Ward was invited to Harvard, in Cambridge, Massachusetts, on the strength of the success of his residency there in 1991. Its culmination was a display that temporarily transformed one of the most notable buildings in Cambridge: King's College Chapel (Fig. 11). Ward arranged for the most powerful theatrical lamps, called—for good reason—brutes, to shine blue light from the Wilkins Building across the court onto the south façade of the chapel in the early evening. At first, sunlight made the blue tint on the stonework scarcely perceptible, but as the sun set and daylight slowly faded, blue took over, accentuating the sense of change—the sky seemed to turn green at one point—giving viewers an alarming intimation of the turning of the Earth. Then the sky was dark and King's College Chapel was evenly and unnaturally quite blue. At that moment the lights went off, and before one's eyes could adjust, all was utterly dark. This display was far more intense than any laser light show. I recall feeling in 1991 that my world had changed, so intensely was I aware of the vertiginous movement of the Earth through space, and its mutability at every moment. Ward repeated the work eight years later, in 2003.

Cast radically undercut the stability of the external scene—cityscape, landscape, seascape—on a huge scale. Paradoxically, such an artwork demonstrates that any distinction between art and the rest of the world dissolves in the process of its making and display. Not only do we realize that display—whether ostensibly static (which no display can be) or performative—never occurs in isolation, but, more broadly, that nothing shown to us—nothing humans view—is isolated, ultimately, from the turning of the Earth.

6
Agency?—Beware!

Where is agency in all this? The agency of humans who contrive displays such as we have been examining is different in kind from the actions attributable to natural forces, such as the world turning on its axis, and different again from the agency ascribed to inanimate things as a way of articulating the otherwise apparently inexplicable effects they appear to have on humans. Agency is a term subject to what Willard Quine terms semantic ascent.[31] As Ian Hacking points out, such terms work at a level different from that of words for objects in the world. He calls them 'elevator words.'[32] One of their key characteristics is that they exhibit instability of sense, making them difficult to use accurately and consistently. All too often, careless thinkers elide the distinctions among the various senses of what is actually not a single predicate but a number of them identically termed, leading to the erroneous assumption that their respective properties are interchangeable.[33] King's College Chapel cannot exhibit agency in respect of David Ward or anyone else who views it when turning blue in the same sense that David Ward can exhibit agency when he turns King's College Chapel blue.

If agency is many things—some, at least, presumably mutually incompatible in their signification—for now we may only be able to point out, not what agency might be in totality, but what is not agency. Mutability is not agency. 'The unimaginable touch of Time,' to use William Wordsworth's words, is not agency: it is metaphor in the form of a residual personification.[34] Agency might at times be literal, and at times metaphorical to

30 Derrida, quoted in Brunette and Wills, 'The Spatial Arts,' 1994, p. 17; quoted in Holly, *The Melancholy Art*, 2013, p. 111. **31** Quine, *Word and Object*, 1960, passim. **32** Hacking, *The Social Construction of What?*, 1999, pp. 22–24. **33** I repeat this claim from my 'Diptychs—What's the Point?,' 2006. **34** Wordsworth, 'Mutability,' 1822; Hutchinson (ed.), *Ecclesiastical Sonnets*, 1974 [1904], Part 3, 34, p. 353.

the point of catachresis; that is, users of the term can find no literal alternative to denote the phenomenon in question so adopt a term for something else and apply it metaphorically. Simultaneously, I acknowledge the agency of certain things in terms derived from the predominant usage of a community that invests those things with agency as part of its belief system. For instance, such things can have agency in the sense of having properties associated with volitionally imbued beings: Orthodox icons, for example, or Māori *taonga*. I do so in accordance with principles articulated within feminist standpoint epistemology and Indigenous standpoint theory.[35] Indeed, such is the complexity of agency as a variety of literally, metaphorically, and catachrestically related phenomena that scholars are beginning to avoid the term.[36]

7
Envoi

In chasing display across the art world, and in the sand dunes, backwoods, and backyards of New England, we have seen distinctions between art and the rest of the world lose coherence and relevance. It seems fitting, therefore, that I should give the final word not to a New Englander, but to the seventeenth-century Chinese poet, Zhang Dai, one of many over the centuries who has contemplated the celebrated 'Ten Scenes of West Lake' at Hangzhou, marked by stelae and shoreline pavilions. In such places, humans may contrive a display, but in doing so they demonstrate that any distinction between art and the rest of the world dissolves in the process. Zhang Dai expressed it thus in a poem on West Lake, *Glow of Sunset upon Thunder Peak*:

> The ruined pagoda at home on the banks of the lake,
> Shambolic as a drunken old man.
> Extraordinary feelings are to be found here amidst the shards,
> What need does it have for the arts of man?[37]

35 See, in the first instance: Harding, *The Feminist Standpoint*, 2004, passim. **36** At the symposium, *Conserving Active Matter*, at Bard Graduate Center, New York City (27–28 November 2017) at which historians, Indigenous scholars, materials scientists, and philosophers spoke, the term *agency* was not used once in the nineteen papers delivered, nor in discussion. **37** 'Ten Scenes of West Lake: Poems by Zhang Dai,' trans. by D. Campbell, *China Heritage Quarterly*, 28 (2011): http://www.chinaheritagequarterly.org/features.php?searchterm=028_poems.inc&issue=028 (last accessed 17 March 2017). I am grateful to Gao Shiming and Cao Yiqiang for their kind invitation to the China Academy of Art, Hangzhou in fall 2016.

Bibliography

B. Atkinson (ed.), *Walden and Other Writings of Henry David Thoreau* (The Modern Library, 1992).

P. Brunette and D. Wills, 'The Spatial Arts: An Interview with Jacques Derrida' in P. Brunette and D. Wills (eds.), *Deconstruction and the Visual Arts: Art, Media, Architecture* (Cambridge University Press, 1994), pp. 9–32.

J. Derrida, *La vérité en peinture* (Flammarion, 1978).

J. Dewey, *Art As Experience* (Minton, Balch & Co., 1934).

J. Dewey and A. C. Barnes et al., *Art and Education* (Barnes Foundation Press, 1947 [1929]).

D. H. Fischer, *Albion's Seed: Four British Folkways in America* (Oxford University Press, 1989).

A. Gell, *Art and Agency. An Anthropological Theory* (Clarendon Press, 1998).

I. Gaskell (ed.), *Canopy/David Ward/A Work for Voice and Light in Harvard Yard: With a Poem by Seamus Heaney and Texts by Parveen Adams and Ivan Gaskell* (Harvard University Arts Museums & The Office for the Arts, 1997).

I. Gaskell, 'Diptychs—What's the Point?,' *Journal of Aesthetics and Art Criticism*, 64 (2006), pp. 325–332.

I. Gaskell, 'Museums and Philosophy—Of Art, and Many Other Things,' *Philosophy Compass*, 7 (2012), pp. 74–102.

I. Gaskell, 'Art, Theory, Poetry, and an Airplane Above Some Trees,' *Brooklyn Rail* (February 2014), pp. 8–10.

I. Gaskell, 'The Museum of Big Ideas' in V. S. Harrison, A. Bergqvist and G. Kemp (eds.), *Philosophy and Museums: Essays on the Philosophy of Museums* (Cambridge University Press, 2016), pp. 55–75.

I. Hacking, *The Social Construction of What?* (Harvard University Press, 1999).

S. Harding (ed.), *The Feminist Standpoint Theory Reader* (Routledge, 2004).

S. Heaney, *Human Chain* (Faber & Faber, 2010).

M. A. Holly, *The Melancholy Art* (Princeton University Press, 2013).

T. Hutchinson (ed.), *Ecclesiastical Sonnets in Wordsworth: Poetical Works*, revised by E. de Selincourt (Oxford University Press, 1974 [1904]).

B. Latour, *Reassembling the Social. An Introduction to Actor-Network-Theory* (Oxford University Press, 2005).

E. Lemire, *Black Walden: Slavery and its Aftermath in Concord, Massachusetts* (University of Pennsylvania Press, 2009).

S. Lubar, *Inside the Lost Museum: Curating, Past and Present* (Harvard University Press, 2017).

M. Maek-Gérard (ed.), *Johannes Vermeer: der Geograph und der Astronom nach 200 Jahren wieder vereint* (Städtische Galerie im Städelschen Kunstinstitut Frankfurt am Main, 1997).

W. V. Quine, *Word and Object* (M.I.T. Press, 1960).

H. Repton, *Fragments on the Theory and Practice of Landscape Gardening* (T. Bensley & son for J. Taylor, 1816).

R. W. Robbins, *Discovery at Walden* (The Thoreau Society, 1999 [Barnstead & Son, 1947]).

H. D. Thoreau, *Walden; Or Life in the Woods* (Ticknor & Fields, 1854).

W. Wordsworth, 'Mutability' in W. Wordsworth, *The Poetical Works of William Wordsworth* (Longman, Hurst, Rees, Orme & Brown, 1827 [first published in *Ecclesiastical Sketches* (Longman, Hurst, Rees, Orme & Brown, 1822)]), vol. 3, p. 431.

Websites:
http://www.acehardware.com/product/index.jsp?productId=81344026&cp=2568443.2568445.2598565.2598660.1971658.

https://www.amazon.com/Adirondack-Plain-Chairs-Fences-Decorations/dp/B00IZIYOSI/ref=sr_1_1?ie=UTF8&qid=1508870905&sr=8-1&keywords=adirondack+chair%2BDarice.

https://www.artforum.com/picks/id=68853.

https://www.barnesfoundation.org/whats-on/collection.

http://www.capabilitybrown.org/event/landscape-lancelot-capability-brown-alnwick-castle.

http://www.chinaheritagequarterly.org/features.php?searchterm=028_poems.inc&issue=028.

http://colonialmexicoinsideandout.blogspot.com/2017/07/new-mexican-gem-of-taos-high-road.html.

http://www.hup.harvard.edu/catalog.php?isbn=9780674971042.

https://www.potterybarn.com/products/pb-classic-adirondack-painted-chair.

http://whtsnxt.net/040.

ELSJE VAN KESSEL

The Street as Frame: Corpus Christi Processions in Lisbon prior to João V

In early modern Europe, art was not only displayed in houses, palaces, galleries and churches, but also taken outside into the street. The architecture, paintings, sculptures, tapestries, banners, silverwork, and precious clothing that were the materials of festival culture could be purpose-made, but could also be given on loan or rented out. Indeed, pre-existing paintings, sculptures, textiles and other forms of visual art were commonly taken outside on such occasions, loaned by their upperclass owners, or leased by businesses that existed for this purpose. As Thomas Crow pointed out, the most important example of the display of the arts in the street Europe-wide (and we might add worldwide) was the feast of Corpus Christi. As he put it: it 'is the feast during which the church is, in effect, turned inside-out.'[1] Focussing on these religious festivals in the little-studied case of early modern Lisbon, I will aim in this paper to examine what happened when these objects were taken off their pedestals, so to speak, into the outdoors. How did art objects function with the street as framing device?

Portuguese festivals have, of course, been the object of extensive study, and I build on this body of work here, including Fernando Checa Cremades's and Laura Fernández-González's work on Spanish Habsburg festivals, and Teofilo Ruiz's book *The King Travels*.[2] The urbanism of early modern Lisbon has recently proven to be a fruitful field of investigation, and I want to mention especially Annemarie Jordan Gschwend's and Kate Lowe's *The Global City: On the Streets of Renaissance Lisbon*, which has been crucial in furthering our understanding of the cosmopolitan nature and vibrant street life of the largest city in

1 The research presented in this chapter was made possible by a Research Grant for Foreigners from the Fundação Calouste Gulbenkian. I thank CHAM – Center for the Humanities at the Universidade Nova de Lisboa for their hospitality while I carried out my project. Crow, *Painters and Public Life*, 1985, p. 82.
2 Checa Cremades and Fernández-González (eds.), *Festival Culture*, 2015; Ruiz, *A King Travels*, 2012. See further, among others: Castel-Branco Pereira et al. (eds.), *A arte efémera em Portugal*, 2000; Ferreira, *Os têxteis chineses em Portugal*, 2011; Paiva, 'As festas de corte em Portugal,' 2002; Torres Megiani, *O rei ausente*, 2004; Vale et al. (eds.), *Lisboa e a festa*, 2009.

Portugal.[3] This scholarship has enabled me to incorporate Lisbon into my wider research on the display of art in the early modern street.

The subject of this paper may seem to be familiar: ephemeral art, or the art of festivals. However, I believe that these categories are not very helpful for the problems that concern me, and that this volume addresses. All too often, the ephemeral art of festivals and permanent art such as easel paintings and sculptures are studied as separate phenomena, while they were in fact so much interlinked that such a separation is difficult to maintain. We know, of course, that the most prominent artists were involved in the making of festivals, and that these displayed similar stylistic trends as did permanent art. However, what has received markedly less attention is the ubiquitous use of existing art objects within festivals, objects that would temporarily move into the streets, and later be returned to their owners. Conversely, permanent art was much less permanent than we might think. Even within the palaces and churches that housed them, works of art would be moved around, ornamented, covered and uncovered, kissed and touched constantly.[4] Until well into the eighteenth century, artworks were not necessarily made to be hung on a wall and silently contemplated. Even Goethe argued for the importance of keeping art collections moving and changing, lest they turn into graveyards.[5] What I am interested in, then, is the constantly changing nature of display in the early modern period, and from this perspective, the category of ephemeral art obscures rather than enlightens.

In this paper I will analyse the display of art objects in Corpus Christi processions on the streets of sixteenth- and seventeenth-century Lisbon, and ask how their framing in this particular setting impacted their agency. An important concept in this analysis will be *presence*, primarily as it is developed in the work of literary theorist and philosopher Hans Ulrich Gumbrecht. This volume sets out to approach the expressiveness of objects not in semiotic terms, nor as a power inherent in the object itself, but rather by proposing a third way: namely, to focus on the object's *situation*. As I will demonstrate, presence is well-suited to tackle the object's *being situated*, as it aims to be an alternative to semiosis, and moves away from the object towards the *interaction* between object and recipient. If my case study of Portuguese processions is to lead me to reflect on the implications of a presence-based approach to the display of art in Portugal more broadly, a first step has to be to examine the background and origins of the idea of presence itself.

3 Jordan Gschwend and Lowe (eds.), *The Global City*, 2015. See also the exhibition catalogue: Jordan Gschwend and Lowe (eds.), *The Global City*, 2017. **4** See: van Kessel, *The Lives of Paintings*, 2017. **5** Goethe, 'Winckelmann und sein Jahrhundert,' 1988 [1805], p. 368. **6** Gumbrecht, 'Epiphany of Form,' 1999. See also: Cruz Santo, 'Unidade e diversidade,' 2001. **7** Gumbrecht, 'Epiphany of Form,' 1999, p. 355. See also: Gumbrecht, *Production of Presence*, 2004. **8** For Ankersmit's engagement with the concept of 'presence' in and beyond Gumbrecht's work, see: 'Presence and Myth,' 2006, as well as other publications.

Meaning and Presence

Gumbrecht formulated his ideas on presence in, among other publications, an essay from 1999 titled 'On the Beauty of Team Sports,' in which he searched for a critical concept with which to analyse the attraction of sports in contemporary culture.[6] Most concepts in the humanities, he points out, are hermeneutic: they deal with the analysis of meaning, signification, mimesis, and representation. Yet to come to terms with the power team sports hold over many of us, such concepts are insufficient. This is where Gumbrecht brings in the notion of presence: derived from the Latin *producere,* the production of presence means 'putting things into reach so that they can be touched.'[7] Presence thus has much to do with spatial proximity. It is an effect that watching a sports game, reading a literary text, or seeing a work of art can have on us: different as these cultural phenomena may be, they have in common that they can touch us physically and emotionally to the point where there is temporarily no boundary between ourselves and the thing.

Gumbrecht's most important reference for the production of presence in Western culture is the Catholic understanding of the Eucharist. The Eucharist is not a case of mimesis, for the host is not the signifier, and Christ is not the signified. Rather, Christ is *present in* the host, he *is* the host, and the faithful share in his presence by participating in the ritual of the Mass. The eating of Christ's body is, of course, an ultimate example of presence. Gumbrecht draws further parallels with the medieval theatre, which depended on audience participation, and, also like sports, was not structured by content-based plots but rather by loose choreographies.

For the modern mind it is difficult to think in terms of the kind of presence produced by the Eucharist. Since the Reformation, signification always imposes itself upon us, as Frank Ankersmit explains, and it becomes nearly impossible to imagine the bread as partaking in God, rather than merely signifying him.[8] To a modern subject, the experience of presence can only be fleeting. Presence itself is a modern concept that *we* need in order to begin to understand something that to medieval people was entirely self-evident.

In this paper I examine the usefulness of this idea of presence in making sense of the display of art in Portuguese processions, and in particular that of Corpus Christi. In doing so I may be seen to commit circular reasoning: I seek to apply a concept inspired by the Eucharist, back onto the Eucharistic practice of the procession. However, I think that, precisely because presence is a contemporary concept, it can help to articulate things that would otherwise remain under the radar. Furthermore, it strikes me that it is extremely relevant to display and the agency of the frame: presence is emphatically about situations, convergences between things and viewers, and as such is an alternative not only to language-based models (that see agency as exclusive to human subjects) but also to mystical takes on agency that attribute it exclusively to objects.

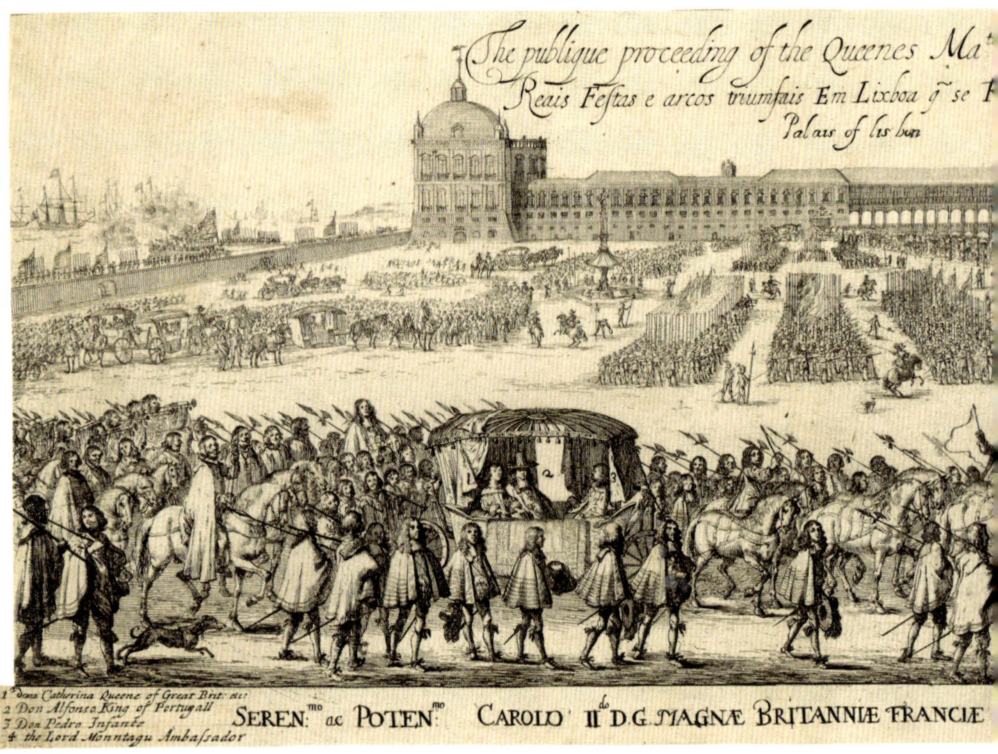

Figure 1:
Dirk Stoop, *The publique proceeding of the Queenes Majestie of Greate Britaine through the City of Lisbone the 20th day of Aprill 1662*, 1662, etching on paper, 18.2 × 55 cm. Amsterdam, Rijksmuseum.

Corpus Christi: The Festival and Its Sources

Before we take a closer look at the kind of art produced for and carried in processions, I want to stress the importance of processions in Portuguese religious and political life of the period. An important source is Inácio Barbosa de Machado's *História Critico-Chronologica de Instituiçam da Festa, Procissam, e Officio do Corpo Santissimo de Christo No Veneravel Sacramento da Eucharistia [...]* (Critical-Chronological History of the Institution of the Festival, Procession, and Mass of the Holiest Body of Christ in the Venerable Sacrament of the Eucharist).[9] Machado, a prominent historian and magistrate, wrote this book for king João V in 1719, the year the Corpus Christi procession was dramatically transformed and which therefore stands as a natural ending point for my inquiry. The author is keen on stressing the importance of the ritual to the Portuguese people: '[O]ur fervour and devotion for the cult of the Sacrament are such that without exaggeration one can affirm that in this aspect of Religion Portugal exceeds all the Provinces of the world.'[10] Lisbon's Municipal Chamber, the country's monarchs and their chroniclers all took a strong pride

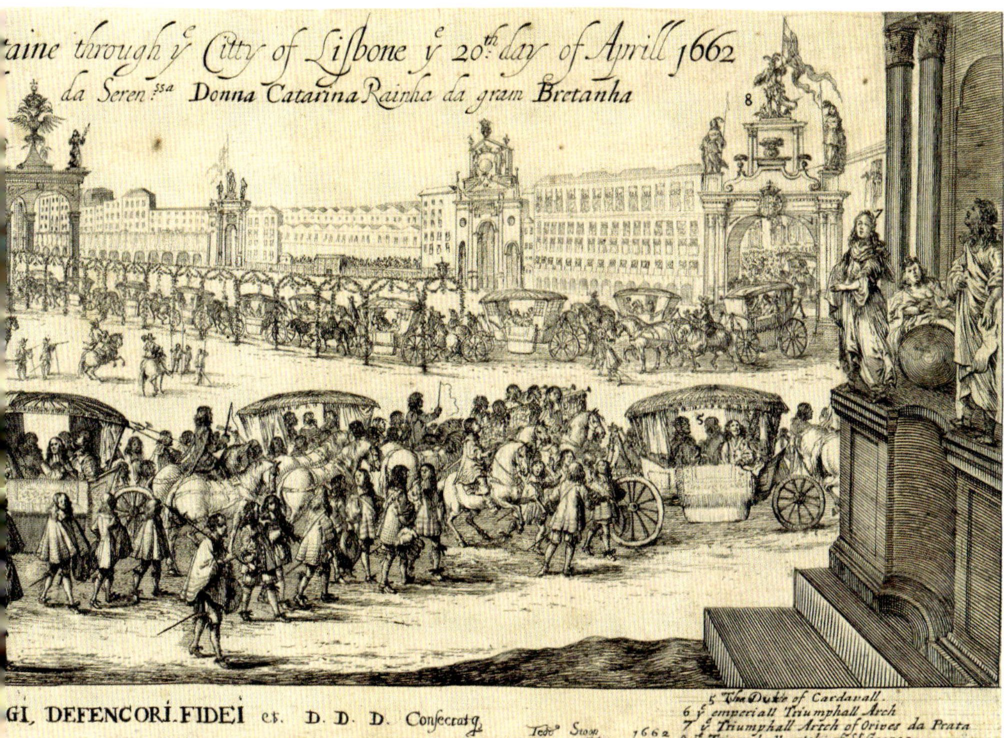

in the tradition of processions, with Corpus Christi prime among them, and they considered their lavish and devout character typical of their country and its capital. Accounts of foreign visitors are also insightful. The Italian witness Giovanni Battista Confalonieri, who spent three years in Lisbon at the end of the sixteenth century and wrote an elaborate description of the city, was generally underwhelmed by Lisbon's art and architecture, but devoted considerable attention to describing and analysing various processions, which, he said, the people of Lisbon loved and on which they spent large sums of money.[11] King Philip II of Spain, who was also king Philip I of Portugal, surely got his share of processions and other festivals touring the various corners of his realm, yet he remarked in a private letter to his daughters that the Corpus Christi procession in Lisbon surpassed his already high expectations.[12]

Next to the ample quantity of textual sources for the festival, the scarcity of visual representations stands out. There is not a single image that depicts the Corpus Christi procession in Lisbon before the eighteenth century (and even after there are very few).

9 Machado, *História Critico-Cronologica*, 1759. **10** Machado, *História Critico-Cronologica*, 1759, p. 128. **11** Confalonieri, *Grandezza et magnificenza*, 2005, p. 216. **12** Bouza Álvarez et al. (eds.), *Cartas para duas infantas meninas*, 1999, p. 161. See also: Ruiz, *A King Travels*, 2012.

This is remarkable in comparison with the situation in other European urban centres, where rituals and spectacles were often depicted, especially in the medium of print. Of the few known representations of processions, court ceremonies and spectacles, many were made by foreign, northern artists, a dominant presence in Lisbon's artistic scene, such as a series of prints by Dirk Stoop (for example, Fig. 1).[13] Despite the small scale of Portugal's early modern art world overall, the absence of Corpus Christi in paintings and prints remains enigmatic.

During the long scope of my research—the sixteenth and seventeenth centuries—the feast of Corpus Christi endured, while political and economic circumstances changed. Most important among these were the various changes of royal power: for a period of sixty years (1580–1640), Portugal was ruled by the Spanish Habsburgs; this so-called Union of the Crowns began and ended in war and was marked by economic decline.[14] Another dominant factor was Portugal's vast overseas empire, which reached its zenith around 1600; in subsequent decades, particularly in Asia, the Portuguese gradually lost their grip on sea routes and trading posts.[15] Commentators on Corpus Christi globally have pointed out that it was the occasion *par excellence* to connect the worldly authority of government with the spiritual authority of the Eucharist; it has also been stressed how popular the feast was in Iberian colonial contexts, where the feast negotiated the relation of the colony to the metropole and of the colonizer to the colonized.[16] In Lisbon, Corpus Christi similarly was a festival that could be adapted to the circumstances with some flexibility. Rather than as a reflection of a given context, I see it as a material and social agent that could intervene in political, economic, or social developments.

What did a typical Corpus Christi procession look like? Documentary sources convey that the starting point of the procession was the Sé (the cathedral), from where the *cortège* would slowly make its way through the city's narrow medieval streets westward. It would pass through the Rua Nova dos Mercadores, the city's main commercial artery, the widest street in Lisbon at the time, and regarded by many as its most beautiful.[17] In some years, the ending point was the convent of São Domingos at the northern end of Rossio Square, while in others the procession returned to the Sé, ending where it had begun. The *cortège* would have been roughly divided into two parts: first came the more playful elements, including the so-called inventions produced by the city's artisans; then came the more solemn elements, heralded by the image of St George, Lisbon's patron saint, and culminating in the Holy Sacrament itself, carried in a precious ark under a canopy. It is not easy to sum up all the things a viewer of the time would have seen, heard, and smelled: a parade of a few thousand people, many in precious dress, walking, dancing, making music;

13 For representations of Lisbon, see also: Jordan Gschwend and Lowe, 'A representação da Lisboa global,' 2017. **14** Curto, *A cultura política*, 2011. **15** The literature on this topic is vast. See especially: Pinto, *The Portuguese and the Straits of Melaka*, 2012; Subrahmanyam, *The Portuguese Empire in Asia*, 1993. **16** Muir, *Ritual in Early Modern Europe*, 1997, p. 74 and further; Cruz Santo, 'Unidade e diversidade,' 2001; Dean, *Inka Bodies and the Body of Christ*, 1999. **17** Jordan Gschwend, 'Reconstructing the Rua Nova,' 2015, p. 109.

banners, burning torches, carts with scenes presenting religious mysteries, figures of demons, dragons, giants, war machinery, ships, a sculpture of the city's patron saint on the back of an actual horse, surrounded by a group of equally mounted boypages; silver crosses, more torches, and eventually God himself, in the form of the host. This short enumeration excludes the decoration of the streets and buildings on the route, enriched with temporary arches, flowers, and precious textiles.[18]

The Limits of Meaning

In trying to make sense of the multifaceted artwork that was the Portuguese procession, as well as of the individual objects that were its components, we might seek recourse to textual interpretations and propose a critical reading. Of course, this will get us somewhere. The most promising strategy here is to examine descriptions of the processions from the period in which they were held. A festival booklet like the one published for a procession held in 1582 (the same one witnessed by king Philip II) proves to be helpful.[19] Written by a Spanish courtier, Isidro Velázquez Salmantino, this account models the procession on the history of salvation, beginning with the Fall of the Rebel Angels and taking the reader from the Old Covenant, via the New Covenant, to the history of the Catholic Church.[20] On the basis of this text, the procession appears as a conventional Christian world history in which the Catholic faith triumphs over evil. Within this framework, the role of art objects such as sculptures of saints and carts with paintings and *tableaux vivants*, is to narrate this story.

However, even in the textual source itself there are elements that do not so easily fit this approach. Isidro Velázquez's account is a hundred and eighty pages long and only a part of these recount the history of salvation. Many more evoke the lavish outfits worn by saintly statues and human participants alike. These extensive descriptions of clothes and jewellery appear elusive if exclusively addressed in terms of narrative content. For instance, the figure of Abel, son of Adam and Eve, impersonated by a boy, was dressed in what Velázquez describes as a pastoral outfit, to which he nevertheless devotes over a page: according to the account the boy wore a robe made of white velvet decorated with gold and pearls all over, a chain with a particularly large pearl on his chest, a hat made out of the same white velvet and ornamented with gold, precious stones, pearls, and boots likewise covered in pearls, whereby the white colour of the outfit as a whole apparently demonstrated the boy's youthful innocence.[21] These and many other lengthy, highly evocative passages on outfits and accessories go beyond signification in making present to the reader, within the limitations of language, the rich effects of precious fabrics and stones.

18 This overview is based on: Confalonieri, *Grandezza et magnificenza*, 2005, pp. 216–220 and pp. 232–234; and Oliveira, *Elementos*, 1882–1911, vol. 1, pp. 421–429. **19** Velázquez, *La orden*, 1582. See also the shortened Portuguese edition of da Silva, *Relaçam da solemne procissam do Corpo de Deos*, 1731. For an elaborate analysis of Velázquez's account see my article in preparation 'The Making of a Hybrid Body.' **20** Velázquez, *La orden*, 1582. **21** Velázquez, *La orden*, 1582, pp. 34r–35r.

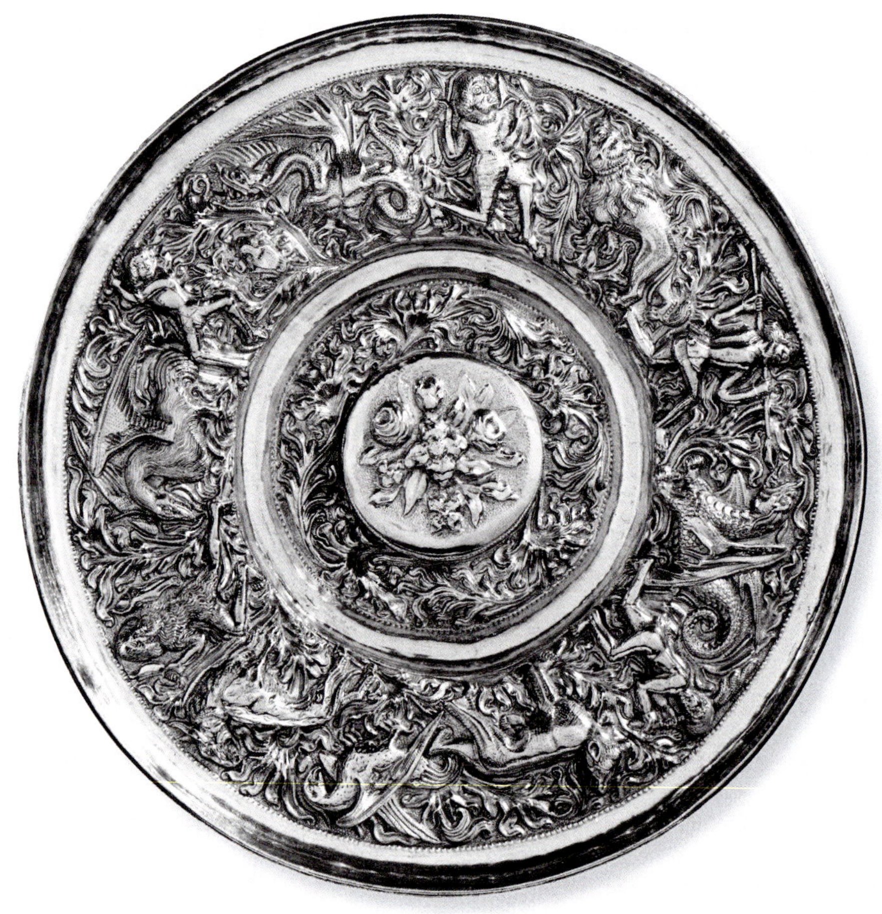

Figure 2:
Porto, *Dish*, c. 1480–1499, silver-gilt, d. 25 cm. London, Victoria & Albert Museum.

Dances and Dishes

Zooming out, as it were, and looking at Lisbon's Corpus Christi tradition over a longer period of time, a more traditional quest for its meaning similarly fails to help us understand the full import of this artwork. Other commentators have pointed out as much. Diogo Ramada Curto, for example, addresses the frequent reuse of certain forms and acts within Portugal's festive tradition, and asks what implications this reuse has for the signification of these elements.[22] I want to take a closer look at some examples here. Singled out by Curto are the dances that were a standard ingredient of Portuguese festivals, including: Corpus Christi and other annually returning processions; the Carnival; incidental celebrations of saints and martyrs; and festivals in celebration of the monarchy.[23] Authorities, participants and spectators alike considered the dances a crucial ingredient of the Portuguese tradition, if a much contested one (in fact, they were common in Iberian festivals broadly speaking). There were times when their elimination was attempted, because of their unorthodox and potentially lascivious nature.[24] In Corpus Christi, they would typically be located at the beginning of the *cortège*, and would be accompanied by loud music produced by string instruments, trumpets and drums; the dancers would also sing, in loud and high-pitched voices.[25] These dances, mainly the *mourisca*, *pela*, and *folia*, would depend on and display the participation of various ethnic groups.[26] Foreign eyewitnesses often described the dances as wild and speculated on the madness and inebriation of the performers.[27]

These events are evidently lost forever, but traces of them remain in objects with which they shared iconographies. We can get an idea of what this part of the procession looked like from Portuguese silverwork of the period, in particular a group of salvers. To discuss but one of these (Fig. 2): a circular silver dish embossed with two bands of foliage, wherein the outer band contains figures of wildmen hunting ferocious beasts. Armed with spears and the like, they are confronted with lions, dragons and other fearful animals and monsters that appear in the midst of the vegetation. Indeed, surrounding all other creatures are plants, their lush leaves suggested by generous lobes of silver and creating a sense of restless movement that is further enhanced by the circular, unending shape of the dish. This sculpted parade reflects the dances within Iberian festivals: the wildmen were a popular feature that could represent the other, that is, the exotic, mythical creatures from far-away parts of the world, but could also represent the evil, the chaotic, the primordial within oneself.[28] The wild dances and accompanying uplifting music were less about the coherent narration of a story and more about creating atmosphere, excitement and a temporary loss of self, as this silver dish illustrates, facilitating a situation in which boundaries between individuals dissolved and a collective emerged.

Used in the nobility's ritual of the tasting of the wine, the silver salvers invited associations with the domain of Dionysos, yet they, like the dances within the feast of Corpus Christi, also had Eucharistic connotations. This is beautifully shown in a painting of the *Last Supper* by Gregório Lopes, where a scene in the background depicts a salver in use (Fig. 3).[29] A second salver, only half visible, is put on display and stands out against an opulent red wall hanging. The circular shape of the dish, which, of course, mirrors the

22 Curto, *A cultura política*, 2011, p. 106. **23** Curto, *A cultura política*, 2011, p. 106. **24** Ribeiro (ed.), *Dissertações chronologicas e criticas*, 1810–1836, vol. 4, part 2, pp. 199–201. See also: Oliveira, *Elementos*, 1882–1911, vol. 11, p. 193. **25** Bouza Álvarez et al. (eds.), *Cartas para duas infantas meninas*, 1999, p. 154; Confalonieri, *Grandezza et magnificenza*, 2005, pp. 216–217. **26** See: Tinhorão, *Os negros em Portugal*, 1988, p. 154 onwards. **27** Confalonieri, *Grandezza et magnificenza*, 2005, pp. 218–219; Sassetti, *Lettere da vari paesi*, 1970, pp. 232–233. **28** D'Orey (ed.), *Inventário do Museu Nacional de Arte Antiga*, 1995, pp. 140–155. **29** D'Orey (ed.), *Inventário do Museu Nacional de Arte Antiga*, 1995, pp. 140–155.

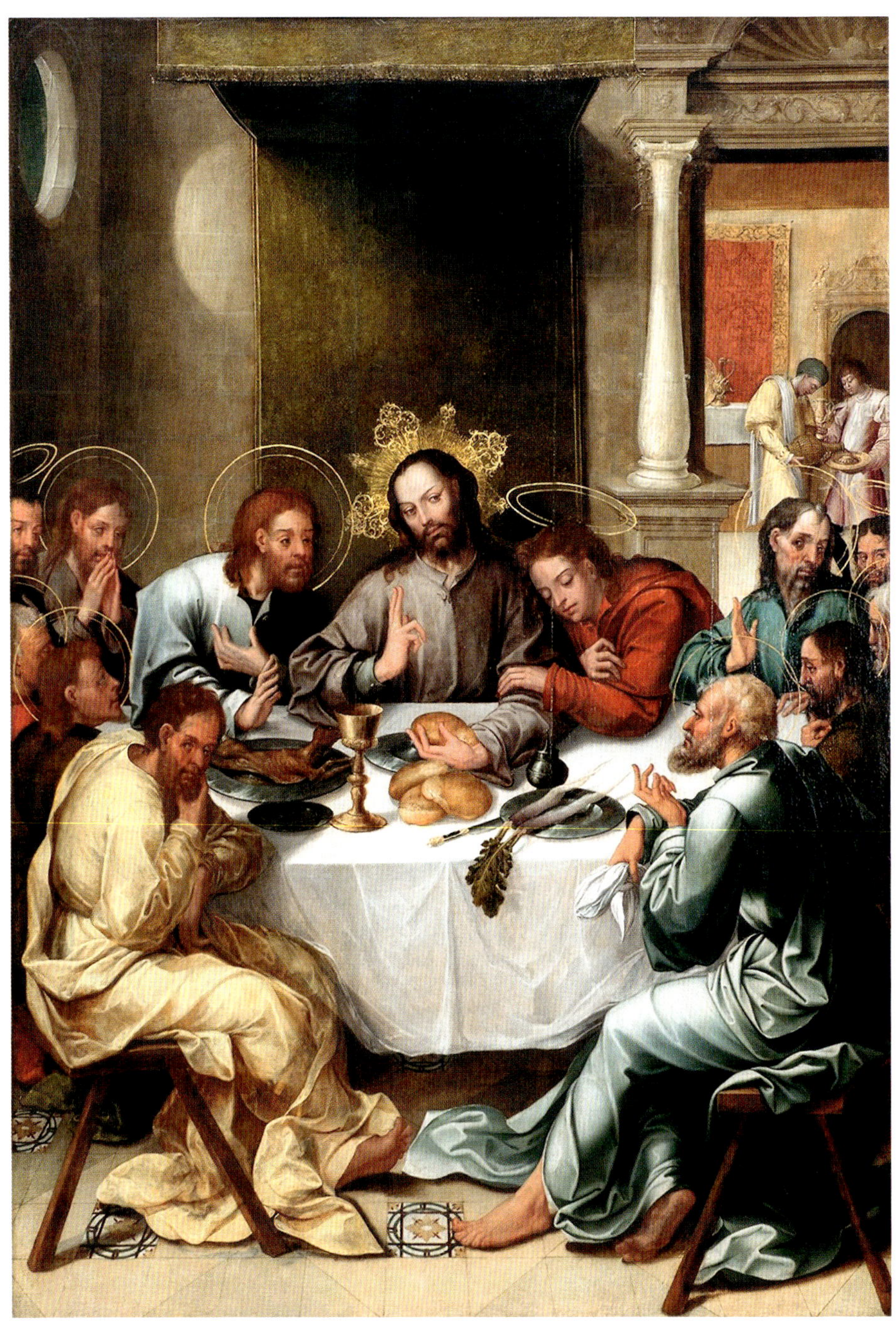

Figure 3:
Gregório Lopes, *The Last Supper*, c. 1520–1530, oil on wood, 170 × 125.5 cm.
Tomar, Igreja de São João Batista.

shape of the host, returns everywhere in the painting: there are the haloes of the apostles, the light projected on to the wall by the circular window, the plates on the table, the bread, the decorated floor tiles, and the circular arrangement of the apostles. The shape of the circle is the communion with the divine, like a procession that ends where it began and that embraces everyone.

Textiles

The wall hanging in Lopes's painting, of what looks like precious red with gold-rimmed silk damask, brings me to another element of Portuguese festivals that is difficult to understand in terms of signification, and easier to grasp when thinking in terms of efficacy and presence: textiles. To describe hangings, precious clothing and other uses of textiles as mere 'decoration' would be misguided. I have already mentioned Velázquez's interest in clothing in his festival account, and there are many other sources pointing to the crucial role of textiles. Perhaps the best-known illustration of the presence of textiles in processions is the panel *The Arrival of the Relics of St Auta at the Convent of Madre de Deus* (Lisbon, Museu Nacional de Arte Antiga), which shows a richly dressed female saint in front of an equally 'dressed' procession. All that is important in the scene is covered in precious textiles, and the effect of this is that the unity between the humans, saint, relics, and buildings is stressed. This complies with the picture arising from archival documents. Richly decorated fabrics made of expensive and sometimes exotic materials were everywhere in processions: as clothes on the bodies of participants and sculptures, in the canopy above the Holy Sacrament, and on the façades of buildings on the route. Dwellers were obliged by law to embellish their windows and balconies with appropriate hangings, as demonstrated by a decree from the Municipal Chamber from the year 1592:

'[S]ix days before the solemnity of the procession of Corpus Christi, the concert of the streets, windows, doors, and pillars was discussed, which are located in the streets where the procession passes, and it was agreed that it should be said that all the people who dwell in the houses of those streets, keep their doors, windows, balconies, and pillars at the front very well set up and dressed in silk, brocade, rich carpets and tapestries of wool and other hangings and gold and gilded ornaments, and any other ornament that needs to be added for the demonstration of devotion, with which the said procession, in which goes the Lord, needs to be venerated and celebrated.'[30]

If textiles were seen to be lacking in quality or splendour, inhabitants could even be fined. If we can gather anything from the immense importance attached to the 'dressing' of buildings of which this document speaks, it is that, because of the textiles, the street as the space in which the procession unfolded was very much already part of the work.

30 Oliveira, *Elementos*, 1882–1911, vol. 1, p. 432.

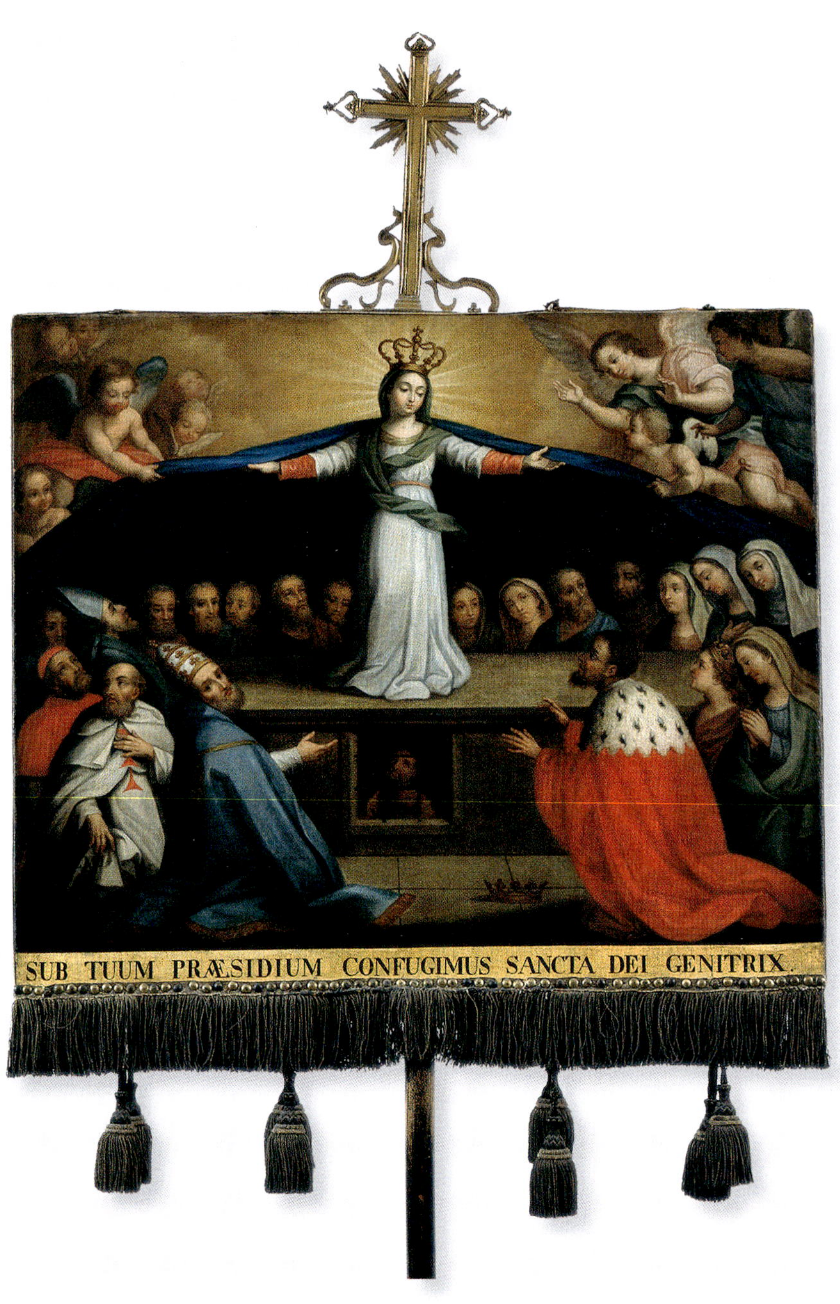

Figure 4:
Bernardo Pereira Pegado, *Banner of Santa Casa da Misericórdia de Lisboa* [front], 1784, oil on canvas, 67 × 87 cm. Lisbon, Museu de São Roque.

When we think of the street as a frame, and the procession as that which is framed, then the textiles make clear that such a distinction is difficult to uphold: indeed, the textile-clad street as frame was already incorporated into the art work.

This last point also leads me to another. The street as part of the procession shows that, within the Corpus Christi procession, it is problematic to distinguish between inside and outside. It was emphatically not a spectacle with an audience, and this is yet another reason why aiming to read it is not the best approach. Rather, everyone took part. In fact, all strata of society were represented. At the top was the king, accompanied by ecclesiastical and worldly officials. All the city's lay confraternities participated, walking with the banners and standards of their institutions, as did all the guilds, who produced carts with *tableaux vivants* and the many figures subsumed under the term inventions. Ethnic minority groups would be involved, as we have seen, in the dances. And, as Maria João Ferreira has shown, other more marginal groups had a share: groups of nuns produced some of the textiles.[31] More than working towards the creation of any final product, the ritual of the Corpus Christi procession was about doing it together in the present, and the various artworks used within it served this greater purpose. Perhaps we can understand the dearth of visual records, signalled above, from this perspective: such representations would have spectacularized the processions in a way that would have been deemed unnecessary.

Presence and Display

In the final part of this paper, I want to think about the implications of this presence-based approach for the study of the display of art in early modern Portugal more broadly. As I pointed out earlier, ephemeral art on the one hand, and the permanent art forms of painting, sculpture, and architecture on the other, which are usually studied quite separately, actually have much in common. Permanent artworks were used in ephemeral events, and also vice versa—see, for example, an eighteenth-century procession banner of the Santa Casa da Misericórdia (Fig. 4), Portugal's most powerful charity institution, surviving until this day in the Museu de São Roque in Lisbon. This work is a quasi easel painting in oil on canvas that, at the same time, contains the elements necessary for its use as a moveable object: a standard, a cross at the top, and frills and eight tassels at the bottom that would have moved and shimmered at every step. Just as ephemeral art works such as this have permanent qualities, the display and use of permanent works were likely to undergo change, so much so that, I would argue, a common approach is justified and necessary: objects in fact often travelled between the two categories.

Let us take a closer look at precious textiles in this context. I have dwelt on their use in processions, but interiors were also commonly clad in textiles. These textiles could be extremely valuable and of foreign origin: through Portugal's maritime empire, not only

31 Ferreira, 'O protagonismo,' 2009, p. 165.

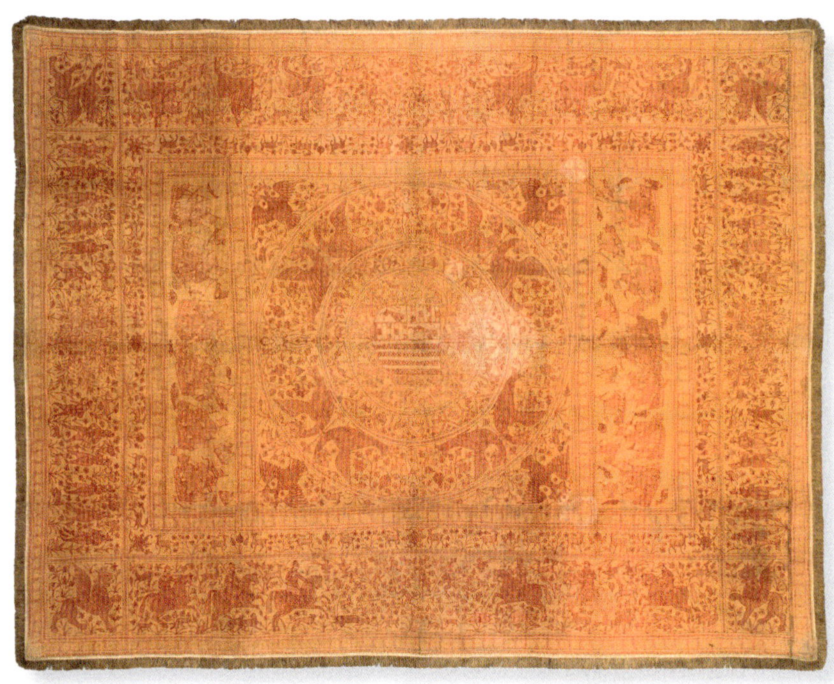

Figure 5:
Southern Bengal, *Coverlet with the Arms of the Lima da Villa Nova da Cerveira Family*, first quarter of the seventeenth century, cotton quilted and embroidered with red silk, 320.3 × 250.3 cm. London, Victoria & Albert Museum.

raw silk but also high quality finished objects such as bedspreads, pillow cases, tablecloths, and wall hangings from Goa and Macau reached Lisbon in a steady stream.[32] These textiles combined local with European motifs and it was not unusual for them to include the coat of arms of the family that had ordered them (for example, Fig. 5). They would be put on display by their owners, in the sense that they were allocated a place in the house (or indeed, as occasion demanded, on its façade) in which they would be seen. Foreign visitors often commented on the Portuguese habit of wrapping churches from floor to

32 See, among others: Peck (ed.), *Interwoven Globe*, 2013, including Ferreira, 'Chinese Textiles for Portuguese Tastes,' pp. 46–55. **33** Confalonieri, *Grandezza et magnificenza*, 2005, p. 213. **34** *Commentarii per Italia, Francia, Spagna e Portogallo*, Lisbon, Biblioteca da Ajuda, MS 46-IX-5, f. 262r. **35** Crespo, 'Global Interiors on the Rua Nova in Renaissance Lisbon,' 2017. **36** Ferreira, 'Asian Textiles in the "Carreira da Índia",' 2015, p. 153.

ceiling in costly hangings, so that 'you do not see a palm of white wall.'[33] To these layers of textiles could then be added further pictures. Others point to what they describe as the unremarkable materials and designs of palace architecture in Lisbon yet praise the 'truly magnificent' adornment of palace interiors with damask and beautiful gilt leather.[34] However, Hugo Crespo has recently argued that Asian textiles (and also Chinese porcelain) in many Portuguese housholds were not being placed on a literal or figurative pedestal, but rather put to use.[35] Ferreira connects the omnipresence of textiles in interiors to the prevalence in Portugal of Mediterranean-Islamic building styles that, as she points out, rely on additional and ephemeral ornamental elements to adorn and structure interior spaces.[36] It therefore seems difficult, in these cases, to distinguish between the work itself and its framing device; rather we may ask how living with such things created presence, and what presence is in such a case.

Conclusion

The music, banners, dances, figures of monsters, giants, serpents, saints, *tableaux vivants*, and hangings that, with human participants and the Holy Sacrament, made up the Lisbon Corpus Christi procession, produced presence: a heightened, physical sense of coming together that goes beyond meaning and that united participants with each other and the divine. Thinking about frames and presentation, it is clear that only in the presentation, could a work of art like the Corpus Christi procession come into being. There seems to be a connection here between the production of presence, the immediacy of the experience, and the procession's participatory nature: helping it unfold over time, there were no boundaries between artist and art work. As in the sports matches that were Gumbrecht's object of study, being there as the procession happened was an important precondition for the sense of presence (watching a game through the framing device of the television hardly diminishes this sense, as long as it happens *live*).

My paper has reflected on the idea of the street as a framing device, and questioned the possibility, within a presence-based model, of separating the object from its frame. As I have proposed, this inseparability may also apply to the presentation and display of what we would see as more permanent types of art. In Corpus Christi, there was no outside from which one could look in; rather, the integration of work and frame gave the procession its remarkable agency.

Bibliography

F. R. Ankersmit, 'Presence and Myth,' *History and Theory*, 45 (2006), pp. 328–336.

F. Bouza Álvarez et al. (eds.), *Cartas para duas infantas meninas: Portugal na correspondência de D. Filipe I para as suas filhas (1581–1583)* (Dom Quixote, 1999).

J. Castel-Branco Pereira et al. (eds.), *A arte efémera em Portugal* (Museu Calouste Gulbenkian, 2000).

F. Checa Cremades and L. Fernández-González (eds.), *Festival Culture in the World of the Spanish Habsburgs* (Ashgate, 2015).

G. B. Confalonieri, *Grandezza et magnificenza della città di Lisbona (1593–1596)* (Nicolodi, 2005).

H. M. Crespo, 'Global Interiors on the Rua Nova in Renaissance Lisbon' in A. Jordan Gschwend and K. Lowe (eds.), *The Global City: Lisbon in the Renaissance* (Museu Nacional de Arte Antiga, 2017), pp. 121–130.

T. Crow, *Painters and Public Life in Eighteenth-Century Paris* (Yale University Press, 1985).

B. Cruz Santo, 'Unidade e diversidade através da festa de Corpus Christi' in I. Jancsó and I. Kantor (eds.), *Festa: Cultura e sociabilidade na América Portuguesa* (Hucitec; Edusp; FAPESP; Imprensa Oficial, 2001), vol. 2, pp. 521–544.

D. R. Curto, *A cultura política no tempo dos Filipes (1580–1640)* (Edições 70, 2011).

C. Dean, *Inka Bodies and the Body of Christ: Corpus Christi in Colonial Cuzco, Peru* (Duke University Press, 1999).

M. J. P. Ferreira, 'O protagonismo dos têxteis nas celebrações realizadas em Lisboa por ocasião das canonizações de Santo Inácio de Loyola e São Francisco Xavier (1622)' in T. L. M. Vale et al. (eds.), *Lisboa e a festa: Celebrações religiosas e civis na cidade medieval e moderna* (Câmara Municipal, 2009), pp. 155–168.

M. J. P. Ferreira, *Os têxteis chineses em Portugal nas opções decorativas sacras de aparato (séculos XVI–XVIII)*, unpublished Ph.D. thesis, Universidade do Porto (2011).

M. J. P. Ferreira, 'Chinese Textiles for Portuguese Tastes,' in A. Peck (ed.), *Interwoven Globe: The Worldwide Textile Trade, 1500–1800* (Metropolitan Museum of Art, 2013), pp. 46–55.

M. J. P. Ferreira, 'Asian Textiles in the "Carreira da Índia": Portuguese Trade, Consumption and Taste, 1500–1700,' *Textile History*, 46 (2015), pp. 147–168.

J. W. von Goethe, 'Winckelmann und sein Jahrhundert' in J. W. von Goethe, *Sämtliche Werke nach Epochen seines Schaffens* (Hanser, 1988 [1805]), vol. 6:2, pp. 195–401.

H. U. Gumbrecht, 'Epiphany of Form: On the Beauty of Team Sports,' *New Literary History*, 30 (1999), pp. 351–372.

H. U. Gumbrecht, *Production of Presence: What Meaning Cannot Convey* (Stanford University Press, 2004).

A. Jordan Gschwend, 'Reconstructing the Rua Nova: The Life of a Global Street in Renaissance Lisbon' in A. Jordan Gschwend and K. Lowe (eds.), *The Global City: On the Streets of Renaissance Lisbon* (Paul Holberton, 2015), pp. 100–119.

A. Jordan Gschwend and K. Lowe (eds.), *The Global City: On the Streets of Renaissance Lisbon* (Paul Holberton, 2015).

A. Jordan Gschwend and K. Lowe (eds.), *The Global City: Lisbon in the Renaissance* (Museu Nacional de Arte Antiga, 2017).

A. Jordan Gschwend and K. Lowe, 'A representação da Lisboa global' in A. Jordan Gschwend and K. Lowe (eds.), *The Global City: Lisbon in the Renaissance* (Museu Nacional de Arte Antiga, 2017), pp. 14–31.

I. B. Machado, *História Critico-Cronologica* (Na Officina Patriarcal de Francisco Luis Ameno, 1759).

E. Muir, *Ritual in Early Modern Europe* (Cambridge University Press, 1997).

E. F. de Oliveira, *Elementos para a História do Município de Lisboa* (Typographia Universal, 1882–1911).

M. L. d'Orey (ed.), *Inventário do Museu Nacional de Arte Antiga: A colecção de ourivesaria* (Instituto Português dos Museus, 1995).

J. P. Paiva, 'As festas de corte em Portugal no período Filipino,' *Revista de História da Sociedade e da Cultura*, 2 (2002), pp. 11–38.

A. Peck (ed.), *Interwoven Globe: The Worldwide Textile Trade, 1500–1800* (Metropolitan Museum of Art, 2013).

P. J. Pinto, *The Portuguese and the Straits of Melaka, 1575–1619: Power, Trade, and Diplomacy* (NUS Press, 2012).
J. P. Ribeiro (ed.), *Dissertações chronologicas e críticas sobre a História e Jurisprudencia ecclesiástica e civil de Portugal* (Academia Real das Sciencias, 1810–1836).
T. Ruiz, *A King Travels: Festive Traditions in Late Medieval and Early Modern Spain* (Princeton University Press, 2012).
F. Sassetti, *Lettere da vari paesi: 1570–1588* (Longanesi, 1970).
J. R. da Silva, *Relaçam da solemne procissam do Corpo de Deos, que aos dous de setembro de 1582 fez a Irmandade do Santissimo Sacramento da Freguesia de S. Julião desta Cidade* (Joseph Antonio da Sylva, 1731).
S. Subrahmanyam, *The Portuguese Empire in Asia, 1500–1700: A Political and Economic History* (Longman, 1993).
J. R. Tinhorão, *Os negros em Portugal: uma presença silenciosa* (Caminho, 1988).
A. P. Torres Megiani, *O rei ausente: Festa e cultura política nas visitas dos Filipes a Portugal, 1581 e 1619* (Alameda, 2004).
T. L. M. Vale et al. (eds.), *Lisboa e a festa: Celebrações religiosas e civis na cidade medieval e moderna* (Câmara Municipal, 2009).
E. van Kessel, *The Lives of Paintings: Presence, Agency and Likeness in Venetian Art of the Sixteenth Century* (De Gruyter, 2017).
E. van Kessel, 'The Making of a Hybrid Body: Corpus Christi in Lisbon, 1582' (in preparation).
I. Velázquez, *La orden que setuuo enla solenne procession que hizieron los deuotos cofrades del sanctissimo Sacramento, de la iglesia de S. Iulian, en la ciudad de Lisboa, celebrando la festiuidad de su cofradia, Domingo, dos de Septiembre, de 1582* (Manuel de Lyra, 1582).

Archive materials:
Commentarii per Italia, Francia, Spagna e Portogallo overo relazione del viaggio de Signori Cavalieri Tron e Lippomani [...],
Lisbon, Biblioteca da Ajuda, MS 46-IX-5, f. 262r.

HANNAH WILLIAMS

Staging Belief:
Immersive Encounters and the Agency of Religious Art in Eighteenth-Century Paris

Religious art, perhaps more than any other category of artwork, has phenomenal potential to act upon its beholders. From depictions of saints that inspire devotion, to objects that actively perform miracles for the faithful, art's ability to affect exists somewhere in the relationship between the object and its beholder. But in the churches and ecclesiastical spaces of eighteenth-century Paris, an object's potential was often artfully amplified through external conditions. Framing devices, controlled modes of encounter, intentionally orchestrated viewpoints, and dynamic displays of choreographed objects all served to imbue artworks with a powerful agency. Indeed at their most dramatic, these spaces could be designed to incorporate the beholder, drawing them into immersive phenomenological experiences where they might encounter the supernatural happenings and complex mysteries of the Catholic faith.

This essay explores the agency of objects and the mechanisms of such interactive strategies in three eighteenth-century spaces: the refectory of the Abbey of Saint-Denis, the Dominican church of the Jacobins (now Saint-Thomas-d'Aquin), and the parish church of Saint-Roch. Each space presents different kinds of objects and strategies of display, from single artworks activated by their site-specific locations, to multiple objects staged in diorama-like settings, or multimedia installations where art and architecture work together to invite viewers to activate the scene. But despite their differing modes of operation,

1 Research for this essay was funded by The Leverhulme Trust through an Early Career Research Fellowship held at Queen Mary University. Thanks to Caroline van Eck, Johannes Grave, and Valérie Kobi for their valuable comments on this essay. My explorations in this essay are drawn from a larger project investigating the role of material culture in religious experience in a book provisionally entitled *Art and Religion: Inside the Parish Churches of Eighteenth-Century Paris*. For important re-engagements with the vastly underexplored terrain of eighteenth-century French religious art, see: Schieder, *Au-delà des Lumières*, 2015 and Gouzi and Leribault (eds), *Le baroque des Lumières*, 2017. **2** On the physical alterations to the canvas, see Gouzi, *Jean Restout*, 2000, p. 225.

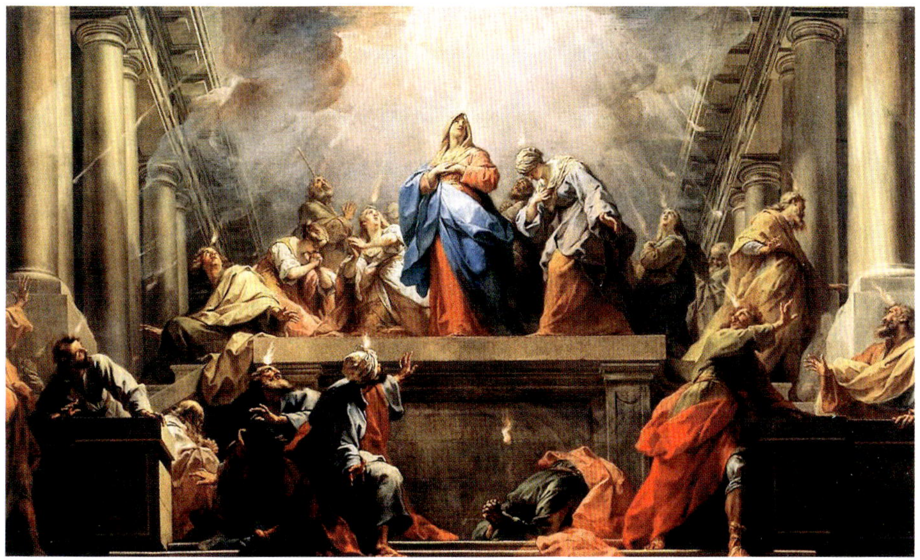

Figure 1:
Jean Restout, *Pentecost*, 1732, oil on canvas, 465 × 778 cm. Paris, Musée du Louvre.

what these spaces share is their creation of a situation that changes the way objects work. Drawn together here as case studies of 'framed' or 'displayed' objects, these religious spaces are also intended more generally as three examples to think with, that is, three examples through which to engage with the broader methodological imperatives of this book. How can frames and displays change the meaning of objects? And beyond even that, how can these external conditions give inanimate things active and performative roles, allowing them to enact ideas and create experiences for, and with, their beholders?[1]

Pentecost in the Refectory

Jean Restout's *Pentecost* (Fig. 1) was painted in 1732 for the refectory of the Abbey of Saint-Denis. Long since removed from its original setting, the *Pentecost* hangs today in the Louvre, where—magnificent as the grand format painting remains—it is difficult for any museum-goer to grasp its full effect. On one hand, this is due to later physical alterations, the canvas having been cut down and reshaped; but on the other hand, it is because the object has been unwittingly broken by its display—broken in the sense that it no longer 'works' like it once did.[2] Now displayed at eye-level on a museum wall, hanging opposite windows that plunge it into raking light in the afternoon sun, Restout's dramatic illusionism is lost and with it the simulated phenomenological encounter that it once promised.

For its 'engaged spectators' (to borrow John Shearman's term), those residents of the Abbey of Saint-Denis for whom the artwork was originally intended, Restout's painting worked not so much as an illustration of the Pentecost, but as a vision of it.[3] It did not simply depict the events of the Pentecost as described in the Acts of the Apostles, but rather simulated something of the experience of this event: not only conveying what happened, but also triggering comparable feelings of awe, unease, surprise, and even fear.[4] Designed to be hung high on the refectory wall, Restout's illusion worked by making the viewer look up.[5] With single-point perspective constructed around a hidden vanishing point, existing somewhere beyond the picture plane, Restout conjured a plunging cavernous space, unfathomable from where we stand below. But with *di sotto in su* architecture and foreshortened figures, he established spatial continuity between this pictorial realm and ours, a continuity reinforced by our shared imagined encounter with its figures. Like the Apostles in the foreground, we witness the scene from below, involuntarily emulating their strained dizzying actions of looking up towards the dissolving ceiling.

How Restout's illusion worked is best understood by imaginatively returning the painting to its original setting in the refectory of Saint-Denis (Fig. 2). Housed in the southern wing of the cloisters beside the basilica, the hall still serves as a refectory, though now for the private girls' secondary school, the Maison d'Éducation de la Légion d'Honneur. Restout's *Pentecost* was painted for the arched space at the far end of the refectory, which, as is evident from the doorways beneath, was over two metres from the ground. This already offers some sense of the beholder's corporeal condition—how the body had to be in order to see the *Pentecost*: whether standing or sitting, the neck would be craned, the eyes directed aloft, and perhaps a foot or a hand would be placed behind to support the backwards tilt of the body. The beholder would, in other words, be forced to share the corporeal condition, and so something of the bodily experience, of those painted witnesses within the scene.

Envisaging the *Pentecost* back in its refectory arch, it is clear that the bodily experience of the painting's actors and spectators is not all that was shared between the world-within the painting and the world-without. Imaginatively reconstructing the painting in that hall, we find a continuity not just between the bodies, but also between the spaces. At one level there is an inherent functional resonance in this site-specific location. After all, the Pentecost supposedly took place in the Cenacle or Upper Room, an upstairs space in Jerusalem frequented by the Apostles, which in Christian tradition is also the location of the Last Supper. Given the Upper Room's association with the act of sharing meals, the Pentecost, like the Last Supper, is an entirely concordant subject to adorn the wall of a refectory (most famously in the case of Leonardo da Vinci's *Last Supper* in the refectory of the convent of Santa Maria delle Grazie in Milan).

3 On Shearman's notion of the 'engaged spectator' and displays of religious art that address, embrace, reposition and are completed by their intended viewers, see: Shearman, *Only Connect*, 1992. **4** The events of Pentecost are recounted in the New Testament in Acts 2:1–31. **5** For further exploration of this mechanism of immersion designed around encouraging the viewer to look up, see: Williams, 'Witnessing Illusion,' forthcoming.

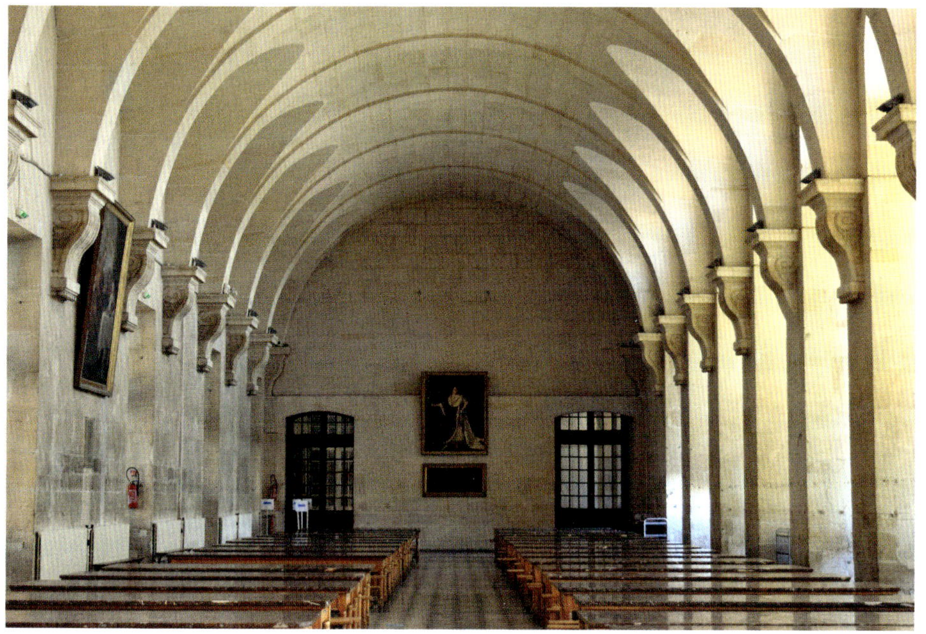

Figure 2:
Original location of Restout's *Pentecost* in the former refectory of the Abbey of Saint-Denis, Saint-Denis, Maison d'Éducation de la Légion d'Honneur.

At another level, there is also a marked visual resonance between the space within the painting and the space in which the canvas resides. That resonance echoes both in materials and in forms: from the bare smooth stone that constructs both the ledge and columns of Restout's Upper Room and the walls and ceiling of the refectory; to the recurring architectural elements, like Restout's line of columns that repeats the refectory's window embrasures, or the corbels supporting the refectory's vaulted ceiling that find a formal corollary in the corbels supporting the stone ledge upon which the Virgin stands. Almost in the spirit of a *trompe l'œil*, Restout pushes his illusion to the edge to merge the space of the beholder with that of the scene beheld. In its original state, moreover, that merging would have been even more complete. Before the later alterations, the canvas was not only larger but also shaped to fit its arched space. And in its shady refectory niche away from the window, Restout's illusion was safe from the raking light that might threaten to rupture its depth as it does now in the Louvre. Filling its wall, framed by the ceiling itself, Restout's *Pentecost* would have blended almost seamlessly with the room around it, extending the space of the hall through the wall, like a vision through to the Upper Room, where the ceiling was breaking open for this dramatic event to occur.

In terms of its display strategies, Restout's *Pentecost* mobilizes the simplest mechanism of the three examples offered here: a single painting designed to hang in a large, relatively empty hall.[6] But the simplicity of the strategy certainly belies its effectiveness. Through its site-specific location and those bodily and spatial continuities between the object and its setting, the framing devices and mode of encounter set up an illusionistic relationship, moving the painting beyond merely addressing the beholder to instead actually implicate them in the scene depicted. Standing in that space, looking up at Restout's *Pentecost*, the inhabitants of the abbey would have found themselves in the path of those rays of light descending as tongues of flame, craning upwards to see for themselves what the Apostles saw, and perhaps even sensing an inkling of what they felt. What was created in this installation in the refectory of Saint-Denis was no mere decorative adornment, but rather an encounter with an empirically unknowable moment, a chance for the faithful spectator to *almost*, if not quite, experience what it was like when the Holy Spirit descended to earth.

Transfiguration in the Chapel

In 1723, François Lemoyne painted the *Transfiguration* on the ceiling of a Jacobin chapel just off Rue du Bac. Now the parish church of Saint-Thomas-d'Aquin, re-designated as such following the diocesan reorganisation during the French Revolution, the church is unusually small and architecturally simple for a Parisian parish church, due to its original function as a chapel for this French branch of the Dominican Order. When first constructed in the seventeenth century, the building comprised only a short nave, a transept, and a tiny choir, but in the 1720s an additional chapel (now the Chapel of Saint-Louis) was built as an annex behind the choir to make more space for the growing order. It was on the ceiling of this chapel that Lemoyne painted his *Transfiguration*, which, thanks to the large aperture at the back of the choir, is visible from the nave of the main building (Fig. 3).[7]

As an example of an object activated by the framing devices and modes of encounter of its architectural situation, Lemoyne's *Transfiguration* is in some ways similar to Restout's *Pentecost* at Saint-Denis: an installation revolving around a single painted surface. But this time the architectural setting is more elaborate—not an empty hall, but a set of interlocking spaces with multiple viewpoints—and far more is demanded of the beholder to make the *Transfiguration* work in its entirety.

Understanding how the display strategies of Lemoyne's *Transfiguration* worked does not in this instance require any imaginative reconstruction, for the work is still in situ and the building has undergone no significant changes. Any visitor to the church of Saint-Thomas-d'Aquin is thus able to experience the work in much the same way as it was

6 Restout's *Pentecost* originally had a pendant, *Moses Receiving the Tablets of the Law*, hanging at the other end of the refectory. This painting is lost and was possibly destroyed during the French Revolution. With no sketches or reproductions, it is now impossible to reconstruct the effect the two works may have had together, but from the brief descriptions that remain, it certainly seems that it would have provided a comparable illusion at the other end of the hall. On Restout's *Moses Receiving the Tablets of the Law*, see: Gouzi, *Jean Restout*, 2000, p. 224. **7** On Lemoyne's artistic practice, see: Bordeaux, *François Lemoyne*, 1984.

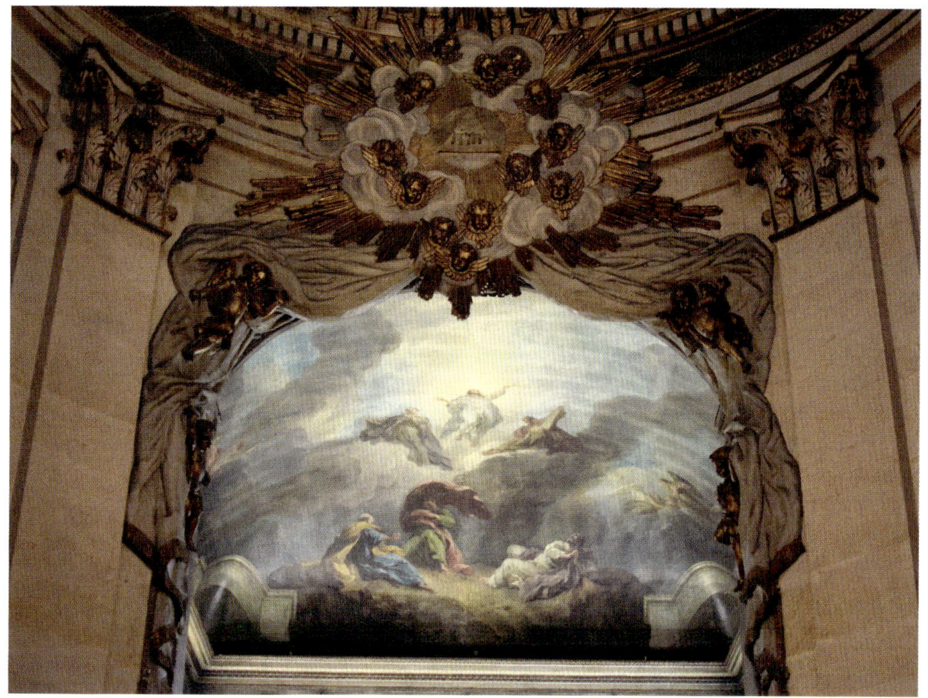

Figure 3:
François Lemoyne's *Transfiguration of Christ* (1723) seen from transept looking through to Chapel of Saint-Louis in the former church of the Jacobins. Paris, Church of Saint-Thomas-d'Aquin.

originally intended. This encounter begins quite soon after entering the church, when, from the start of the nave, the *Transfiguration* can first be glimpsed. At this point, all that can be seen is the very base of the mountain and the feet of the Apostles, but this is just enough to pique interest and draw the beholder onwards. As the beholder walks along the nave towards the choir, more and more of the illusion is gradually revealed. By halfway, the bodies of the three Apostles are almost entirely visible, the colours of their garments iconographically identifying at least two of them—Peter in his customary blue and yellow, John in his customary pink and green, and James in white and purple. By three-quarters of the way along, the Apostles are fully resolved and it is clear from the glimpse of the trailing garments of the prophets that something is happening above their heads. Then finally, upon reaching the transept and the edge of the choir, the full Transfiguration is revealed with the shimmering body of Christ flanked by the prophets, Moses and Elijah.

In this space, where the painting changes constantly as the beholder moves through the church, viewing Lemoyne's *Transfiguration* feels more like attending a theatrical performance than looking at a painting. The ambulation required to activate the scene gives the experience something of the embodied liveness of the theatre, or perhaps more accurately, it is like an inversion of a magic lantern show: instead of a series of static images moved at speed before a stationary viewer, this animation is comprised of a single static image and a moving beholder, who activates an unfolding narrative by walking up the nave. The theatricality of Lemoyne's *Transfiguration* is, moreover, intensified by the proscenium arch that frames the action (Fig. 3). The arched aperture between choir and chapel is adorned by sculpted curtains (complete with tasselled fringes), pulled back by gilded putti to reveal the painted stage where the painted actors perform their parts in the miracle: Christ shining with light, the prophets conversing, and the Apostles witnessing. In fact, the frame even becomes part of the action. According to the account of the Transfiguration in the Gospel of Luke, as Christ's body was transformed, his raiment white and glistering, the prophets appeared to converse with him 'in glory.'[8] True to the word, 'glory' also makes an appearance here, thanks to the explosion of stucco and gilded wood at the very top of the curtained arch. With the triangle of the Trinity at its centre, rays of light projecting outwards, and the seraphic heads of angels floating in clouds, this is a Counter-Reformation church ornament known in French as a *gloire* (glory). A common feature of Parisian churches in the eighteenth-century, here the *gloire* plays not only a symbolic or decorative role, but a narrative one, presiding over the scene to become the glory in which this vision of the Transfiguration takes place.

For its original beholders, the Jacobin friars, the Transfiguration was a particularly significant event. According to the writings of the great Dominican theologian, Thomas Aquinas, the Transfiguration was the greatest of Christ's miracles because this was the act that had allowed the Apostles to witness the glory of God and the perfection of heaven from here on earth.[9] Witnessing was thus paramount in a theological sense and became fundamental also in the dramatizing display that unfolded in their own church, where the illusionistic installation permitted a simulation of that witnessing experience. But in fact, standing at the edge of the choir in the main church, looking through that curtained arch, this witnessing experience was far from over.

Even though the theatrically framed view through the arch confirms that this is the ideal viewing position, from this vantage there is something troublingly odd about the painting's composition (Fig. 3). The Apostles' bodies certainly look distinct and in proportion, but the body of Christ is strangely foreshortened, and the Apostles are difficult to distinguish. Luring the beholder deeper in, the chapel promises a reward for anyone continuing their journey through a side passage and into the space itself, where they discover yet another ideal viewing position. Inside the chapel, standing directly below the figures, Christ's body corrects itself, the prophets resolve into clear bodily forms, and the entire illusion of Christ's Transfiguration is even more impressive than before. Thus in his painting of the *Transfiguration*, what Lemoyne managed to construct was a single composition with two different perspectives and so two separate ideal viewing positions. In the

8 The presence of 'glory' is mentioned twice in Luke's account. New Testament, Gospel of Luke, 9:31–32. **9** Healy, *Thomas Aquinas*, 2003, p. 100. **10** New Testament, Gospel of Matthew, 17:6. **11** Aquinas, *The Summa Theologica*, 1914, p. 260.

first, the viewing point is in the transept, the vanishing point is somewhere behind the Apostles, and it is the lower register of the composition that is organized around it. In the second, the viewing point is in the chapel itself, the vanishing point is above Christ's head, and it is the upper register of the composition that is organized around it. Lemoyne's compositional feat was achieved by minimising the use of linear perspective and so avoiding any disrupting dividing lines between the two spatial structures. Instead the two perspectives are created through the relative foreshortening of bodies and the two spaces are held together through the nebulous substance of cloud, which allows for a seamless join.

For the beholder, this interactive experience of the *Transfiguration* is like a game, a treasure hunt to complete the picture. But this is a game with a spiritual objective. In his compositional feat of constructing two separate perspectives, Lemoyne has also created two simultaneous realms—earthly and heavenly—on a single surface. From the transept, where the Apostles' bodies look correct, we find the earthly side of this experience: through the theatrical arch, we watch the Apostles witnessing Christ's transfiguration and get just a glimpse of their vision. Then, from the chapel, where Christ and the prophets are properly resolved, we switch from a detached view to an active one, no longer watching others watch, but instead seeing what they saw. In this climax of the game, once again with head thrown dizzyingly back, the beholder is drawn into a simulation of the phenomenological encounter. Looking up at Christ, the beholder takes on the Apostles' positionality (literally and figuratively), becoming witnesses through them. In fact, even their compositional instability in this second perspective (the fact that they now look perilously close to toppling down the mountainside) adds to this experience, because it echoes the volatility and uncertainty of their encounter with Christ's transfigured body and the voice of the Holy Spirit emanating through the cloud. As the Gospel of Matthew recounts, when the disciples heard the voice, 'they fell on their face and were sore afraid.'[10]

What is created in this church—through an illusionistic painting, framing devices, intentionally orchestrated viewpoints, and controlled modes of encounter—is an interactive experience where spectatorship is enhanced to the level of simulation: where art and architecture work to produce comparable effects in the beholder as the actual event had caused in its original witnesses. For its original Jacobin audience, this simulated experience had particular import. The gradual unfolding of the miracle that played out through the beholder's movement through the building can be understood as an enactment of Thomas Aquinas's interpretation of the act of witnessing that took place at the Transfiguration. In explaining why Christ brought only three disciples, Aquinas claimed that such 'lofty mysteries should not be immediately explained to everyone, but should be handed down through superiors in their proper turn.'[11] With its sequential viewpoints and the increasing clarity and understanding that comes with each vision, Lemoyne's *Transfiguration* thus plays out in a distinctly Dominican way. Indeed this whole illusion—a wondrous vision simulating the bodily, emotional, and cognitive experience of Christ's miracle—made this Jacobin church an ideal setting for the spiritual observances of an order who privileged ecstatic experience as a way of knowing God.

A Theological Ambulation

By far the most complex of the three examples in this essay is found in the parish church of Saint-Roch. Involving most of the church, with multiple objects and spaces working together, the entire material fabric of the building mobilizes a display strategy that we might call a theological ambulation: a treatise of theological ideas that reveal themselves as the beholder moves through the church. A much more elaborate building than the simple Jacobin chapel, Saint-Roch is composed of a series of connected and interlocking spaces (Fig. 4): a long cruciform housing the nave, transept, choir, and an ambulatory; a rotunda housing the circular Chapel of the Virgin with a continuation of the ambulatory around it; another rotunda behind that housing the Communion Chapel; and finally an additional annex built in the 1750s to accommodate the Chapel of Calvary.[12] Through these spaces, the images and objects staged within them, and the framing devices between them, the beholder was invited to experience some of the most complex mysteries of the Catholic faith, materialized in immersive other-worldly encounters and interactive theological trajectories.

Many of the artworks and spaces at Saint-Roch remain in situ and intact, but there have also been losses and changes—objects removed during the Revolution and after, replacements made to fill gaps, and architectural alterations to accommodate shifting liturgical customs. It is still possible, however, to reconstruct something of the original experience of moving through Saint-Roch's enfilade of vistas, its spaces, the passages between them, and the interacting artworks passed along the way. Upon entering the church, the beholder is immediately offered this enticing path. Standing at the far end of the nave and looking straight up the central aisle, the beholder consumes a vista through the entire building, right to the back of the Chapel of Calvary. This visual trajectory along the church's central axis is an ideal path that does not in fact map onto any actual navigable path through the building, but instead serves to establish a series of desired destinations. Glimpses of enticing objects and curious changes in light—from natural, to a golden, bright warmth, and then a distant cool glow—all draw the viewer forward. But the path, tantalizingly promised through the open apertures along the central axis, is quickly denied by both the structure of the building and by ritualized restrictions to movement.

Setting out along the central aisle of the nave, the first obstacle reached is the choir. Though physically accessible, entry to this sacred space was only permitted to clergy, making this the furthest point along the visual trajectory that an ordinary parishioner could attain. But even from here, the sights glimpsed earlier can already be seen in more detail: the warm light resolves into gilded golden rays, and the far-off pale glow begins to take on a more definite sculptural form. For those with privileged access, these sights

12 On the architectural design of the church, see: Violle, *Paris son Église et ses églises*, 2004, pp. 300–302. The main part of Saint-Roch was based on plans by Jules-Hardouin Mansart; the Chapel of Calvary was designed by Louis-Étienne Boullée.

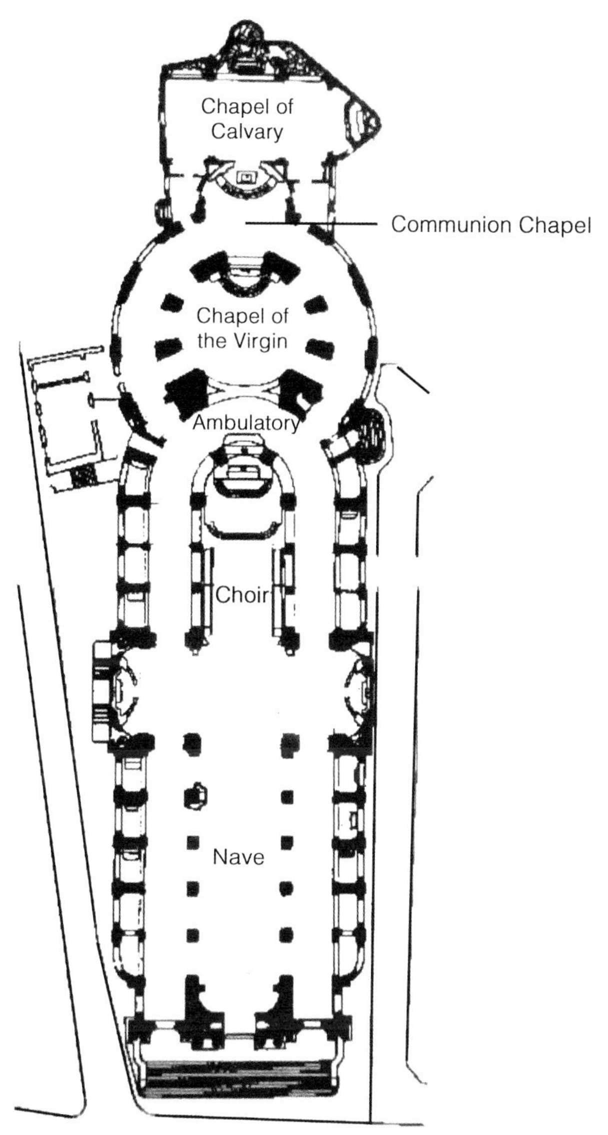

Figure 4:
Floor plan of the church of Saint-Roch, Paris.

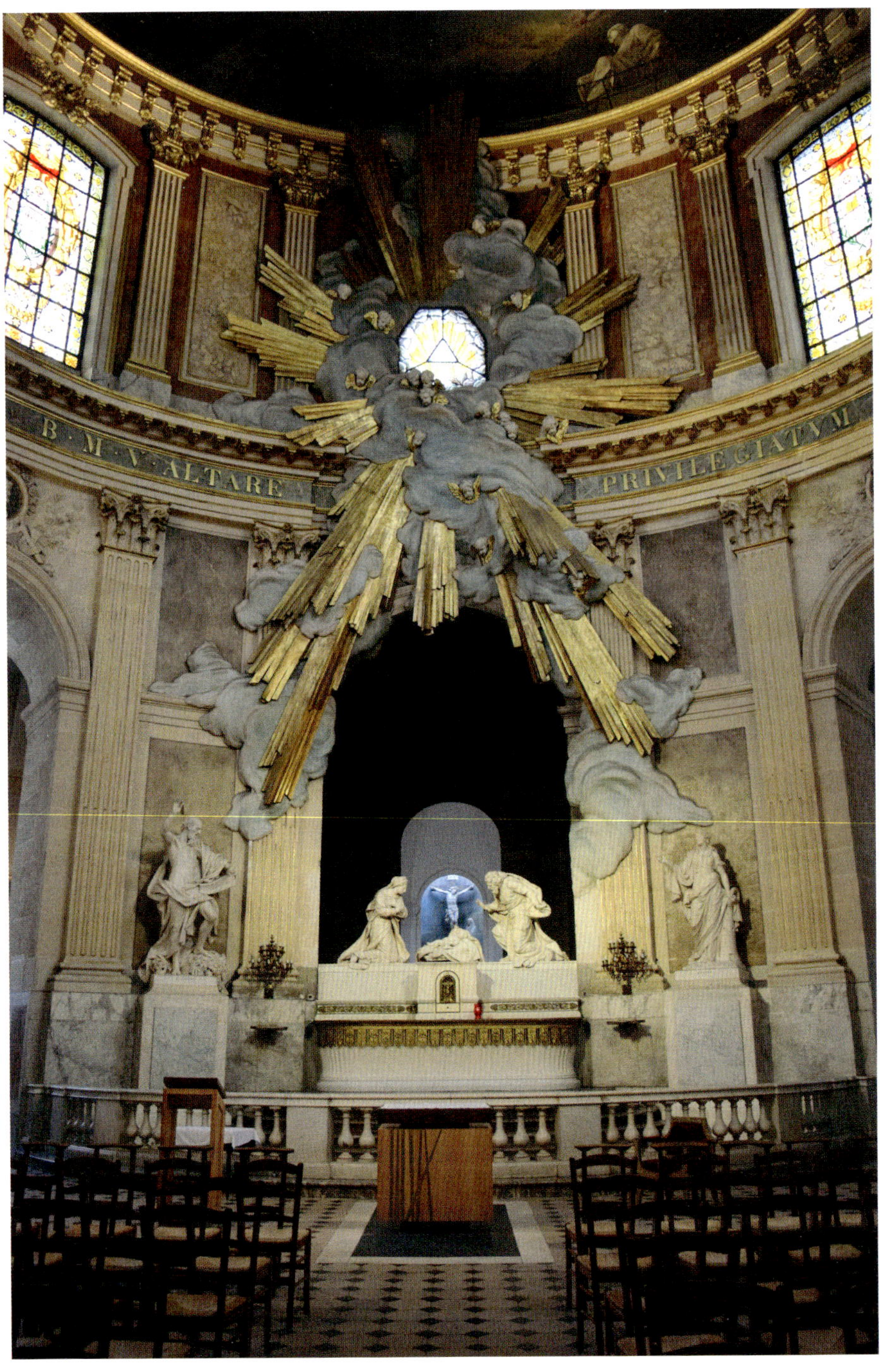

Figure 5:
View down central axis of Saint-Roch from the Chapel of the Virgin through to the Chapel of Calvary. Paris, Church of Saint-Roch.

become clearer still from the end of the choir, but this is the absolute limit of the navigable portion of the visual trajectory. At this point, blocked by the end of the choir, any further discovery requires backtracking and circumnavigation. The only walking path involves leaving the central axis and going either right or left around the choir through the ambulatory. In these side passages, the desired visual destination becomes momentarily completely hidden, coming slowly into view the further along the beholder reaches. Then finally, the central axis is regained at the entry to the Chapel of the Virgin and the beholder is rewarded with a full, unimpeded view of the first destination sought (Fig. 5).

In the Chapel of the Virgin, Saint-Roch's first mystery of the faith—the Incarnation—is unfurled in a material explosion. The warm glowing object glimpsed from the outset is revealed as a soaring *gloire*, the work of the sculptor Étienne-Maurice Falconet, with rays of gilded wood extending at varying lengths, pulling the eye in every direction, while clouds of moulded plaster emanate through the light, bearing the heads of angels. Its real illusionistic mastery, however, comes from the embedded window bearing the symbol of the Trinity. At the centre of this explosive boom, the window's stream of natural light not only activates the gilded rays, but also makes the entire object appear like a burst of celestial light breaking through the wall, a theatrical effect reinforced by those organic clouds that engulf the walls and disrupt its architectural elements. While the *gloire* is relatively intact, the scene below has changed completely since the Revolution. Where we now find Michel Anguier's *Nativity* group of the Virgin, Joseph, and the infant Christ, the eighteenth-century beholder would have encountered an *Annunciation*, also sculpted by Anguier.[13] Much of the original meaning and spectacle is therefore lost, but by imagining an Annunciation scene the relations between all the material parts are reactivated. On the ledge, a marble Angel Gabriel once announced to a marble Virgin that she would bear the son of God, while pointing upwards to Falconet's *gloire*, which slipped seamlessly from decorative device to narrative actor as the Holy Spirit descending to play its part in the Incarnation of Christ. Like a diorama, these interacting objects were thus set in a permanent static performance of this fundamental mystery—the moment when God the son became truly human.

Without doubt, the Chapel of the Virgin is a dramatic peak in Saint-Roch's theological ambulation, but as established by the initial visual trajectory, it is not the final destination. With the central axis once again blocked, the beholder's course continues by returning to the ambulatory and skirting around either side of the chapel, to reach the incredibly underwhelming space behind it. Even in the eighteenth-century, the Communion Chapel was the most subdued, but it did have more coherent decoration than its present state would suggest. Not surprisingly, given its Eucharistic function, the mystery embodied here was that of Transubstantiation, the Catholic belief that during the Mass,

13 The current *Nativity* group was originally made for the Church of Val-de-Grâce; it was moved to Saint-Roch around 1800. On the Annunciation as a subject in Parisian churches, see Gouzi, 'L'Annonciation dans l'espace ecclésial parisien,' 2013, pp. 128–149.

the bread and wine become the body and blood of Christ. As the site for the distribution of the Host, the Communion Chapel was inherently devoted to this mystery, but physical changes to the space make it difficult to retrieve precisely how this worked materially. From guidebook descriptions, we know that an altar and tabernacle stood where the nineteenth-century ones now stand, flanked by two large angels sculpted by Paul-Ambroise Slodtz, and the chapel was crowned with a scene of *The Triumph of Religion*, painted on the dome by Jean-Baptiste-Marie Pierre.[14] But none of these objects or artworks remain today. What the chapel does retain is its position on the central axis, offering the beholder a final unimpeded vista along the visual trajectory and the most detailed glimpse so far through to the ultimate destination in the final chapel.

Entering the Chapel of Calvary, the beholder is confronted with the magnitude of Christ's sacrifice on the cross. This phenomenological encounter with the Crucifixion materializes the final mystery on this theological ambulation, the complex and crucial mystery of Redemption, in which the death of Christ brings human salvation through deliverance from sin. The Chapel of Calvary is now inaccessible to the public and, once again, substantially altered, but enough remains to give some sense of the extraordinary experience it once presented. Designed by the architect Louis-Étienne Boullée and Falconet, this highly theatrical space was an immersive recreation of the site of Christ's Crucifixion. More like a stage-set than a chapel, the scheme once again took existing sculptures by Anguier and set them in a dioramic performance. A marble *Christ on the Cross* with a *Penitent Magdalene* (now replaced by another Anguier Crucifixion and a nineteenth-century Virgin) stood in a niche with a blue-green backdrop to evoke a dark outdoor setting, painted by Pierre-Antoine Demachy, an artist known for his theatre set designs. Beneath this sculptural group was the mountain of Calvary, formed from plaster moulded and painted to become the craggy rocks of the hill, with a grotto-like cave in which the altar stood. The scene was completed by Boullée's ingenious lighting trick of a hidden skylight over the niche of the Crucifixion, which bathed the scene in that cool ethereal glow that was glimpsed from the very beginning.

Despite its later transformations, some sense of the immersive experience that the Chapel of Calvary once offered can be gleaned from contemporary representations. Best known of these is a striking painting by Nicolas-Bernard Lépicié, *The Chapel of Calvary at the Church of Saint-Roch* (1756, Musée Carnavalet, Paris), in which the painter succumbs so entirely to Boullée and Falconet's illusion that we hardly seem to be in a church at all, but rather a subterranean cave.[15] Yet in other ways Lépicié's depiction is probably quite accurate, including many details mentioned in eighteenth-century guidebook descriptions, such as: two sculpted soldiers on one side; sculpted tree trunks on the other with a serpent snaking among them; and an altar of blue marble in the form of an antique tomb, adorned

14 The chapel is described in Dulaure, *Nouvelle description*, 1791 [1785], vol. 2, pp. 340–341. **15** On this work, see Rosenberg, 'Une énigme résolue,' 1978, pp. 23–28. **16** For a description of the chapel see Dulaure, *Nouvelle description*, 1791, vol. 2, p. 341. **17** Dulaure, *Nouvelle description*, 1791 [1785], vol. 2, p. 341.

with urns producing perfumed smoke, and a tabernacle in the form of a broken column.[16] Clearly, the Chapel of Calvary was an immersive spectacle designed to prompt an affective response. It certainly did for the proxy visitors depicted in Lépicié's painting, their bodies arched back in awe or thrown forward in grief, and the guidebooks warned potential visitors that 'the shadowiness of the place, the low height of the vaults, its solidity, and the silent air that reigns, all penetrate the soul with sorrow.'[17]

From the moment one enters Saint-Roch and glimpses the pale glow of Christ's body in the distance, the Chapel of Calvary becomes the ultimate destination, just as salvation is the ultimate goal of the Catholic faith. What the building and art works in Saint-Roch permitted for parishioners was thus not so much an explanation of these mysteries, but an experience of their material unfolding, as they physically played out their relationship with each other, and their relationship with the devotional practices that took place here. In other words, the visual trajectory maps onto a theological trajectory, related in the vistas between and through those mysteries. Looking from the Chapel of the Virgin through to the Chapel of Calvary (Fig. 5), for instance, Redemption is understood in relation to the Incarnation. Christ's death was, after all, only possible because the immortal son of God became mortal in his human nature, born of the Virgin. Meanwhile the sacrifice that this death fulfilled was only sufficient satisfaction because Christ's divine nature made it proportional to the offence of the original sin. Redemption is thus dependent on Incarnation, and the Incarnation is the pre-destined path to Christ's ultimate sacrifice. Beholding the *Crucifixion* through the *Annunciation*, at Saint-Roch, these events were not just two moments in a narrative (beginning and ending Christ's life on earth), but two entwined doctrinal concepts, following from and leading to each other, just like the path through the church.

Another theological trajectory is revealed in the vista between the Communion Chapel and the Chapel of Calvary, where Transubstantiation is conceived in relation to Redemption. Every Christian Mass is a re-presentation of Christ's sacrifice on the cross, but through Transubstantiation, the Mass makes present that sacrifice at the climax of the liturgy when the priest says the words: 'Take, eat, this is my body' and 'Take, drink, for this is my blood, shed for you and for many for the remission of sins.' In Saint-Roch's Communion Chapel, with its aperture through to the Chapel of Calvary, when the sacraments were held aloft at this crucial moment of the rite, they were silhouetted before the sacrificed body of Christ hanging on his cross. That distinctively Catholic belief that the Mass was not simply recalling Christ's sacrifice, but rather making that sacrifice truly present through the transformative act of Transubstantiation was thus materialized powerfully in the vision of the crucified body beyond. Here and throughout Saint-Roch, the building and its objects served as far more than mere decoration or even explanation. Through sophisticated strategies of display, complex theological ideas were encountered through phenomenological experiences, and the intricate connections and interdependencies between these ideas were made manifest through framing devices, lines of vision, interactions between objects, and navigable pathways through spaces.

Conclusion

Though drawing on the particularities of religious objects and spaces in eighteenth-century Paris, the intention of this essay was to offer three examples to think with more generally: three cases where the display of images and objects not only transformed their meaning, but also imbued these inanimate things with an active agency, acting on and for their beholders, drawing them into interactive exchanges, and rewarding the viewer's efforts with affective encounters. By way of conclusion, this essay gathers some of those thoughts, ideas and discoveries that have emerged from an exploration of three ecclesiastical spaces and the strategies of display that they so deftly deployed.

Perhaps the most striking conclusion to be drawn from this examination of framing devices is the overwhelming impression that artworks in the eighteenth-century were not limited to the role of aesthetic objects. Despite eighteenth-century Paris's associations with the birth of modern art exhibitions, with the Académie Royale's Salons and the emerging museumification of artworks, art was still frequently called upon to be far more than an object presented for the judgement of an art-critical audience. Demonstrating as much connection to, as evolution away from, modes of spectatorship associated with medieval or renaissance spaces, these examples disrupt that prevailing image of an Enlightenment art world of connoisseurs and consumers. In Paris's churches, artworks could escape the metaphorical confines of their wooden frames and stone plinths to be re-framed and re-positioned in new contexts, where their external conditions transformed them from objects for aesthetic contemplation into dynamic agents for liturgical acts and theological enlightenment. In these choreographed situations where objects interacted across spaces, art was no longer contained, but existed instead with permeable edges and ambiguous boundaries.

Another observation is the implications that this activation of art had for the beholder. In Saint-Denis's refectory, the Jacobin chapel, and Saint-Roch, art became a demanding interlocutor. Far from restful, art became something to walk into, move around, or pass through, refusing to let the viewer stand still and instead forcing interactions and kinetic exertions. As the depicted beholders in Lépicié's *Chapel of Calvary at the Church of Saint-Roch* remind us, art was not something 'over there' expecting to be looked at, but something all around insisting that the beholder become part of it. More installation than object, more experience than image, these situations transformed art from a passive object waiting to be enjoyed into an activity demanding to be experienced.

Just as these situations held implications for the beholder, so too were there consequences for the objects themselves. In their immersive settings with ambulant spectators, art was no longer necessarily static. The images depicted may have been still, but resonances with the material fabric of their settings (like the continuities between Restout's *Pentecost* and the architecture of the refectory), or the physical movement of their beholders (like the beholder walking up the nave to complete Lemoyne's *Transfiguration*), could turn still images into animated performances or illusionistic simulations. These dynamic display strategies also reveal the playful interaction across media and the creative use and re-use of objects. Cross-media interaction is nowhere more evident than in the narrative role that the decorative *gloires* were called to play, both in the Jacobin chapel and at Saint-Roch. Their sculpted, stuccoed, and gilded forms could interact with a painted ceiling to become the presence of glory in Lemoyne's *Transfiguration*, or with marble sculptures to become the Holy Spirit descending in Anguier's erstwhile *Annunciation*. This latter example was already an instance of creative appropriation: when Falconet and Boullée designed the Chapel of the Virgin, they took Anguier's seventeenth-century sculptures and restaged them to create an eighteenth-century religious diorama. Arising from all this material interaction and re-use, we find intriguing questions on many fronts. What might its implications be for an understanding of artistic authorship in the eighteenth century? How strict were the hierarchies of media beyond the art-theoretical world of the Academy, given the interdependency of all these art forms? And for a period so often characterized by competition between artists, might collaboration not be as important a relationship for understanding artistic production?

A final thought from these explorations brings the dismantling of yet another eighteenth-century stereotype, namely that rationality was always the order of the day. This may have been the 'age of reason,' but in all the examples examined here, there is an undeniable impetus to make the beholder 'feel.' Though perhaps not as viscerally or melodramatically as some of their Italian baroque predecessors, all of these situations were, nevertheless, efforts to affect those who experienced them. Even in Saint-Roch's theological ambulation, arguably the most cerebral of the three examples, knowledge is only granted through empirical experience of the materialized mysteries: the beholder has to sense these ideas, visually, kinetically, in order to understand them. Within the emotionally conservative context of Enlightenment Paris, these were emotive spectacles. Whether it was wonder, awe, fear, surprise, grief, love, gratitude, or devotion, these immersive displays were designed to elicit an affective response.

Strategies of display not only changed the meaning of objects in Paris's ecclesiastical spaces, but transformed them into active performers with the agency to compel, act, initiate, affect, enlighten, and inspire. An examination of Restout's *Pentecost*, Lemoyne's *Transfiguration*, or any of the artworks in Saint-Roch's theological ambulation that isolates these objects from their external conditions, could never capture the dynamism with which they were intended to work. For those framing devices, controlled modes of encounter, illusionistic interactions, and intentionally orchestrated viewpoints were not peripheral to the artworks, but an inherent part of their overall design.

Bibliography

T. Aquinas, *The Summa Theologica of Saint Thomas Aquinas* (R&T Washbourne, 1914).
J.-L. Bordeaux, *François Lemoyne and His Generation, 1688-1737* (Arthena, 1984).
J. A. Dulaure, *Nouvelle description des Curiosités de Paris* (Chez Le Jay, 1791 [1785]).
C. Gouzi, *Jean Restout 1692–1768* (Arthena, 2000).
C. Gouzi, 'L'Annonciation dans l'espace ecclésial parisien au XVIIIe siècle: liturgie française et modèle italien,' *Studiolo*, 10 (2013), pp. 128–149.
C. Gouzi and C. Leribault (eds), *Le baroque des Lumières. Chefs-d'œuvre des églises parisiennes au XVIIIe siècle* (Paris Musées, 2017).
N. M. Healy, *Thomas Aquinas: Theologian of the Christian Life* (Ashgate, 2003).
P. Rosenberg, 'Une énigme résolue: La Chapelle du Calvaire de l'église Saint-Roch,' *Bulletin du Musée Carnavalet*, 31/2 (1978), pp. 23–28.
M. Schieder, *Au-delà des Lumières: La peinture religieuse à la fin de l'Ancien Régime* (Éditions de la Maison des sciences de l'homme, 2015).
J. Shearman, *Only Connect... Art and the Spectator in the Italian Renaissance* (Princeton University Press, 1992).
B. Violle, *Paris son Église et ses églises* (Les Éditions du Cerf, 2004).
H. Williams, 'Witnessing Illusion: Looking Up in the Churches of Paris,' in M. Castor and K. Dickhaut (eds.), *La vraisemblance ou les enjeux de la représentation: Le théâtre et la peinture dans les discours académiques (1630–1730)* (Garnier, forthcoming).

MECHTHILD FEND

Order and Affect.
The Museum of Dermatological Wax Moulages at the Hôpital Saint-Louis in Paris

Dermatological wax moulages tend to be excessively framed.[1] The image of a condition taken from a sick person's body is held and labelled by a number of devices, it is fitted into a cabinet and kept behind glass (Fig. 1). In its vitrine, the moulage blends into a larger display that puts skin diseases in order and dermatology in place. A lot is done to moulages in order for them to do something for the establishment of a discipline. But the waxen casts surpass a mere medical purpose. As a group—circa 4800 in the case of the Hôpital Saint-Louis in Paris—the mute representatives of the sick, greeting visitors as they enter the museum, have an overwhelming presence (Fig. 2).[2] The waxen reliefs are reproductions of conditions that affect the skin, the human body's protective border, and they prompt an affective reaction. Their lifelikeness is shocking, and it is hard to look at them without getting one's own body involved, without the sensation of an itch or the feeling of disgust.

Despite this potential for discomfort, there is a curious fascination. It is spurred by the lure of lifelikeness that images made of wax have provoked for a long time, from ancient waxes and early modern ceroplasty via medical models to the waxen celebrities

1 I would like to thank the research project *Parerga und Paratexte—Wie Dinge zur Sprache kommen* and notably Christiane Holm, for inviting me to join them as an external member. This article's section on labels much benefitted from our discussions. Part of the research on wax moulages was done during a stay at the Max Planck Institute for the History of Science in Berlin in spring 2014, and I am particularly grateful to Lorraine Daston for her insightful comments on the paper that I presented in her department's colloquium. I would also like to thank Silvie Dorison, Chargée du musée-bibliothèque, Hôpitaux Universitaires Saint-Louis, in Paris, for her help and support. **2** The moulages of the Musée des moulages de l'Hôpital Saint-Louis have been completely photographed and digitized. They can be consulted via the image database of the Bibliothèque interuniversitaire de santé (Paris): [http://www.biusante.parisdescartes.fr/histoire/images/index.php] (last accessed 1 May 2018). For a brief history and virtual tour of the museum see the recently updated website: [http://www.biusante.parisdescartes.fr/stlouis/fr/debut.htm] (last accessed 1 May 2018).

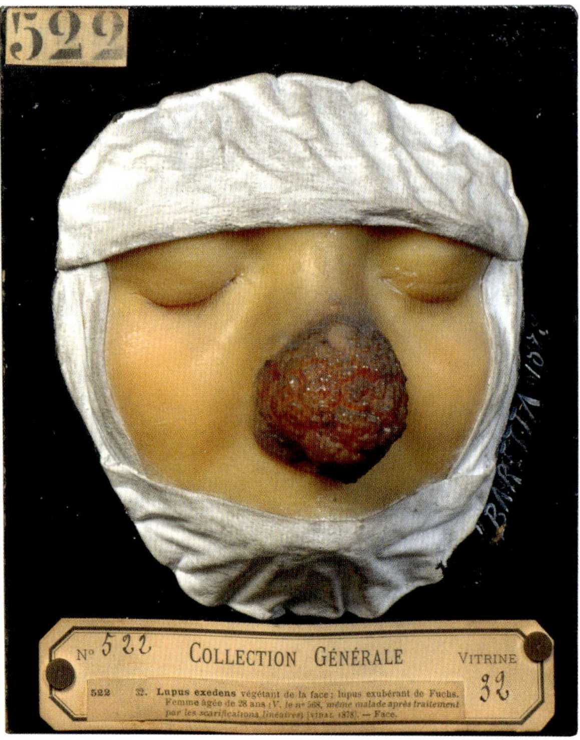

Figure 1:
Jules Baretta, *Lupus exedens de la face*, 1878, wax moulage nº 522.
Paris, Musée de l'Hôpital Saint-Louis.

at Madame Tussaud's or the Musée Grévin in Paris.[3] The main reason for the appeal is the once highly significant role of the wax figure as simulacrum, and—in the case of the early modern effigies of the king—to stand in for the person it represents. Since the nineteenth century, the thrill of confounding representation and represented became part and parcel of the wax museums' entertainment strategies. These effects and associations were felt and known during the nineteenth century, when collections of dermatological wax moulages were built up throughout Europe. The working of these tools of dermatological training and study relied on the material qualities of wax, the power of the imprint and on convincing resemblance. Their use value also depended on the possibility of taking

3 Schlosser, 'Geschichte der Porträtbildnerei in Wachs,' 1910–1911; Schlosser's text remains a seminal study and was translated into English in Panzanelli (ed.), *Ephemeral Bodies*, 2008. The introduction and further essays in this volume provide an excellent survey of recent scholarship on wax. On Madame Tussaud's see: Kornmeier, 'Almost Alive,' 2008; more generally on wax see: Goodie and Grootenboer (eds.), 'Theorizing Wax,' 2013, and especially the introduction 'On the Substance of Wax,' pp. 1–12.

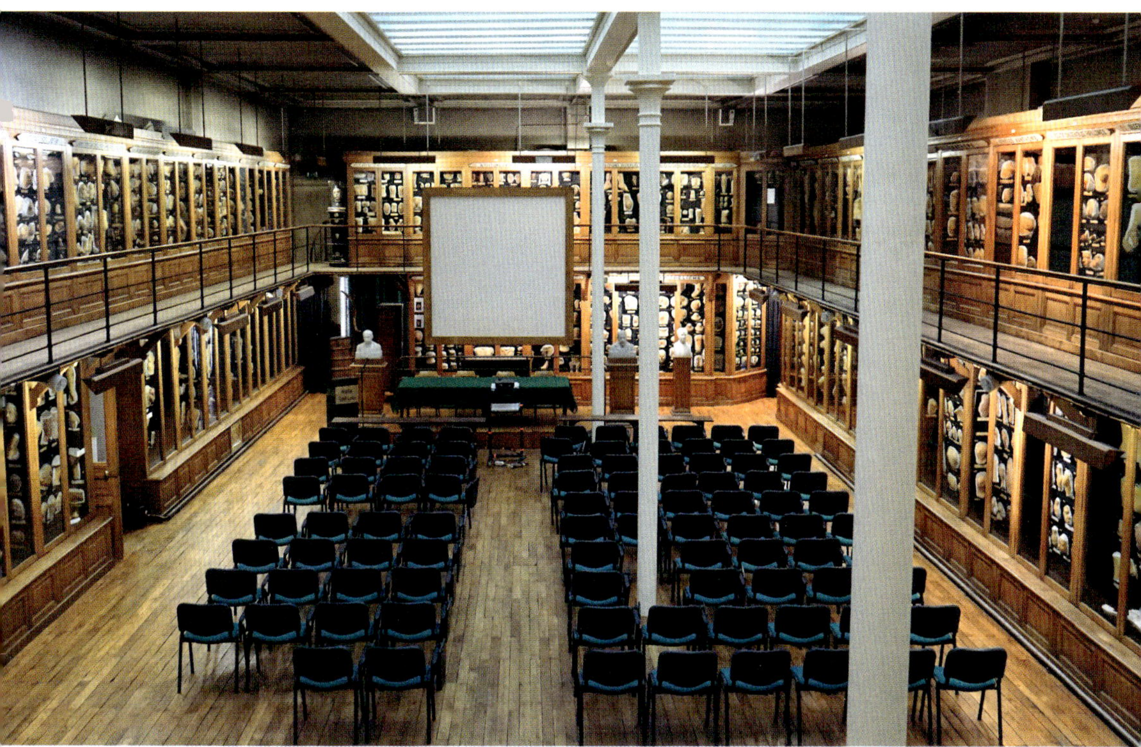

Figure 2:
View of the main hall of the Musée de l'Hôpital Saint-Louis, Paris.

the image for the patient. This brought them dangerously close to their popular counterparts and medical institutions felt pressure to keep this kinship with spectacular displays and associations with magical image practices at bay. This essay will argue that framing and ordering were not only ways of making the growing collection accessible, but also to secure its credibility as a scientific display. Dermatological wax moulages—their commissioning, fabrication, collection and use—formed part of the visual and material culture of nineteenth-century medicine. How they played their role within this culture depended on the specific institution in which they were made, handled and displayed. The focus here is the Hôpital Saint-Louis in Paris, an important institution for the development of modern dermatology. Its Musée des moulages is the largest collection of its kind and still exists today in its late nineteenth-century set up.

The Hôpital Saint-Louis was built during the early seventeenth century outside Paris' city walls as a hospital for the containment of the sick during times of epidemics, initially mainly for plague victims. During the second half of the eighteenth century, the hospital was permanently opened to patients. The building had become incorporated into the growing city and was now situated in the Faubourg du Temple. As one of the medical institutions reformed in the aftermath of the French Revolution, the hospital gradually became a clinic specialising in the treatment of conditions of the skin, which included, at that time, venereal diseases such as syphilis.[4] Due to its unique specialisation, it soon developed into a centre for the study and cure of skin conditions, and a medical mecca for students and physicians from all-over Europe and North America.[5] From the outset, images played a major role at the Hôpital Saint-Louis, and they were crucial for the formation of dermatological ways of seeing the sick and their lesions.[6] In early dermatology, skin diseases were understood as conditions that manifest themselves on the body's surface. They were first and foremost defined by their visual accessibility, and optical inspection formed (and still forms) a significant part of dermatological diagnosis.

The hospital's most important human player in the first decades of the nineteenth century was the physician Jean-Louis Alibert, generally considered the founder of modern dermatology in France.[7] His first major publication, the 1806 *Description des maladies de la peau observées à l'hôpital Saint-Louis*, is a lavish folio atlas illustrated with fifty-two stipple engravings coloured à la poupée, a fairly laborious technique for which the engraver Salvatore Tresca was well known. By putting 'description' first, the title stresses the nosographic approach to the diseases; it makes a claim for visual empiricism ('observation') and underlines the significance of the site: the Saint-Louis Hospital. In the volume's preliminary section, Alibert promotes it as the ideal place to study skin diseases. Alibert presents the hospital as a theatrical space and imagines himself as the spectator who watches a continuous display of morbid appearances in constant transformation.[8] It is as if this physical and performative space in itself turned the observed phenomena into images. The dermatological clinic is both an architectural and an epistemological space in which diseases process and are brought to a halt in order to become visible as clinical pictures.[9]

Alibert stresses both the affective and scientific aspect of the images. In a remarkable paragraph, in which he highlights the significance of the colour prints for his atlas and his entire nosographic enterprise, he points to the 'terrifying colours of the painter' and expresses

4 For early accounts of the Hôpital Saint-Louis's history see: Alibert 'Note sur l'Hôpital Saint-Louis,' 1832, pp. xj–xij; Gougerot and Brodier, *L'Hôpital Saint-Louis*, 1932; and more recently Tilles, 'The Hôpital Saint-Louis,' 2002. Classic general accounts of the formation of modern medicine in France include Foucault, *The Birth of the Clinic*, 1973 [1963] and Ackerknecht, *Medicine at the Paris Hospital*, 1967. More recently, historians of medicine have de-emphasized the role of the French Revolution, arguing for a more gradual development of modern medical practices. See: Hannaway and La Berge, 'Paris Medicine: Perspectives Past and Present,' 1998. **5** Alibert proudly points this out in the introduction to his *Monographie des dermatoses*, 1832, p. xiv. **6** See in more detail: Fend, 'Portraying Skin Disease,' 2013. **7** If not indicated otherwise, I rely for biographies of the Saint-Louis physicians on Tilles, 'The Hôpital Saint-Louis,' 2002, pp. 414–448. **8** Alibert, *Description des maladies de la peau*, 1806, p. i; see also: Jacyna, 'Pious Pathology,' 1998. **9** Fend, 'Portraying Skin Disease,' 2013, pp. 152–153. **10** If not indicated otherwise, translations are mine. The entire paragraph in context is: Alibert, *Description des maladies de la peau*, 1806, p. xxj: 'Pour imprimer un plus grand sceau d'authenticité à ce que j'ai écrit, pour ajouter à l'énergie et à la puissance

the wish 'to strike' his readers with the images. What is more, he posits that accurate description in conjunction with the use of images allows dermatology to become a science. This new method of using images can, he writes, 'introduce more precision into descriptive medicine and free medicine from the reproach of being a conjectural science.' Alibert further hopes that the images 'print [...] a seal of authenticity' onto his case descriptions and 'fortify the impressions' of his words.[10] Associating the imprint with authenticity at the same time as highlighting the affective dimension of images, he almost seems to anticipate the kind of dermatological imagery that only came into use after his death: wax moulages.

It was around the middle of the nineteenth century that the establishment of a collection of waxen reproductions of skin diseases was promoted by the physicians working at Saint-Louis. The material and the technique of casting had already been used to document skin diseases elsewhere,[11] and beyond the immediate diagnostic purposes in line with the earlier visual practices and uses of images, the building of a significant collection was meant to safeguard the status of the Hôpital Saint-Louis, and of France more broadly speaking, as *the* leading centre for dermatology. The Hôpital Saint-Louis, notably Charles Lailler, physician at the hospital between 1863 and 1887, was thus actively seeking an artisan who would be able to provide such lifelike reproductions of skin diseases, and found, in 1863, Jules Baretta, at the time still a manufacturer of *trompe l'œil* fruit made of *papier mâché* with a workshop at the Passage Jouffroy, an arcade in the ninth arrondissement that later also became the home of the Musée Grévin. Apparently, Baretta first familiarized himself with his new subject, and accompanied Lailler on his hospital rounds to learn the basics of dermatology, and—we can assume—an expert way of looking at diseases and diseased. In parallel, he was experimenting with the materials and procedures for his moulages. Like many other mouleurs, Baretta never put the specifics of his practice into writing. However, based on nineteenth-century manuals on the techniques of moulding, third person accounts of Baretta's procedures, more recent reports from mouleurs and technical investigations of some of his moulages,[12] it is possible to make well-informed assumptions about the making of his dermatological moulages.

de mes discours, pour perpétuer et animer en quelque sorte tous mes tableaux, j'ai cru devoir recourir à l'artifice ingénieux du pinceau et du burin. J'ai voulu fortifier les impressions, par l'image physique des objets que je desirois offrir à la contemplation du Pathologiste: j'ai voulu enfin, par les couleurs effrayantes du peintre, instruire pour ainsi dire la vue par la vue, faire ressortir et contraster davantage les caractères des Maladies de la peau, fixer leurs moindres nuances, frapper en un mot les sens des mes lecteurs, et reproduire vivans devant eux les divers phénomènes qui avoient étonné mes regards. Ce nouveau secours peut sans doute introduire plus de précision dans la Médicine descriptive, et l'affranchir désormais du reproche qu'on lui a fait, d'être une science conjecturale.' On the affective dimension see also: Jacyna, 'Pious Pathology,' 1998. **11** For a history of the dermatological wax moulage see: Schnalke, *Diseases in Wax*, 1995. **12** For the production of dermatological moulages see: Schnalke, 'Casting Skin,' 2004. For Baretta's techniques in particular see the technical analysis and re-enactment of the casting and modelling process by Fabien Noirot available at: [www.youtube.com/watch?v=XDsoaWipkko] (last accessed 1 May 2018); see also: Noirot, 'Jules Baretta et les secrets du moulage pathologique,' 2014.

In what I consider a first act of framing, a particular appearance of a disease to be reproduced had to be singled out by one of the physicians, before the patient was sent to Baretta whose studio was located within the premises of the hospital. The patients must have been informed to some extent about the procedures, as their participation was required. They had to keep the plastered body parts immobile, and needed to know that the plaster developed heat when settling.[13] That done, they had to be conveniently positioned before a protective film (possibly made from the skin of animal intestines) was placed on the lesion to be reproduced. This film would reduce potential discomfort or pain for the patient, but also allow for better results as it prevents the moisture of morbid phenomena (like ulcers, pustules) from interfering with the setting of the plaster.[14] Thereafter, fine plaster was spread over the affected region, and mouleur as well as patient had to wait for the material to set. When moulding a person's face, particular precautions needed to be taken, as eyes and mouth had to remain shut. Once the plaster had dried, it was removed, and provided a negative form into which melted wax was poured in several layers to produce the actual moulage. But it was not a mere mechanical reproduction. Baretta's skills were crucial. The practitioner, embedded—to adopt a phrase by Tim Ingold—his 'tactile and sensuous knowledge' of the body's surface and texture and his physical familiarity with the sick in the moulage.[15] The relief of the wax cast was reworked and refined, colour was added with the brush, and, at times, hair was applied. This can be seen, for example, in moulage *number 27*, treating a case of lupus, where actual hair was used to insert eye brows and eye lashes (Fig. 3). These additions had diagnostic value only insofar as their absence might have felt like a lack, like part of a condition. They mainly serve to increase the lifelikeness of the moulage and facilitate, in the case of faces, the engagement with a fragment as if it was a person. With the eyes necessarily closed and the wax piece embedded in white cloth, the faces often look peacefully asleep despite their conditions.

The wax moulage was fully recognized as a scientific tool by dermatologists, and as such they ranked equal with photography, a medium more typically associated with scientific practices and the paradigms of what Lorraine Daston and Peter Galison have termed 'mechanical objectivity.'[16] As for the particular case of the Hôpital Saint-Louis, Jules Baretta was hired around the same time that the dermatologist Alfred Hardy initiated the production and collection of photographs of skin diseases and Arthur de Montméja, an ophthalmologist and photographer, started the campaign. The first published outcome, the *Clinique photographique de l'hôpital Saint Louis*, appeared in 1868 while Baretta finished

13 Advice on the posing of the model is given in Lebrun and Magnier, *Nouveau manuel complet du mouleur*, 1850, pp. 51–57. **14** Noirot, 'Jules Baretta et les secrets du moulage pathologique,' 2014, p. 206. **15** Ingold, 'The Textility of Making,' 2010. **16** Daston and Galison, *Objectivity*, 2007, see in particular pp. 115–190. **17** See for photography: Hardy and de Montméja, *Clinique photographique*, 1868, p. i; for moulages: Lebrun and Magnier, *Nouveau manuel complet du mouleur*, 1850, p. 52. See also: Papet, 'Technique: "saisir la nature sur le fait",' 2001. **18** Devergie, 'Musée de l'hôpital Saint-Louis,' 1876, here p. 393:

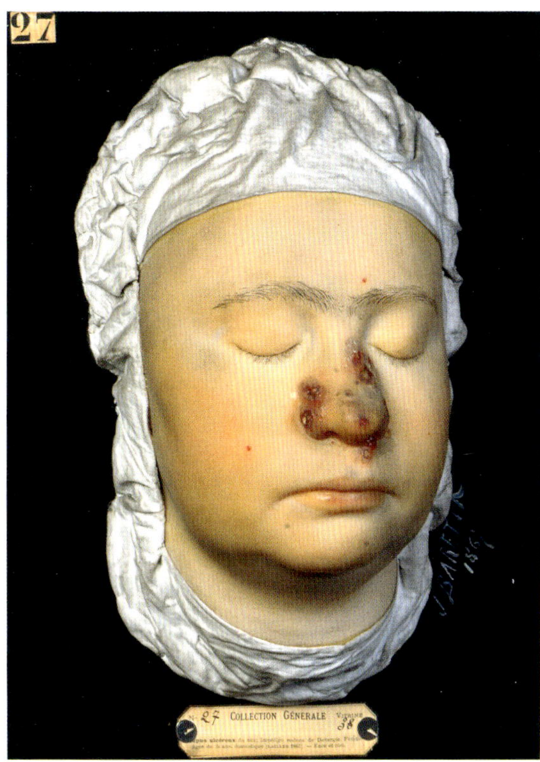

Figure 3:
Jules Baretta, *Lupus ulcéreux du nez*, 1827, wax moulage n° 27.
Paris, Musée de l'Hôpital Saint-Louis.

his first successful moulage in 1867. The rhetoric surrounding photographs and wax moulages was very similar, their value was seen in their quality as imprints. Despite their different looks, they were both considered 'faithful reproductions,' and equally praised for catching 'nature in the very act.'[17] In addition, Alphonse Devergie, physician at Saint-Louis between 1840 and 1867, who was instrumental in the establishment of a dermatological museum, lauded the wax reliefs for their 'natural form and size' and the 'the most perfect morbid colouring.' Only these qualities, not achievable by photography, made them 'reproductions of diseased and disease as complete and truthful as possible.'[18]

'Forme, grandeur naturelle, coloris morbide le plus parfait, en un mot, reproduction aussi complète et aussi vraie que possible du malade et de la maladie. [...] Je dis mouleur, car M. Baretta ne fait pas de modelages en cire coloriée. Il opère à l'aide d'un moule en plâtre dans lequel il coule une matière spéciale à une température de 200 degrés; il fait des dessins avec des pâtes colorées de diverses nuances, de sorte que ses reproductions sont indélébiles.' The information on the temperature can hardly be correct, as wax melts at much lower temperatures.

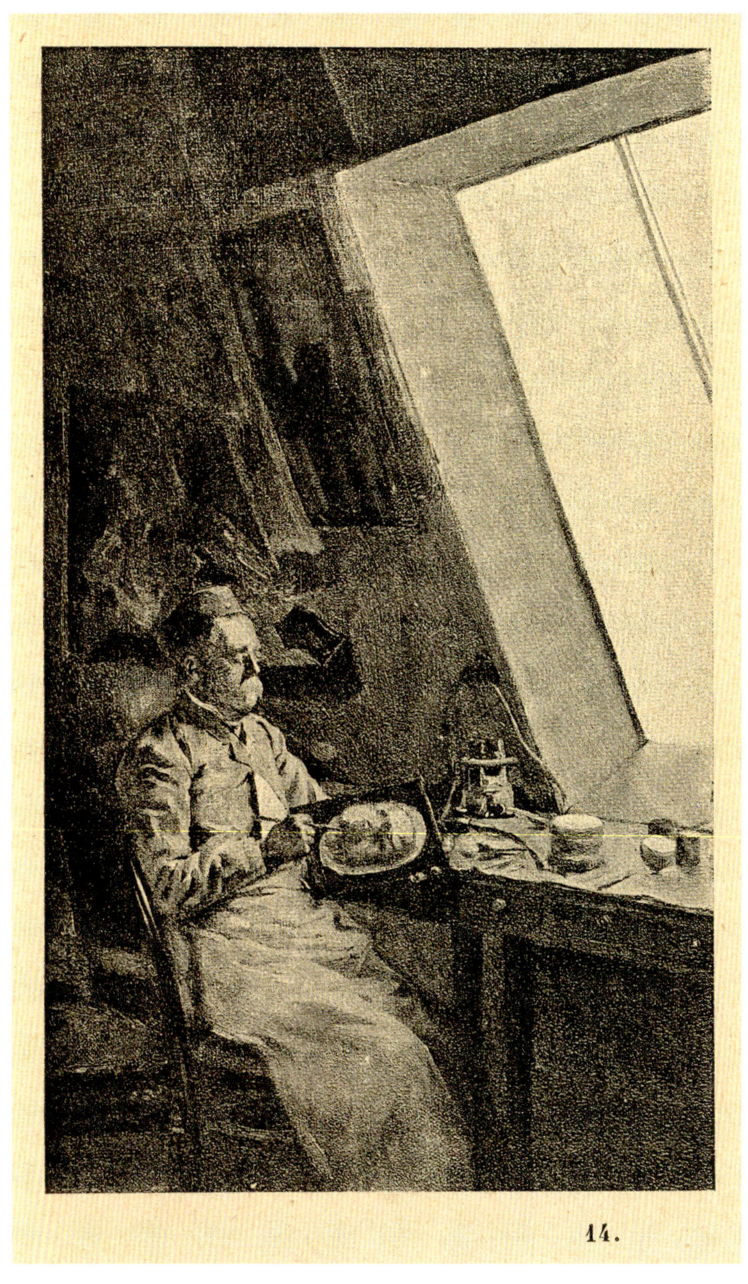

Figure 4:
Baretta colouring a moulage in his studio, engraving by Ch. Petit, in Roger-Milès, *La cité de misère*, 1891, plate 14.

The wax objects were not just visual aids, they were active participants in dermatological practices, fundamental to the establishment of the discipline's diagnostic methods and prestige, as well as for the communication between physicians. But in order for them to fulfil this role, they needed to be more than simply a faithful reproduction of a condition in a wax relief. Complex framing was required to facilitate the functioning of the moulages within a medical collection. This can be demonstrated with one example, the moulage of a case of lupus (Fig. 1). Once the wax cast had been made and the refinement of the relief were completed, the moulage was carefully wrapped in white fabric held in form through the application of liquid plaster. The cloth is neatly wound around the fragment. It conceals the margins of the cast and along with it its status as an artefact rather than body part. It also recalls hospital bed sheets but also resembles the draperies used in anatomical and pathological imagery to conceal cuts—both surgical and visual—and to encourage the viewer to focus on the body part in question. Here it helps to concentrate on the affected nose, placed centrally within the chosen segment of the face. With this wrap the moulage is attached to a black wooden board. As a portrait of the mouleur published in a fictionalized reportage of the hospital, *La cité de misère* by art historian and critic Léon Roger-Milès, suggests, it was only after the relief was fixed that Baretta made finishing touches and applied colours to enhance the likeness and make the lesions more legible (Fig. 4). This kind of framing, the fragmentation and attachment on a board, was pretty much standardized for dermatological moulages and used since the mid-nineteenth century in relevant medical collections throughout Europe. Not all mouleurs signed their casts, but Baretta did so systematically. Written in white paint on black and in capital letters, his name, often accompanied by the date when the moulage was made, is placed obliquely next to the plastered cloth, sometimes nestling against the fragment and following its shape. With the act of signing Baretta takes ownership of the moulage and the condition, it is no more the patient's disease, but Baretta's product. By using a signature, the mouleur also aligns himself with artists and their way of marking and authenticating their work. However, highlighting the madeness of the scientific image was always a dicey enterprise. Mouleurs, not unlike taxidermists, tended to be in a conundrum in the nineteenth century: they liked to stress the artistic qualities and their skills certainly heightened the lifelikeness and efficacy of their three-dimensional images, but this tendency always risked undermining the truth value of the cast or preserved specimen, its ability to be presented as 'nature itself' or as an imprint that mechanically reproduced a morbid phenomenon.[19]

19 This has been highlighted for taxidermy by Lange-Berndt, *Animal Art*, 2005, in particular pp. 26–29; on art history's difficulty with accepting imprints as art see also: Didi-Huberman, *La ressemblance par contact*, 2008, especially pp. 92–111 and 122–135.

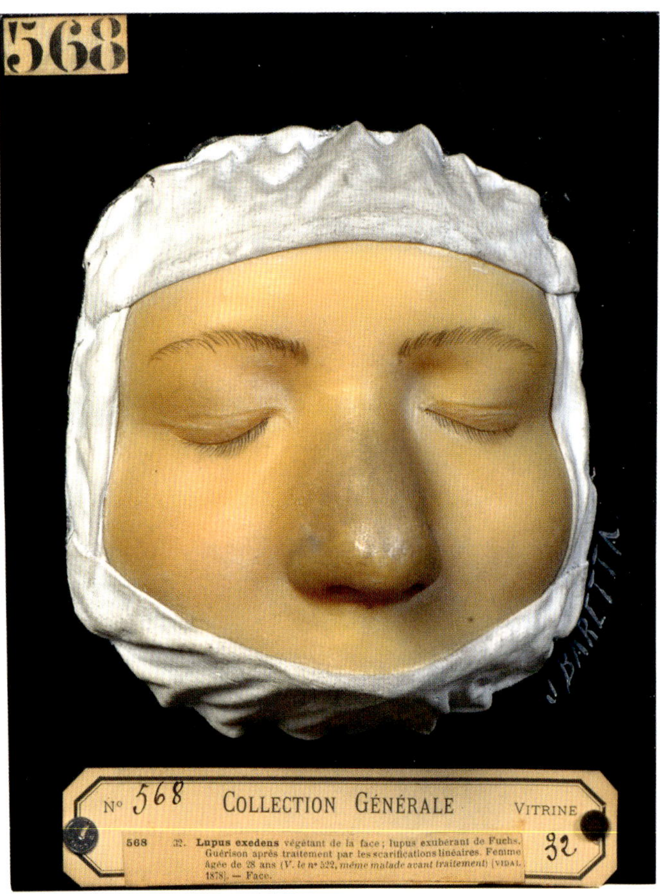

Figure 5:
Jules Baretta, *Lupus exédens végétant de la face*, 1878, wax moulage n° 568.
Paris, Musée de l'Hôpital Saint-Louis.

In Paris, each of the moulages also carry a number on a piece of paper glued onto the black board. This number records the sequence in which the items for a particular collection were made. Here I am focusing on the *Collection Générale*, which was complemented by collections made for individual doctors and grouped in the museum under their name, most notably the collection of the surgeon Jules Émile Péan discussed in detail by Mary Hunter in her book *The Face of Medicine.*[20] The system of sequential numbering for the *Collection Générale* was followed by Baretta and his successors until the last moulage was made by Stéphane Littré in 1958. This number clearly identifies a moulage, and is still used

20 Hunter, *The Face of Medicine*, 2016, pp. 108–165; see also her article: '"Effroyable Réalisme",' 2008.
21 Feulard, *Musée de l'hôpital Saint-Louis*, 1889. **22** Brodier, *Musée de l'hôpital Saint-Louis*, 1922.

today for the reproductive photographs made from the objects and available from the image database of the Bibliothèque interuniversitaire de santé in Paris. The systematic numbering allowed for a system of double-entry filing and a certain mobility of the medical objects. The sequence in which the moulages were made was to some extent accidental or at least arbitrary to the order in which they are shown in the museum. It depended on the interests of the dermatologists at the hospital and on the availability of patients showing exemplary or exceptional manifestations of a given disease.

The ordering of the moulages within the museum display was a different matter—and as will be discussed later on—subject to debate. Let's take for example *number* 522, a moulage showing a case of lupus (a condition explained today as an autoimmune disease), and *number* 568 cast from the same face a few months later (Fig. 1 and 5). Two temporalities come together here, the time of the disease and the rhythm of Baretta's work. In the interval Baretta made forty-four moulages and the patient was cured. At least, the waxen image looks healed, and a smoothly modelled nose has replaced the growth at the centre of the earlier wax relief. Such 'before and after' images are comparatively rare in the collections of the Hôpital Saint-Louis, as were, with many diseases, the chances for a cure. Be that as it may, the two faces of a patient were reunited in one display case—*N° 32*, dedicated to lupus (Fig. 6). These two numbers—the one indicating the sequence in which the moulage was made by Baretta and the other the number of the vitrine—were filled into a preprinted label pinned onto the black board. This label was potentially removable, for example when a symptom was attributed to a different condition, when a clinical picture was re-diagnosed, and a moulage changed display case. The moulages are thus potentially mobile, but remain identifiable by their number. Additional information was glued onto the label. For all moulages commissioned until 1922 it was cut out from the catalogue of the Musée des moulages. During a period of not only busy production of moulages but also intense debate about their ordering and classification, three catalogues were printed. The first catalogue of the collection was assembled by Henri Feulard and published in 1889 jointly with the official opening of the Musée des moulages.[21] The display was installed by 1886 already but the inauguration was delayed until 1889, to coincide with the centenary of the French Revolution, the Paris World Fair and the first gathering of the International society of dermatologists who met in the lecture hall surrounded by the wax moulages. Since ca. 1922, the majority of the moulages have been given labels with cut outs from the third museum catalogue authored by Léon Brodier, a physician and the administrator of the museum and its adjacent dermatological library between 1913 and 1939.[22] It remained the last catalogue of the museum, published nine years after Baretta retired. Even though pathological waxes continued to be produced for another three decades, the fact that the catalogue was never updated again, can be seen as an indication of the declining significance of the wax moulage as a scientific tool. Moulages commissioned after 1922 carry handwritten inscriptions detailing the disorder in question, and provide information about the patient and the doctor in charge.

The older moulages were entirely inventoried in Brodier's catalogue and itemized by serial number. A comprehensive index lists the diseases, and allows for the usage of the catalogue as a dermatological compendium. Each entry and the matching label typically provide the name of the condition, short information about the gender, age and profession of the sick person and a reference to the doctor who treated the patient and studied the condition. In the case of moulage *number* 522 the entry reads as follows:

'522 vit 32. Lupus exedence végétant de la face; lupus exubérant de Fuchs. Femme agée de 28 ans (*V. le n° 568, même malade après traitement par les scarifications linéaires*) [VIDAL 1878.]—Face.'[23]

The information in square brackets refers to the doctor who commissioned the moulage and thus associated himself with the case. Here it is Émile Vidal, a founding member of the *Société française de dermatologie*—established at the same time (1889) as the official opening of the museum—who had lectured on lupus at the Hôpital Saint-Louis the very year the moulage was made. He was celebrated for the method of linear scarification applied—if we can trust the moulages and records—successfully in the case of the 28-year-old woman with lupus.[24]

The moulage in question here was commissioned and made in 1878, the framed and tagged relief was initially put into vitrine *number* 28, first catalogued in 1889,[25] subsequently moved to vitrine *number* 32, and obtained its final paratexts in or shortly after 1922, when the label was updated. Since, it had collected dust, was more recently cleaned and photographed, but remained otherwise physically unaltered and immobile.

The reproduction of a disease carried on her face by a 28-year-old woman was thus doubly marked by an authoritative gesture—that of the maker and that of the medic. Once in a vitrine, itself labelled with the name of a condition, and safely kept behind glass, the coloured wax relief portrays the condition, not the woman. It becomes part of a museum display and the order of diseases. This ensemble of *parerga* and paratexts further turns the cast of a body part—already singled out as an item of dermatological scrutiny—into a scientific object. As such the moulages were instrumental in the institutional setting of the hospital and in the establishment of dermatology as a medical discipline. And they were further entwined with texts. The building in which the museum was housed included not only an out-patient unit on the ground floor, but also a dermatological library adjacent to the collection of moulages to allow for an exchange between objects and texts. While the catalogue entries and labels for moulages *numbers* 522 and 568 make only reference to the commissioning physician, many other tags refer to more extensive case notes published in the dermatological literature, namely the then new specialist journals such as the *Annales de dermatologie et syphiligraphie* founded in 1869.

23 Brodier, *Musée de l'hôpital Saint-Louis*, 1922, p. 33. **24** Vidal, *Exposé des titres et travaux scientifiques*, 1879, pp. 47–48, further on Vidal's biography: Tilles, 'The Hôpital Saint-Louis,' 2002, p. 447. **25** Brodier, *Musée de l'hôpital Saint-Louis*, 1922, p. 26. **26** Latour, 'Visualisation and Cognition,' 1986.

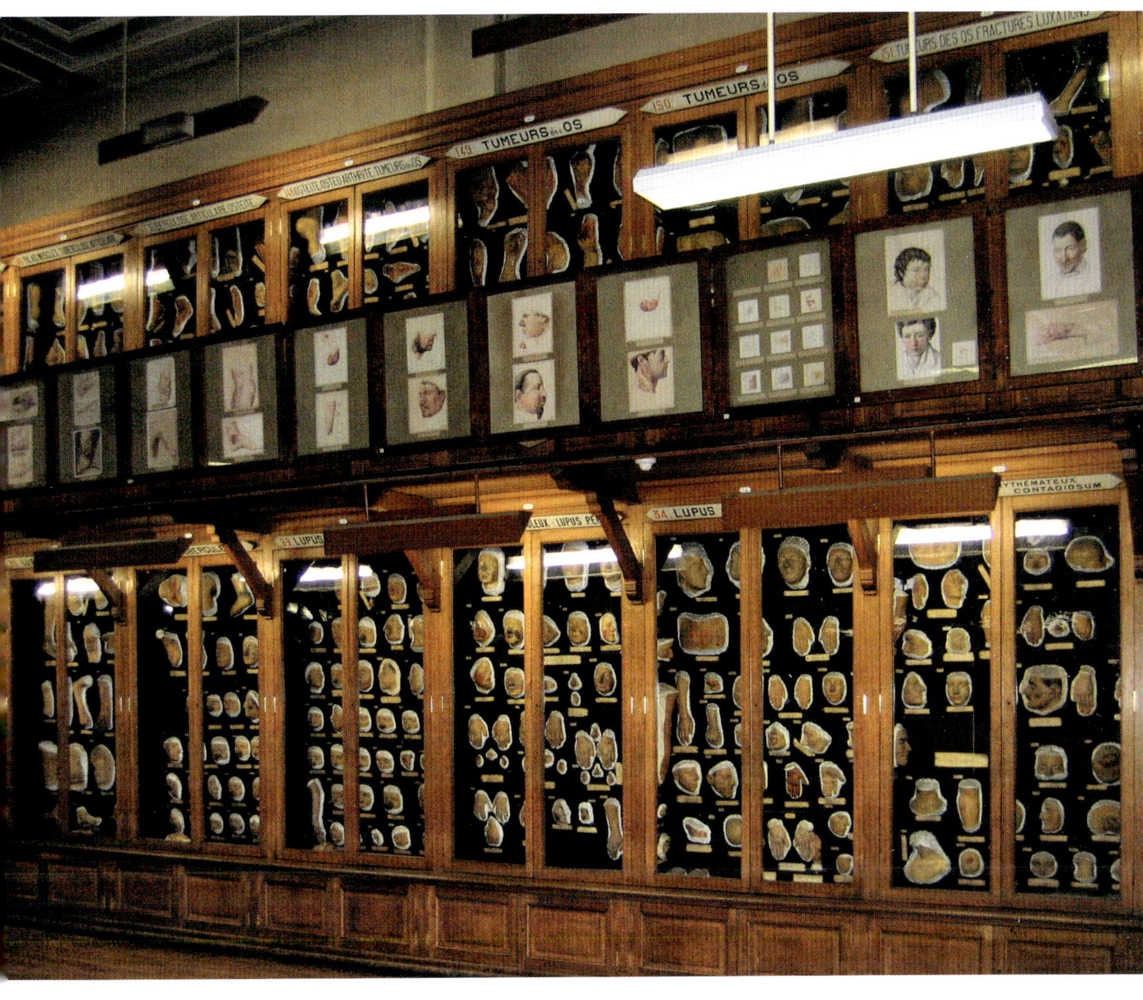

Figure 6:
Vitrine *Lupus*. Paris, Musée de l'Hôpital Saint-Louis.

This extensive network of *parerga* and paratexts is part and parcel of the order established at the hospital's museum, and it is only within this framing that the wax moulages can work—for the nineteenth-century dermatologists—as scientific images that can stand in for individual cases and afford, as a collection, to represent their discipline as a whole. It is this particular constellation that enables the moulages to work as what Bruno Latour has called 'quasi-objects' or 'immutable mobiles.'[26] They help to turn sick people into cases, and make symptoms observable as they are presented in a comparable format unified through a more or less homogenized mode of production, method of framing and system of reference. At the same time, they can be re-arranged in their vitrine or between display cases, and occasionally they travelled further, as they were lent to other teaching institutions or reproduced from the plaster negative and dispatched for display in other medical collections. However, simply ascribing the moulages one form of agency as non-human participants, means seeing only one aspect of them. Waxen simulacra operate on multiple levels. They were made by a skilled practitioner operating hand in hand with medical professionals to fulfil a specific function in dermatological study and teaching. The truth value attributed to them and the resemblance achieved through the casting and moulding process, as well as the colouring and remodelling of the wax relief, allowed them to successfully work as dermatological entities within the Saint-Louis hospital for about hundred years, before they became an embarrassment for a differently understood and practiced medical science and transformed instead into items of historical interest.

The moulages never fully fitted into the order of dermatology. The imponderability starts with the physical disorders themselves. Disease resists standardization. It was defined as an aberration in the nineteenth-century regime of the normal and the pathological, and it is different in every single person. Skin diseases are multiform and the situation of growths, sores and lesions on at times oblique and intimate parts of the body, each required a different form of contact and technical approach. The ordering of the multiple appearances of diseases—and in consequence of the moulages reproducing them—proved itself a challenge. This can be gleaned from the discussions the dermatologists in charge of the museum had about the arrangement of the maladies in wax.

In the years predating the inauguration of the museum the physicians at Saint-Louis vividly debated the question of how to order the waxes, and with them the cutaneous conditions. The arrangement finally developed avoided the potential pitfalls of a particular taxonomy and ranged the diseases alphabetically.[27] This also allowed for the continuous complement of the collection with new cases and waxes, while retaining the initial order. No matter what arrangement the individual dermatologist opted for, they agreed that the initial disorder, a *beau désordre*, as Dévergie put it in 1876, was dissatisfactory and that an appropriate classification was key for the framing of the museum as a scientific institution and educational site.[28] Ten years later, Adrien Doyon, founder of the *Annales de dermatologie et de syphiligraphie*, still worried in an article on dermatological teaching methods that in the current state the unguided student was rather overwhelmed and

27 This is pointed out by Henri Feulard in his introduction to Besnier, *Le Musée de l'hôpital Saint-Louis*, 1895–1897, pp. ii–iii. **28** Devergie, 'Musée de l'hôpital Saint-Louis,' 1876, p. 396: 'C'est donc on peut le dire *un beau désordre*. [...] Vaste travail, travail de patience, travail d'amour de la science et d'amour de l'enseignement; car par ce classement on fera de l'enseignement pour les médecins et les élèves.' See on the significance of taxonomy for the scientific credibility of the Musée des moulages also Hunter, *The Face of Medicine*, 2016, p. 151. **29** Doyon, 'Du mode d'enseignement de la dermato-syphiligraphie contemporaine,' 1883, here part 2, p. 252: 'L'étudiant, n'ayant pas de fil conducteur, errera pour ainsi dire à l'aventure tout autour de ces vitrines renfermant tant de matériaux d'un prix inestimable, et cela sans profit pour son instruction, et à chaque instant découragé par le nombre même des objets qui se disputent son attention. Aujourd'hui déjà on va au musée poussé plutôt par un sentiment de curiosité, qu'en vue de son instruction.' **30** Kornmeier, *Madame Tussaud*, 2006, pp. 268–278; Schwartz, *Spectacular Realities*, 1998, pp. 98–148. **31** The remaining waxes from the Musée Spitzner used to be part of the

discouraged by the sheer number of objects that were 'fighting for the student's attention.' 'Today,' he continues, 'one visits the museum rather driven by a sentiment of curiosity' than with regards to the instruction it has to offer.[29] From the dermatologist's perspective, 'curiosity' is apparently not the right attitude for medical study. It was deemed problematic, I presume, because it recalled older—now outmoded—forms of anatomical or natural history displays in the tradition of cabinets of curiosities, and was associated at the same time with the contemporary wax displays seeking to attract broader Parisian audiences.

The Musée Grévin—only a twenty-minute walk from the Hôpital Saint-Louis—had opened in 1882, aiming to outdo London's Madame Tussaud's by embedding the wax figures into tableaux and dioramas.[30] Spitzner's *Grand Musée d'Anatomie* with its spectacular anatomical displays had opened in Paris in 1856 to an initially male-only audience and continued to enjoy success as a travelling exhibition. On display were large numbers of high-quality wax models and moulages, including dermatological moulages fabricated by Baretta.[31] Very similar wax casts of skin conditions were shown at the Musée Spitzner and at the Hôpital Saint-Louis, but they gained different meanings through their context and paratexts. This proximity made it all the more necessary for the doctors in charge of the hospital's collection to distinguish their newly built museum from these sensationalist wax displays that mixed, in the case of the Musée Spitzner, medical and sexual elucidation with erotic titillation and entertainment.[32]

An 1888 visitor to the Musée des moulages equally experienced mixed feelings upon first sight of the collection. The German dermatologist Paul Gerson Unna left an account of his visit, later translated by Doyon for the *Annales de dermatologie*:

'During a first promenade around the museum, before the detail of the preparations and their comparison with each other demand our full attention, the sentiment oscillates between the admiration for the artistic perfection of the preparations and the surprising experience that the diagnosis works almost as easily and reliably as it does from the life. One feels simultaneously transported into the studio of a remarkable artist and in a veritable hospital hall filled with sick people reuniting typical cases of common and rare dermatoses.'[33]

collections of the Musée Delmas-Orfila-Rouvière at the Faculté de médecine in Paris, and, after a decade in storage, have found a new home in the anatomical collections of the Université de Montpellier. See: Palouzié and Ducourau, 'De la collection Fontana à la collection Spitzner,' 2017. **32** Hunter, *The Face of Medicine*, 2016, pp. 138–139 and 151. **33** The letters were initially published in German as Unna, 'Pariser Briefe,' 1888, here p. 532. Doyon translated and summarized them for the French journal, see Doyon, 'Lettres de Paris par P. G. Unna,' 1888, p. 57: 'Dans une première promenade à travers le musée, avant que le détail des préparations, leur comparaison avec d'autres exige toute notre attention, on ne sait ce qu'on doit le plus admirer de la perfection artistique des préparations ou des procédés surprenants d'après lesquels on peut faire le diagnostic presque aussi facilement et aussi sûrement que sur le vivant. On se sent ici en même temps transporté dans l'atelier d'un artiste remarquable et dans une véritable salle de malades, qui réunit les cas typiques des dermatoses communes et rares.'

This ambivalence is frequently found in the encounter with wax figures, as Unna's perception alternates between seeing the artist's work and the perfect reproduction. These conflicting impressions are superseded by a more stable feeling, that of joy nourished by the 'quiet and serious bliss of scientific study' in which the artifice is forgotten, even though this very artifice enables a kind of concentrated examination not possible when engaging with actual sick persons. For Unna, the value of the museum depends not only on the precision of the reproductions but also on the ordering and labelling. He appreciates what he refers to as 'republikanische Etikettierung' with which the collections stuck (at the time) to the initial diagnosis of the doctor responsible for the case and the commissioning of the moulage, thus also recording its own history.[34]

When blending out the artifice, Unna takes the wax reliefs for the sick, and he was not the only dermatologist who saw the moulages as effective replicas of diseases and diseased. The lifelikeness afforded by the material wax and the technique of casting, allows for the moulages to work for the dermatologist, but there is an animist residue when they act as substitutes for the sick. Not long after Unna was pondering the efficacy of dermatological moulages, another Hamburg scholar, art historian Aby Warburg, was also thinking about wax and lifelikeness. In his famous essay *Bildniskunst und florentinisches Bürgertum* (1901) he stressed the significance of wax figures for the development of Renaissance portraiture.[35] Conjuring the waxen votive sculptures that used to populate the Florentine Church of Santa Maria Annunziata Warburg wrote:

'The interior of the church must have looked like a waxwork museum. On one side stood the Florentines [...] and alongside them the popes. [...] Particular objects of pride, however, were the foreigners who, out of veneration for the Santissima Annunziata, had left their own life-size effigies in wax by way of visiting cards [...]. As late as 1630, there were 600 life-size figures, 22,000 papier-maché *voti*.'[36]

Warburg explains that the waxen simulacra deployed in the church served as intermediaries facilitating the communion between the donors and God.[37] Betraying the Florentines' Etruscian heritage, it was ancient superstition transformed into Christian practice and tolerated by a Church aware of primordial religious beliefs. But Warburg looked both backwards and forward. In his attempt to visualize the historic display, he also drew comparisons with modern cultural practices and visual cultures—the visiting card and the waxwork museum. In a similar manner, I would like to evoke the votive images at Santa

34 Unna, 'Pariser Briefe,' 1888, pp. 532–533. **35** Didi-Huberman, 'Ressemblance mythifiée et ressemblance oubliée,' 1994, especially pp. 410–411. **36** Warburg, 'The Art of Portraiture and the Florentine Bourgeoisie,' 1999 [1902], here pp. 206–207. **37** On Warburg and the 'Agency of Lifelikeness' see also: van Eck, *Art, Agency and Living Presence*, 2015, pp. 183–188. The author (p. 183) likens Warburg's account of the Florentine '*Bildzauber*' with Alfred Gell's concept of 'distributed agency.' **38** Holmes, 'Ex-votos: Materiality, Memory, and Cult,' 2009. **39** Schnalke, *Diseases in Wax*, 1995, pp. 15–23. **40** Lebrun and Magnier, *Nouveau manuel complet du mouleur*, 1850, p. 219: 'M. le docteur Despine fils, a eu l'heureuse idée de présenter une série de faits pris sur nature [...] qui [...] offrissent à l'œil l'état des maladies et celui

Maria Annunziata to look at the late nineteenth-century museum of medical moulages in order to bring out the material histories that still resonate in the modern practices of making, collecting, displaying and viewing medical waxes. The arrangement of reproduced body parts in displays like those at the Hôpital Saint-Louis show remarkable similarities with the display of ex-votos in churches. Like the dermatological moulages, ex-votos—offerings given in gratitude to a deity or saint after the fulfilment of a vow—often come as more or less lifelike imitations of body parts, especially when the vow made relates to a health condition.[38] Not surprisingly, scholars of dermatological moulages have referred to the tradition of votive images before,[39] but they have so far overlooked how close wax moulages and ex-votos came in nineteenth-century France, where hopes of miraculous healings had grown after Saint Bernadette of Lourdes had her Marian apparitions in 1858. Lourdes quickly became a major pilgrimage site and soon several miraculous healings were attributed to the water from the spring close to where the apparition had happened. Votive offerings abound at Lourdes, they mostly take the form of inscriptions and only occasionally that of body parts. Still, the health benefits of spring water, wax moulages and ex-votos were explicitly related in the nineteenth century. The widely circulated handbook for moulders, the *Nouveau manuel complet du mouleur*, reports in a section on 'Wax moulages in thermal baths' of a Dr Despine who had the idea of presenting a series of casts in order to 'offer the eye the state of diseases before and after recovery.' To that end, the industrious doctor produced a number of wax moulages, which he displayed in the establishments of the spa Aix-en-Savoie to demonstrate 'striking cases of healings performed by the thermal waters.' The manual expresses the wish that more thermal baths would form comparable pathological museums, because 'these medical archives would remain like the ex-votos of churches to attest their miraculous healings.'[40] This remarkable desire is followed by a list of conditions already preserved in wax pieces, which includes a number of diseases (such as psoriasis, syphilis or lichen) also treated—and reproduced—at the Hôpital Saint-Louis. Practicing in a spa, Constant Despine certainly treated patients wealthier than those who had to resort to the crowded Hôpital Saint-Louis, and used his moulages as a form of advertisement. His moulages were not primarily made for physicians, but for actual and potential patients. Did the sick treated at the Hôpital Saint-Louis also get to see the casts taken from their bodies? As they were required for their making, they must have witnessed their production up-to the point

de leur guérison. Pour cela, il a formé une collection de pièces en cire, qu'il a déposée dans l'établissement thermal d'Aix-en-Savoie [...]. Cette précieuse collection présente déjà plusieurs cas remarquables de guérisons opérées par les eaux thermales. [...] Il serait à désirer que les autres établissements thermaux, [...] formassent des Musées pathologiques semblables; ces archives médicales resteraient-là comme les *ex-voto* des églises, pour attester leurs miraculeuses guérisons.' The same paragraph (without the added list of conditions) is repeated in the 1887 edition. Constant Despine himself published among others: *L'Été à Aix en Savoie*, 1851, where he mentions his museum (p. 29).

where they served as models during the application of colours. At this moment, when the disease was taken off them and externalised, some of them might well have believed in the magic potential of the waxes, hoping they helped in the cure like votive offerings. Like the Florentine effigies discussed by Warburg, the moulages then became mediators between the sick and whatever divine or spiritual entity they trusted to have power over their medical destiny.

Even within a fairly exclusive medical environment, like that of the Hôpital Saint-Louis, the dermatological wax moulages could not simply shake off religious traditions and magical practices, and they could have quite different significations and affective potentials for doctors and patients. But an affective—and possibly magical—dimension was an intrinsic part of how dermatological moulages worked for physicians as well. Their lifelikeness enabled them to operate in the diagnostic practices of dermatology and to be taken as substitutes for the sick. The affective responses they prompt allowed them to act as mediators between doctors and patients. If their lifelikeness and presence has the effect of engaging viewers then and now, then the ways in which physicians and wax moulages co-operate within the setting of the medical museum and the hospital is historically specific. The historic protagonists testify to a very nineteenth-century interplay of affect and order, in which the moulage first attracts the attention through the spectacular effects of verisimilitude before potentially leading to a more studious dermatological observation. This form of visual examination was encouraged as much by the truth-value of the moulages, which derived both from their lifelikeness and from casting as their mode of production, as by their framing. If this afforded a more detached mode of engagement, which adheres to the virtues of nineteenth-century medical science, dermatological wax moulages are hardly ever detached from the physicality of diseases or from the semantic and actual fluidity of the material wax, the procedures of their making and the complex histories of lifelikeness, ceroplasty and the imprint.

Bibliography

E. Ackerknecht, *Medicine at the Paris Hospital, 1794–1848* (John Hopkins Press, 1967).
J.-L. Alibert, *Description des maladies de la peau observées à l'hôpital Saint-Louis* (Barrois, 1806).
J.-L. Alibert, 'Note sur l'Hôpital Saint-Louis' in J.-L. Alibert, *Monographie des dermatoses où précis théorique et pratique des maladies de la peau* (Chez le Docteur Daynac, éditeur, 1832).
E. Besnier, *Le Musée de l'hôpital Saint-Louis. Iconographie des maladies cutanées et syphilitiques: avec texte explicatif* (Rueff, 1895–1897).
L. Brodier, *Musée de l'hôpital Saint-Louis. Catalogue des moulages coloriés* (Imprimerie typographique de l'École d'Alembert, 1922).
L. Daston and P. Galison, *Objectivity* (Zone Books, 2007).
C. Despine, *L'Été à Aix en Savoie, nouveau guide pratique, médical et pittoresque* (Dauvin et Fontaine, 1851).
A. Devergie, 'Musée de l'hôpital Saint-Louis,' *Annales de dermatologie et de syphiligraphie*, 7 (1876), pp. 390–400.
G. Didi-Huberman, 'Ressemblance mythifiée et ressemblance oubliée chez Vasari: la légende du portrait sur le vif,' *Mélanges de l'Ecole française à Rome. Italie et Méditerranée*, 106 (1994), pp. 383–432.
G. Didi-Huberman, *La ressemblance par contact. Archéologie, anachronisme et modernité de l'empreinte* (Minuit, 2008).
A. Doyon, 'Du mode d'enseignement de la dermato-syphiligraphie contemporaine. Vienne, Paris, Lyon,' *Annales de dermatologie et de syphiligraphie*, 4 (1883), pp. 189–196, 249–256, 309–314.
A. Doyon, 'Lettres de Paris par P. G. Unna,' *Annales de dermatologie et syphiligraphie*, 10 (1888), pp. 57–88.
M. Fend, 'Portraying Skin Disease: Robert Carswell's Dermatological Watercolours' in K. Siena and J. Reinarz (eds.), *A Medical History of Skin* (Pickering and Chatto, 2013), pp. 147–164.
H. Feulard, *Musée de l'hôpital Saint-Louis. Catalogue des moulages coloriés* (G. Steinheil, 1889).
M. Foucault, *The Birth of the Clinic: An Archaeology of Medical Perception*, trans. by A. M. Sheridian Smith (Tavistock, 1973 [1963]).
A. Goodie and H. Grootenboer (eds.), 'Theorizing Wax: On the Meaning of a Disappearing Medium,' Special Issue of *Oxford Art Journal*, 36 (2013).
H. Gougerot and L. Brodier, *L'Hôpital Saint-Louis et la Clinique d'Alfred Fournier* (J. Peyronnet & Cie, 1932).
C. Hannaway and A. La Berge, 'Paris Medicine: Perspectives Past and Present' in C. Hannaway and A. La Berge (eds.), *Constructing Paris Medicine* (Rodopi, 1998), pp. 1–69.
A. Hardy and A. de Montméja, *Clinique photographique de l'hôpital Saint-Louis* (Chamerot et Lawereyns, 1868).
M. Holmes, 'Ex-votos: Materiality, Memory, and Cult' in M. W. Cole and R. Zorach (eds.), *The Idol in the Age of Art. Objects, Devotions and the Early Modern World* (Ashgate, 2009), pp. 159–181.
M. Hunter, '"Effroyable Réalisme": Wax, Femininity, and the Madness of Realist Fantasies,' *RACAR*, 23 (2008), n° 1–2, pp. 43–58.
M. Hunter, *The Face of Medicine. Visualising Medical Masculinities in Late Nineteenth-Century Paris* (Manchester University Press, 2016).
T. Ingold, 'The Textility of Making,' *Cambridge Journal of Economics*, 34 (2010), pp. 91–102.
S. Jacyna, 'Pious Pathology: J. L. Alibert's Iconography of Disease' in C. Hannaway and A. La Berge (eds.), *Constructing Paris Medicine* (Rodopi, 1998), pp. 185–219.
U. Kornmeier, *Madame Tussaud und die Geschichte des Wachsfigurenkabinetts vom 17. bis zum frühen 20. Jahrhundert* (E-doc Humboldt Universität Berlin, 2006) [http://edoc.hu-berlin.de/18452/16199].
U. Kornmeier, 'Almost Alive. The Spectacle of Verissimilitude in Madame Tussaud's Waxworks' in R. Panzanelli (ed.), *Ephemeral Bodies. Wax Sculpture and the Human Figure. With a Translation of Julius von Schlosser's 'History of Portraiture in Wax'* (Getty Research Institute, 2008), pp. 67–81.
P. Lange-Berndt, *Animal Art. Präparierte Tiere in der Kunst 1850–2000* (Silke Schreiber, 2005).

B. Latour, 'Visualisation and Cognition: Thinking with Eyes and Hands,' *Knowledge and Society. Studies in the Sociology of Culture Past and Present*, 6 (1986), pp. 1–40.

M. Lebrun and M.-D. Magnier, *Nouveau manuel complet du mouleur en plâtre, au ciment, à l'argile, à la cire, à la gelatine. Nouvelle édition, revue […] et augmentée de nouveaux procédés de moulage […]* (Roret, 1850).

F. Noirot, 'Jules Baretta et les secrets du moulage pathologique au XIXe siècle. Analyse de la cire n° 1364 au musée de l'hôpital Saint-Louis,' *Histoire des Sciences Médicales*, 48 (2014), pp. 203–208.

H. Palouzié and C. Ducourau, 'De la collection Fontana à la collection Spitzner, l'aventure des cires anatomiques de Paris à Montpellier,' *In Situ. Revue des patrimoines*, 31 (2017) [http://journals.openedition.org/insitu/14142].

R. Panzanelli (ed.), *Ephemeral Bodies. Wax Sculpture and the Human Figure. With a Translation of Julius von Schlosser's 'History of Portraiture in Wax'* (Getty Research Institute, 2008).

É. Papet, 'Technique: "saisir la nature sur le fait"' in É. Papet, *À fleur de peau. Le moulage sur nature au XIXe siècle* (Réunion des musée nationaux, 2001), pp. 74–77.

L. Roger-Milès, *La cité de misère* (Marpon & Flammarion, 1891).

J. von Schlosser, 'Geschichte der Porträtbildnerei in Wachs,' *Jahrbuch der kunsthistorischen Sammlungen des allerhöchsten Kaiserhauses*, 3/29 (1910–1911), pp. 171–258.

T. Schnalke, *Diseases in Wax. The History of the Medical Moulage*, trans. by K. Spatscheke (Quintessence Publishing, 1995).

T. Schnalke, 'Casting Skin: Meanings for Doctors, Artists and Patients' in S. de Chadarevian and N. Hopwood (eds.), *Models. The Third Dimension of Science* (Stanford University Press, 2004), pp. 207–241.

V. R. Schwartz, *Spectacular Realities: Early Mass Culture in Fin-de-Siècle Paris* (University of California Press, 1998).

G. Tilles, 'The Hôpital Saint-Louis from 1607 until 1945' in D. Wallach and G. Tilles (eds.), *Dermatology in France* (Éditions Privat, 2002), pp. 381–458.

P. G. Unna, 'Pariser Briefe,' *Monatshefte für praktische Dermatologie*, 7 (1888), pp. 530–534.

C. van Eck, *Art, Agency and Living Presence. From the Animated Image to the Excessive Object* (De Gruyter and Leiden University Press, 2015).

É. Vidal, *Exposé des titres et travaux scientifiques* (Impr. Émile Martinet, 1879).

A. Warburg, 'The Art of Portraiture and the Florentine Bourgeoisie. Domenico Ghirlandaio in Santa Trinita: The Portraits of Lorenzo de' Medici and His Household' in A. Warburg, *The Renewal of Pagan Antiquity. Contributions to the Cultural History of the European Renaissance*, trans. by D. Britt (Getty Research Institute, 1999 [1902]), pp. 185–221.

Websites:

http://www.biusante.parisdescartes.fr/histoire/images/index.php.

http://www.biusante.parisdescartes.fr/stlouis/fr/debut.htm.

www.youtube.com/watch?v=XDsoaWipkko.

CINDY KANG

The Barnes Ensembles, Again

In 2012 the Barnes Foundation opened its Philadelphia gallery building, relocating its renowned art collection from the suburbs of Merion, PA to an urban center. The installation of the collection replicated the one in Merion, keeping Dr. Albert Barnes's characteristic ensembles—symmetrical displays mixing fine and decorative arts from disparate eras and regions—intact. This relocation and replication have been the subject of acrimonious debate in the courts and in the press, given that the move required a hotly contested deviation from the Foundation's indenture. Typical critical reactions to the reconstructed galleries include one art critic's dismissal of the 'weird downtown Barnes museum' as 'a simulacrum with better lighting.'[1] Others praised the move as a success: '[T]he changes for the most part enhance the viewing experience [...] the recreation is a triumph of meticulousness;' '[e]ntering the re-created spaces is like encountering a friend who just spent time at a spa. The rooms look rejuvenated and fresh, the paintings appear more alive than ever. It is different, to be sure, yet the same.'[2]

Aside from a few studies in the field of architecture, there has been little scholarly reflection on the theoretical implications of the move.[3] For the most part, the legal and financial controversies have dominated discussion of the Philadelphia Barnes. Accepting the relocation as a *fait accompli*, this essay focuses on the replication of the display—what did this recreation of the ensembles achieve or mean in terms of museology, material preservation, and the meaning of these objects within the narrative of art history? Was the original simply destroyed in favor of a simulacrum? Is there another way to look at it?

I will analyze the de-contextualization and re-contextualization of the Barnes ensembles as a flashpoint, exposing set assumptions and attachments to certain ways of thinking about history and authenticity. Interrogating the replication opens up new ways in which to understand originality and its relationship to the agency of display.

1 I would like to thank Laura Leigh Fielding Sevelis for her invaluable assistance in the preparation of this essay and Brendan Sullivan for his incisive comments on an earlier draft. Knight, 'Review,' 2012: http://articles.latimes.com/2012/may/18/entertainment/la-et-barnes-art-review-20120518 (last accessed 27 March 2018). **2** Sozanski, 'Review,' 2012; Saffron, 'The Barnes,' 2012. The reviews cited in this essay, unless noted as websites, were collated and reprinted in an institutional publication, Barnes Foundation, *Philadelphia Opening Media Report*, 2012. **3** Lawrence, 'Preservation through Replication,' 2015; Stuth, 'Continuity, Criticality, and Change,' 2010.

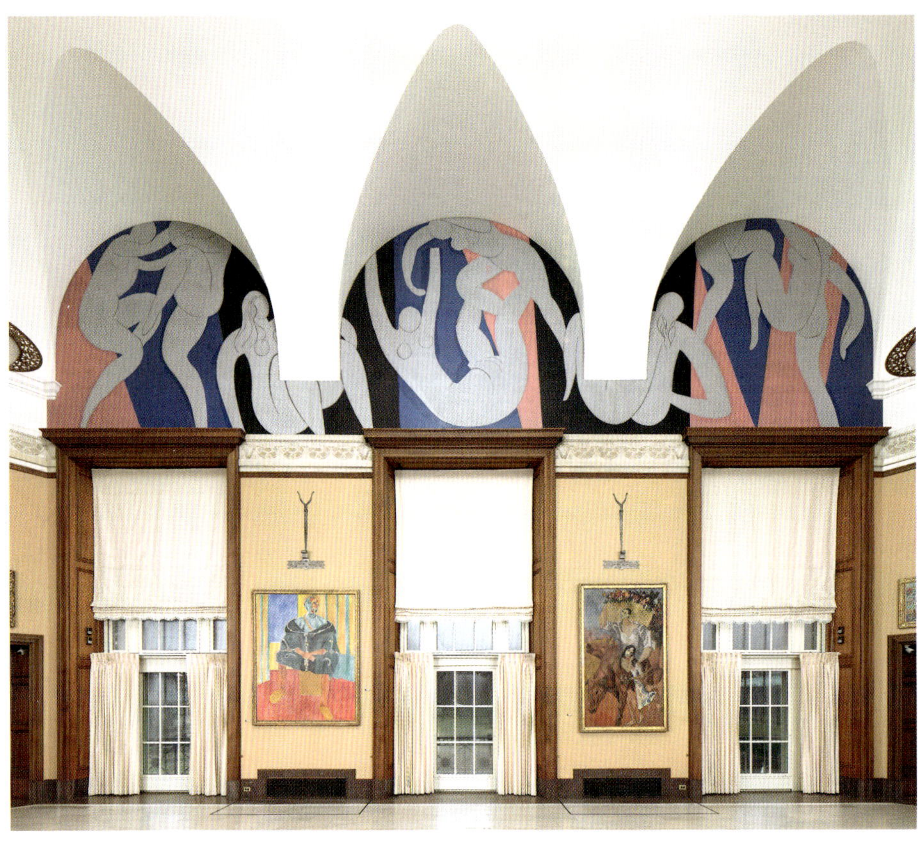

Figure 1:
Barnes Foundation, ensemble view, Main Gallery, south wall, Merion, 2009.

Replication as Repetition

'Replicate is a very scary word. We didn't want to replicate.' —Billie Tsien[4]

Tod Williams and Billie Tsien, the architects of the Philadelphia Barnes, received the difficult brief of reconstructing the installation of the ensembles in a new building. They ultimately produced a self-aware replication of the Merion galleries. The dimensions of the walls and the rooms, as well as the configuration of the ensembles, remains the same. Williams and Tsien reconstructed the symmetry and proportions of the installation, with the spacing between works measured down to 1/16 of an inch; they orientated the galleries to have south-facing windows as they did in Merion; and they selected warm-colored burlap wall coverings to maintain a similar background color and texture for the ensembles.

4 Quoted in Bernstein, 'For the New Barnes,' 2012. In this essay I have favored the term 'replication' over other possible choices, such as 'copy,' 'reproduction,' 'facsimile,' or 'duplication,' primarily because it was the term most frequently used in the discourse surrounding the Philadelphia Barnes. One could argue that 'replication,' more than its synonyms, suggests handiwork over mechanical reproduction, and

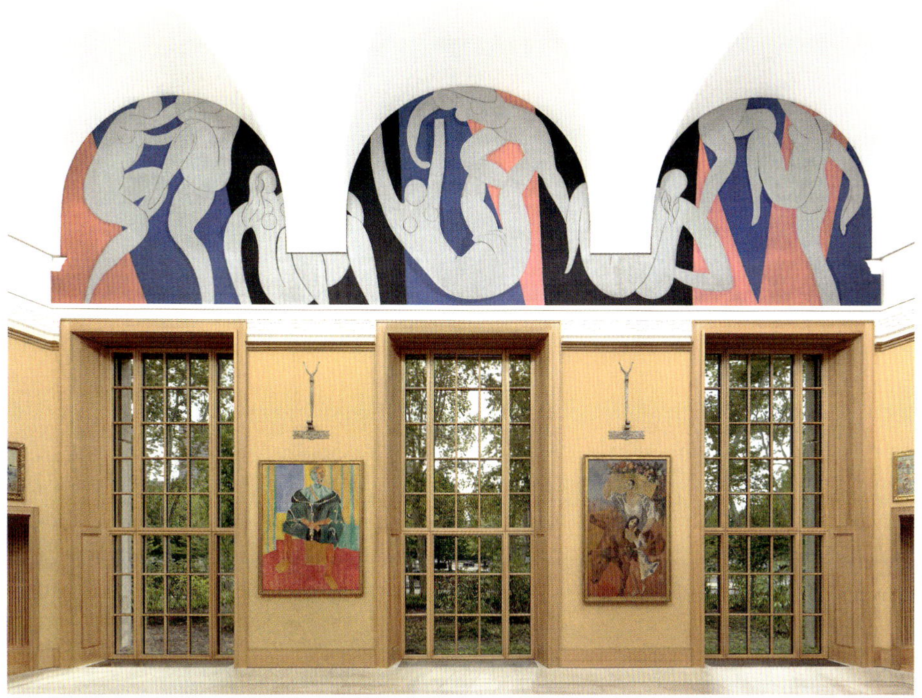

Figure 2:
Barnes Foundation, ensemble view, Main Gallery, south wall, Philadelphia, 2012.

However, the profiles of the moldings, the design of the frieze and the balustrades in the main gallery, the clerestory lighting on the second floor, among other details, are all the work of Williams and Tsien. They are reinterpretations of Paul Philippe Cret's designs for the Merion gallery. These interventions form a modernist frame for the replicated displays, acknowledging the ensembles' placement within a new setting. As a case in point, the notches on the sides of Matisse's *Dance* (1932–1933, 2001.25.50a,b,c), which Williams and Tsien left exposed, attest to where the mural used to be installed around the cornice in Merion (Figs. 1–2).

The presence of the original works of art in the reconstructed installation is, nevertheless, a source of discomfort. One critic lamented: 'In keeping such close company with

allows for more variation among iterations. Replication furthermore carries the connotations of a reply, especially in a legal context, as well as the repeated performance of a scientific experiment in a medical context, both of which are significant contexts for the history of the Barnes.

fake architecture, [the van Goghs, Klees, and Modiglianis] seem in their own right somehow less real.'[5] This comment proposes an interesting reversal of the supposed 'aura' of the original. In this critic's mind, genuine works of art are not necessarily guarantors of authenticity. His statement implies that authenticity is not intrinsic to the original and is instead tied to context, a point to which I will return.

By contrast, other critics felt the replication reached the status of the hyperreal: '[T]he installation is so thoroughly and convincingly replicated that there are times you have to remind yourself that you're on the parkway, not in Merion;' '[i]n several instances, the installation is better in the replica than it was in the suburbs.'[6] Although these viewpoints express a positive response to the replication, they still function within a conceptual structure of authentic versus counterfeit. The hyperreal is a falsehood, an illusion of the real, even if it's a desirable one.

Caught in this binary of real/fake with the only escape route being the revaluation of the hyperreal, 'replicate' does indeed become a scary word. But if not replication, is there another word that might offer a different point of entry? The words of one critic quoted above—'[i]t is different, to be sure, yet the same'—suggests an alternate approach. In *Difference and Repetition*, Gilles Deleuze writes: '[I]n the infinite movement of degraded likeness from copy to copy, we reach a point at which everything changes nature, at which copies themselves flip over into simulacra and at which, finally, resemblance or spiritual imitation gives way to repetition.'[7]

Instead of analyzing how the replication compares to the original, or how the existence of the original determines the life and reception of the replication, we can flip our perspective. We can perhaps consider how the replication gives life to the original, and in a sense, determines its existence. In other words, the replication of the ensembles can be considered a repetition in the Deleuzian sense. He writes: '[Repetitions] do not add a second and a third time to the first, but carry the first time to the "nth" power. [...] [I]t is [...] Monet's first water lily which repeats all the others.'[8] Deleuze points to the idea that repetition creates the original. The original cannot exist as an origin or 'first time' without a repetition, a 'second time' or an 'nth time.'

More importantly for the purposes of this essay, it is the repetition that gives the original value and sense. Repetition makes the original visible, or rather, emphasizes that which is repeated. In the case of the Barnes ensembles, repetition put the emphasis on the installation of the collection and began to distance the discussion from being solely defined by the psychology of the collector. Severing the ensembles from the site of their

5 Hawthorne, 'Barnes Storm,' 2012. **6** Gibson, 'Saving Dr. Barnes's Vision,' 2012; Sozanski, 'Review,' 2012. **7** Deleuze, *Difference and Repetition*, 1994, p. 128. **8** Deleuze, *Difference and Repetition*, 1994, p. 1. B. G. Chang served as a useful interlocutor with Deleuze through his article, 'Deleuze, Monet, and Being Repetitive,' 1999. **9** Wills, 'The Burden of History,' 2012: http://www.architectmagazine.com/design/buildings/the-burden-of-history_o?o=0 (last accessed 27 March 2018). **10** 'The court asked the witness [Kimberly Camp, executive director and CEO] about reproducing the gallery in Philadelphia, if the move

creator frees them to a certain extent to stand on their own, to circulate as ideas, and enter into new contexts and conversations. Repetition allows for reinvention. It changes the temporal valence from *having-been* to *yet-to-come*.

This is not to deny the sense of loss of the original. As one critic expressed: 'Those who made frequent pilgrimages to Merion may well experience [...] an ineffable feeling of loss when they visit the new site.'[9] Loss is built into the logic of repetition. The moment of repetition is the moment when the origin, the 'first time,' can be identified. From this standpoint, the origin can thus only be seen retrospectively, as a historical event already lost to time at the moment of its recognition. For the Barnes ensembles, the lost original perhaps serves as a productive void, its absence allowing the possible futures of its repetition to proliferate. Repetition thus reveals itself to be a generative practice. The ensembles are the same, to be sure, yet different. And this difference in repetition is critically valuable, as it both reveals attitudes towards the notion of origins, and points to other ways of understanding it.

The repetition of the Barnes ensembles made display the defining factor of the institution. The case for the relocation brought before the Montgomery County Orphans' Court in 2004 included the assumption that the displays would be replicated.[10] This, however, was not necessarily the view of the general public. Several critics questioned the reconstruction of the ensembles: 'Now that they've substantially breached the founder's trust indenture, the foundation's curators might just as well rethink his eccentric, thought-provoking but sometimes vexing installation,' proposed one; '[o]nce we've so clearly blown off Barnes's stated aims for his foundation [...] there may not be much point in preserving his notions on how art should be hung,' complained another.[11]

Nevertheless, the decision to replicate the ensembles and its precise execution ensured that the installation of the collection characterized the institution as much as the objects in the collection themselves. It affirmed the ensembles' importance as cultural and intellectual heritage. Consequently, the replication encourages reflection on museum display in general—as a strategy, an argument, a way to make sense and create order out of heterogeneous objects. Display, in short, is a means of structuring and communicating knowledge.

The history of display remains a fruitful area of research. Gail Feigenbaum's introduction to *Display of Art in the Roman Palace, 1550–1750* stands as a cogent and vital contribution to this field. She argues that 'display emerges as a nonverbal discourse on art;' elaborating further, 'display constitutes a form of art-historical narrative to be considered

is authorized [...] Ms. Camp was emphatic that the gallery must be replicated exactly, and the issue is nonnegotiable.' (N.T. vol. X, 73), *Opinion*, n. 58788 (O.C. Montg. Dec. 13, 2004) (Ott, J.). **11** Rosenbaum, 'Bogus Barnes Foundation,' 2012: https://www.huffingtonpost.com/lee-rosenbaum/bogus-barnes-foundation-f_b_1531230.html (last accessed 26 March 2018); Gopnik, 'Philadelphia's Reopened Barnes Foundation,' 2012: https://www.thedailybeast.com/philadelphias-reopened-barnes-foundation-puts-its-masterpieces-in-a-better-light (last accessed 26 March 2018).

on an equal footing with the kind of written texts that have been so attentively unpacked by scholars.'[12] The Barnes ensembles were certainly a 'nonverbal discourse on art.' More than his book, *The Art in Painting* (first published in 1925), the ensembles encapsulated and expressed Dr. Barnes's methodical approach to a formalist analysis of art based on the properties of light, line, color, and space.

Barnes continually changed his displays, rearranging the ensembles and adding to them as his collection grew and his theories on art and art education developed. It was a living text, or as he conceived of it, a scientific laboratory.[13] The galleries were spaces for hands-on experimentation, where students learned to look at and analyze art. Interestingly, Feigenbaum describes the Baroque Roman palace as 'a laboratory for catalyzing an interaction among sculpture, painting, furniture, and the decorative arts.'[14] I will not push this comparison too far, however, as the display strategies of the elite in Baroque Rome cannot be directly correlated to those of a newly wealthy twentieth-century American with radical democratic ideas. Indeed, Feigenbaum also claims that in these palaces 'it was through display, as much as any other mechanism, that such a new category of "fine art" came into being.'[15] Barnes's ensembles were specifically meant to reintegrate the fine with the decorative arts in order to overturn traditional hierarchies and reveal the universal expression of aesthetic principles.

The repetition of the ensembles in Philadelphia has, however, shifted the meaning and reading of the display. If previously they were primarily pedagogical tools, their modernist framing within a new building has allowed them to simultaneously be interpreted as a historical display of taste and aesthetic philosophy. They have become an art historical presentation, ripe for unpacking. Unlike a typical public art museum, the Barnes had never intended to present a historical, museological narrative. Given that it was not founded as a museum, this is not surprising. The Barnes was instead conceived as an educational institution for the appreciation of art and horticulture; its display was at the heart of a stridently democratic approach to art education. Unfortunately, Dr. Barnes's ambition for his method to revolutionize art education in America was never realized.

Scholars and critics have consistently described the Barnes ensembles as 'idiosyncratic,' a characterization that serves to particularize and trivialize them.[16] They have viewed the ensembles as exceptional, rather than the universal pedagogical system Dr. Barnes was trying to create. However, the relocation and repetition has opened up new possibilities, which at least one art critic apprehended: '[H]is quirky institution is suddenly on the verge of becoming the prominent and influential national treasure that it has long

12 Feigenbaum with Freddolini (eds.), *Display of Art*, 2014, pp. 17 and 1. I would like to thank Dario Gamboni for pointing me to this reference. **13** Wattenmaker, *American Paintings*, 2010, pp. 2 and 39. **14** Feigenbaum with Freddolini (eds.), *Display of Art*, 2014, p. 17. **15** Feigenbaum with Freddolini (eds.), *Display of Art*, 2014, p. 17. **16** See for example: Newhouse, *Art and the Power of Placement*, 2005, p. 23; Goldberger, 'The New Barnes Foundation,' 2012; Huxtable, 'The New Barnes,' 2012; see also note 18. **17** Smith, 'A Museum,' 2012. **18** Dobrin, 'Barnes Move to Parkway,' 2012: http://www.philly.com/philly/entertain-

deserved to be. It is also positioned to make an important contribution to the way we look at and think about art.'[17] By shifting the viewpoint of the displays from representing the personal and idiosyncratic to being institutional and historicized, the relocation and repetition has allowed the ensembles to be visible again, to be re-inscribed into a museological and art historical narrative.

Rethinking Original Context

With this theoretical framework in mind, I want to turn back to the issue of original context and explore how repetition might suggest a new understanding of the notion of origins. The media criticism of the Barnes relocation was rife with arguments about site specificity. Understandably, the fascination with collection institutions like the Merion Barnes or the Isabella Stewart Gardner Museum, for example, is partly based on their direct relationship with their founders—this is the site they selected, this is the building they built, these are the halls they haunted. The collection institutions that remain *in situ*, like the Gardner, share with historic house museums these reverential ties to a place and person, affording them the status of a relic.

By contrast, the replication of the ensembles in Philadelphia severs the galleries from their indexical connection to the founder, the larger-than-life personality that was Dr. Barnes, releasing them into unknown interpretive territory. This is no longer the place where he walked, the benches he sat on, the walls he obsessively rearranged, even though these are still the same objects he touched. One journalist lamented: '[V]isitors will never again have [...] the powerful feeling of being led around the museum by the hand of its founder.'[18]

Others focused less on the body and personage of Dr. Barnes and more on the site and space: 'To separate artwork from its context is the worst sacrilege of all, particularly for an idiosyncratic collection like Barnes, which was meant to be seen in a specific setting;' 'the collection is [...] an artifact now displaced from its historical roots. In Merion, it felt grounded in its natural environment;' and the most extreme comment, '[t]o have ripped out of its original context one of Matisse's most important works—a work especially designed for that wall in that building on that street—is fairly astonishing [...]. To experience *The Dance* in Merion was to experience it in the precise spot on Earth for which Matisse intended it.'[19]

The history of this argument about original context goes back to an even more notorious and massive relocation at the dawn of the museum age—Napoleon's requisition

ment/arts/20120520_Barnes_move_to_Parkway_is_progress__but_a_quirky_something_has_been_lost.html#ixzz1vQnKElaF (last accessed 27 March 2018). **19** Aldredge, 'Re-Branding the Barnes: Has a 25-Billion-Dollar Art Collection Been Disneyfied?': https://www.gwarlingo.com/2012/re-branding-the-barnes/ (last accessed 20 March 2018); Sozanski, 'Review,' 2012; Perl, 'The Barnes Foundation's Disastrous New Home,' 2012: https://newrepublic.com/article/106435/barnes-foundation-move-philadelphia-tod-williams-billie-tsien (last accessed 27 March 2018).

and transfer of art from Italy in 1798 to create his Musée Napoleon.[20] During this process, the influential arts administrator and theoretician Antoine Chrysostome Quatremère de Quincy wrote a series of letters protesting the installation of the spoliated art works in a French museum, separated from their original context in Rome.

Quatremère de Quincy argued that the whole of Rome was a museum, using language that prefigures the comments of the journalists cited above: '[T]he museum of Rome was placed there by the very order of nature, which intended that it should exist only there; the country itself is part of the museum.' This museum was inclusive of the 'mountains, quarries, ancient roads, the respective positions of the ruined towns, geographic connections,' etc. Works of art derived their power and significance from their integration with the land, climate, and country in which they were made: 'What artist has not experienced in Italy the penetrating harmony between the work of art, the sky that illuminates it, and the landscape that is its background [...]?'[21] Ripping the works from their natural environment would render them senseless fragments that could only serve as decoration, or as a political or financial commodity. Quatremère de Quincy's advocacy did eventually lead to the return of the spoliated works from the Louvre to Italy in 1815.

Nevertheless, Quatremère de Quincy was not a hard and fast defender of leaving works of art *in situ*, and he acknowledged the complexities of the situation. In 1817, the British ambassador to the Ottoman Empire, Lord Elgin, transferred sculptural fragments from the Parthenon in Athens to London. The Elgin Marbles, as they are known, were put on permanent display in the British Museum. Quatremère de Quincy subsequently wrote a text in the form of correspondence addressed to the sculptor Antonio Canova admitting to the advantages of the relocation and installation. He enthused: '[We] can enjoy it no doubt even better than on the Parthenon itself, where it was feebly lit and placed farther from the eye.' As an interesting parallel, the one consistent improvement over the Merion Barnes that critics pointed out was the new lighting in the Philadelphia galleries.

In Athens, Quatremère de Quincy claimed that the sculptures were endangered by the neglect of the government: '[T]heir native land [...] had become their tomb.' In the British Museum, properly displayed, the Elgin Marbles could 'once again [...] serve as a model for the taste of artists and the endeavors of art,' as well as 'an inexhaustible source of theories, scholarly discussion, and instructive comparison.' He argued that 'they would have never produced this or any other effect on the taste of the moderns had they not so fortunately been brought to Europe.'[22] Quatremère de Quincy thus recognized that the new museum context was beneficial to the works and not simply destructive.

As Dominique Poulot has argued, the apparent contradiction in Quatremère de Quincy's position in his *Letters to Miranda* versus his *Letters to Canova* can be explained by 'political

20 Gamboni, 'Déplacer égale détruire?,' 1997; Gamboni, 'The Museum As a Work of Art,' 2005; Newhouse, *Art and the Power of Placement*, 2005, chapter 1. **21** Quatremère de Quincy, *Letters to Miranda*, 2012 [1796, 1836], pp. 101 and 107. **22** Quatremère de Quincy, *Letters to Miranda*, 2012 [1796, 1836], pp. 129, 132 and 144. **23** Poulot, 'The Cosmopolitanism of Masterpieces,' 2012, pp. 34 and 57–59. **24** Poulot, 'The Cosmo-

geography.'[23] Rome in the eighteenth century was a center of art and archaeology. It formed part of the cosmopolitan Enlightenment community of Europe. Removing art works from Rome amounted to destroying the heritage with which this European elite identified. Greece under the Ottoman Empire, however, was a country on the outer reaches of civilization, an Orientalized 'other' in a state of decay. The transfer of what was regarded as universal heritage from such a site to England was an act of preservation. Similar arguments were made for and against the relocation of the Barnes's collection from Merion to Philadelphia, although the situation was not exactly analogous. Critics of the move raised the specter of the destruction of cultural heritage. Advocates of the move claimed that in Merion, the art was inaccessible, and the building was not adequately maintained. Relocation to Philadelphia was the best way to preserve the collection.

More germane to this parallel is Poulot's further observation: 'The two series of letters therefore offer, surely for the first time in heritage history, the spectacle of cost-benefit analysis being undertaken before new institutions are created. In calculating the benefit of transfer relative to the *status quo* [...] it was the advantage or disservice to the collectivity that was being measured.'[24] The rhetoric surrounding the relocation of the Barnes emphasized exactly these considerations of the benefits to the collectivity. Moving to an urban center with expanded facilities, advocates argued, would increase access to the art for the general public, students, and tourists. The language and reasoning behind the move was thus prefigured in late-eighteenth/early nineteenth-century France. The limits of original context are intrinsic to the birth of the museum as an institution.

How can the concept of repetition offer a different perspective on this issue? With the repetition of the ensembles, an alternate model of origins emerges. Instead of the original context of production, the process and systems used to fabricate the work take on primary value. This model is already part of cultural practice in other parts of the world. In Japan, for instance, the Ise Grand Shrine located in the Mie prefecture on the main island of Honshu presents an illuminating example. At this site, multiple structures are rebuilt every twenty years using the same types of materials and techniques established in the seventh century CE. Thus the buildings, while physically new as structures, are considered to be ancient because of the origins of their construction process.

In the history of western art, Minimalist artists attempted to use this alternate model of originality to distance the work of art from the auratic hand of the artist. Instead of privileging the made object, artists like Donald Judd sometimes sold the conceptual plan. The instructions for fabricating the object then became the work of art, even attaining the status of the original.[25] The objects themselves, produced in serials, hold equivalent status as neither copy nor original, but multiple.

politanism of Masterpieces,' 2012, p. 36. **25** Of course, the controversy over the Panza Collection complicated this issue. Donald Judd, who signed letters of agreement and certificates between 1974–1976 granting Count Panza rights to fabricate and/or reconstruct the works he purchased, subsequently protested against Panza's reproductions according to the plans sold to him.

One final example closer to the subject of this essay is the reconstruction of the Frankfurt Kitchen in the Museum für Angewandt Kunst, Vienna (MAK). Designed by the Austrian architect Margarete Schütte-Lihotzky in 1926, this modernist, rationalist kitchen was installed in approximately 10,000 newly constructed apartments in Frankfurt as part of an ambitious municipal building project. The kitchen, a largely pre-fabricated plan with some customizable details, was meant to save women time by making housework more efficient. Examples of this kitchen, salvaged from buildings in Frankfurt, entered the collections of the Museum of Modern Art, New York and the Victoria & Albert Museum, London.

The MAK, however, did not acquire a Frankfurt Kitchen from a Frankfurt apartment building slated for demolition. Instead, they hired the architect Gerhard Lindner to work with Lihotzky herself to construct a new Frankfurt Kitchen for the museum in 1990. The result is a fascinating interrogation of the concept of originality. While based on the same plans and ergonomic principles of the 1926 design, MAK's reconstructed Frankfurt Kitchen uses different materials and paint colors than those originally used and available in Frankfurt in the 1920s.

The MAK's modern recreation thus de-emphasizes the importance of original context. Although the involvement of Lihotzky served as a guarantor of authenticity, the process of the reconstruction simultaneously suggests another way to consider originality. The repeated proportions, color harmonies, and concept of the design also function as markers of authenticity; seen from the perspective of repetition, they become the defining characteristics of the Frankfurt kitchen. Like the Philadelphia Barnes, MAK's modern period room without an original demonstrates the agency of display, that is, its critical capacity to upend accepted ideas about the origins of a work of art or architecture.

A Modern Period Room?

'Replicating the hang was really difficult—we are modernist architects and we didn't want to end up with period rooms.' –Billie Tsien[26]

Is the Barnes one giant period room, as a colleague remarked to me one day? The period room has survived the vicissitudes of taste in museological practice, from its celebration in the 1920s as the most innovative form of museum display, to the late 1990s and early aughts, when Ivan Gaskell described them as the 'hated stepchildren' of American art museums.[27] While Tsien's quote above demonstrates that distaste for period rooms has not completely faded, current scholarly and curatorial interest would suggest this mode of display is being resuscitated with new eyes and new perspectives.[28]

26 Quoted in Loos, 'Vogue's First Look,' 2012. **27** Gaskell, 'Costume, Period Rooms, and Donors,' 2004, p. 617. **28** Costa, Poulot and Volait (eds.), *The Period Rooms*, 2016; Philadelphia Museum of Art (ed.), 'Period Room Architecture in American Art Museums,' special issue of *Winterthur Portfolio*, 46/2–3 (Summer/Autumn 2012); Bryant, 'Museum Period Rooms,' 2009; Sparke, Martin and Keeble (eds.), *The Modern Period Room*, 2006; recent renovations of period rooms in museums include those in the

Julius Bryant generously and succinctly defines the period room as 'a reconstructed historic interior that is in some way representative of its past owner, era and/or region.'[29] Whether they are transported from an endangered structure to the museum setting or recreated after an original, period rooms generally attempt to assemble fine and decorative arts, visual and material culture from a similar time and place. They attempt to create an experience of history—documenting either daily life in a certain place at a certain time, or the history of taste and styles in the decoration of interiors.

The reconstructed galleries of the Philadelphia Barnes do not endeavor to create a fiction of history. And yet in their modernist architectural frame, the ensembles become a historical fragment representative of the taste of a very specific person, place, and time. Incidentally, it was during the heyday of period rooms that Dr. Barnes established (1922) and opened (1925) his foundation. His ahistorical mix of fine and decorative arts, a display strategy that he developed in the 1930s, was in a sense an anti-period room. The installation was organized not according to historical eras and styles, but according to formal properties. Now repeated, this installation becomes a kind of period piece in itself and a significant case study in the history of display.

As a useful point of comparison, the Robert Lehman Collection at the Metropolitan Museum of Art is a period display housed in its own wing. Lehman's bequest of his exceptional collection of fine and decorative arts after his death in 1969 included the stipulation that it be installed to evoke the ambiance of his family's townhouse. The Lehman home in midtown Manhattan was not dismantled for the relocation of the collection and is still extant and privately owned, like the Merion gallery building.

In the Metropolitan's Lehman wing, Old Master paintings hang over fireplace mantels and Renaissance furniture, and plush red furnishing fabric decorates the walls. While not a meticulous reconstruction like the Barnes, the Lehman wing does present a suite of rooms displayed according to the wishes of the donor, and in a separate structure appended to the larger museum. It is akin to the rectangular block housing the Barnes Collection, which is attached to and yet distinct from the rest of the building.

The Lehman wing, with its domestic display loosely grouped by chronology and geography, is in line with the period room typology. It furthermore represents the taste in art and interiors of a wealthy American class. By contrast, the replicated displays of the Barnes do not comfortably serve as a document of historical style. Although the collection does represent the taste of its owner, the ensembles as a display strategy do not relate to the history of interiors. They juxtapose objects from vastly different cultures and periods that were not usually displayed together in neo-aristocratic American private collections—for

Museum of the City of New York, 2015; the Europe galleries, Victoria & Albert Museum, London, 2015; American rooms, Museum of Fine Arts, Boston, 2010; and the Minneapolis Institute of Art as well as the Musée Carnavalet, Paris are currently renovating their period rooms. **29** Bryant, 'Museum Period Rooms,' 2009, p. 75. See also: Aynsley, 'The Modern Period Room,' 2006, pp. 9–10.

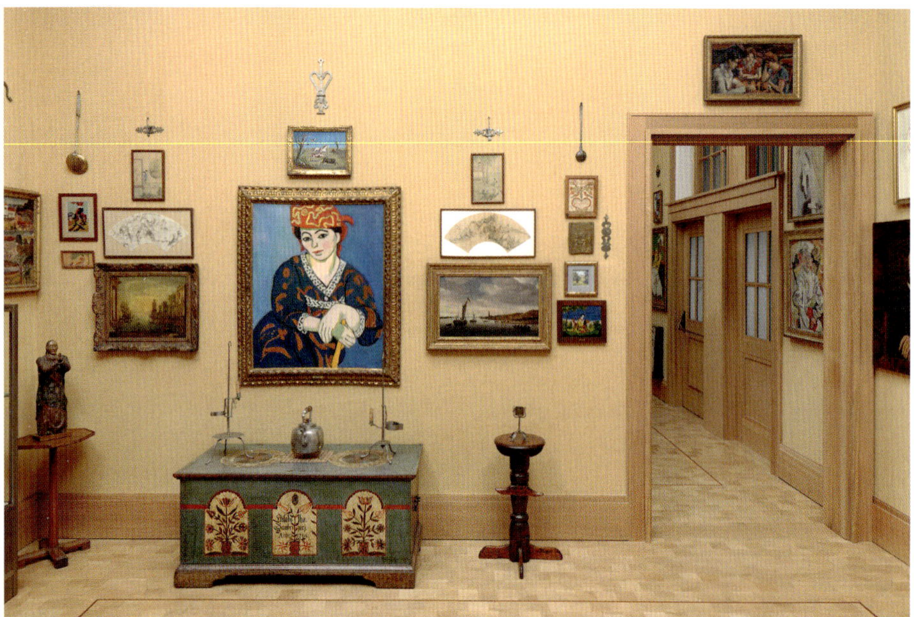

Figure 3:
Barnes Foundation, ensemble view, Room 15, south wall, Philadelphia, 2012.

example, Henri Matisse's *Red Madras Headdress* (1907, BF488) next to a Ming dynasty fan (BF2510), or a Fang reliquary guardian head (nineteenth century, A124) below an eighteenth-century Dutch pewter flagon (01.22.23) (Figs. 3–4). Despite the domestic scale and inclusion of utilitarian objects, the display was never part of a domestic setting.

The Philadelphia Barnes is perhaps more comparable to the recreated artist's studio, painstakingly reconstructed to its condition at the time of the artist's death.[30] The artist's studio is a space that valued process and experimentation, like the gallery-laboratory of the Foundation. Indeed, Dr. Barnes is sometimes described as a collector-artist, though that analogy may not be as valid for him as it is for other early twentieth-century private collectors like Isabella Stewart Gardner.[31] Moreover, the ensembles were arbitrarily fixed after Barnes's unexpected death in 1951 from an automobile accident, similar to the state of some reconstructed artists' studios, like that of Francis Bacon in the Hugh Lane Gallery, Dublin.

A more apt comparison for the Barnes is Constantin Brancusi's studio, reconstructed twice in the plaza of the Centre Georges Pompidou. The first reconstruction consisted of a replica of the entire building Brancusi occupied on the impasse Ronsin in the Montparnasse neighborhood of Paris. Visitors could enter the building and stand in a cordoned

30 Vere, 'Authentic the Second Time Around?,' 2012; Barthel, 'The Paris Studio of Constantin Brancusi,' 2006. **31** Dolkart, 'To See As the Artist Sees,' 2013, p. 23; Gamboni, 'The Museum As a Work of Art,' 2005, p. 22. **32** Barthel, 'The Paris Studio of Constantin Brancusi,' 2006, p. 42. **33** See Meijers, 'The Museum and the

path. The sculptures were installed just as Brancusi placed them before he died. Towards the end of his life, Brancusi had used his studio as an exhibition space, and had determined the exact positioning and placement of his works to create the visual and artistic relationships he desired. The installation was recreated after period photographs. Unfortunately, the replicated studio flooded in 1990 and closed down.

The Renzo Piano Building Workshop was subsequently engaged to entirely reconceive the project. They decided to replicate the dimensions, wooden framework, and installation of the studio, but to house it in a larger building that did not attempt to reconstruct the original Montparnasse building. In conceiving the Philadelphia Barnes almost two decades later, Williams and Tsien would follow a very similar tactic. For Brancusi's studio, RPBW designed an intimate walled garden near the entrance to suggest the sheltered ambiance of the impasse Ronsin. Likewise, Williams and Tsien inserted garden spaces into the Barnes galleries as a nod to the arboretum in Merion. Brancusi's studio was reinstalled in the plaza of the Centre Georges Pompidou in 1997. Critics of the studio's various reconstructions raised the well-established arguments about original context.[32] Nevertheless, the repetitions of Brancusi's installation have allowed it to be seen and re-seen, re-inscribing it into a museological narrative.

The Barnes Ensembles, Again

The repetition of the Barnes ensembles has allowed them to enter into this fruitful theoretical terrain of reconstruction and the modern period room; it also serves to place them in a broader conversation about exhibition display. Rather than a one-off experiment, the ensembles' juxtapositions of varied objects from varied eras and regions can be seen as part of a larger intellectual dialogue. As a case in point, the radical Swiss curator Harald Szeemann installed the exhibition *Ahistorical Sounds* at the Museum Boijmans van Beuningen, Rotterdam in 1988. In an expansive, modernist, 'white cube' space, Szeemann mixed historical and contemporary works from different regions—a Bruce Nauman sculpture, a Hieronymus Bosch painting, a sixteenth-century Venetian glass dish. He attempted to find empathy (Einfühlung) between the objects and express some essential utopian link between the arts.

Other exhibitions and curators in the 1980s had similar aims.[33] Although their installations and theories were not equivalent to the Barnes ensembles, there is clearly a resonance between these disparate projects. The repetition of the ensembles has underscored their contribution to modernist and subsequently postmodernist thinking about art. It has given new context and opened new interpretive territory to their ahistorical mixing of diverse objects.

"Ahistorical" Exhibition,' 1996. The Getty Research Institute's recent exhibition *Harald Szeemann: Museum of Obsessions* (February 6 – May 6, 2018) and accompanying publications are evidence of current scholarly interest in this history of exhibition display.

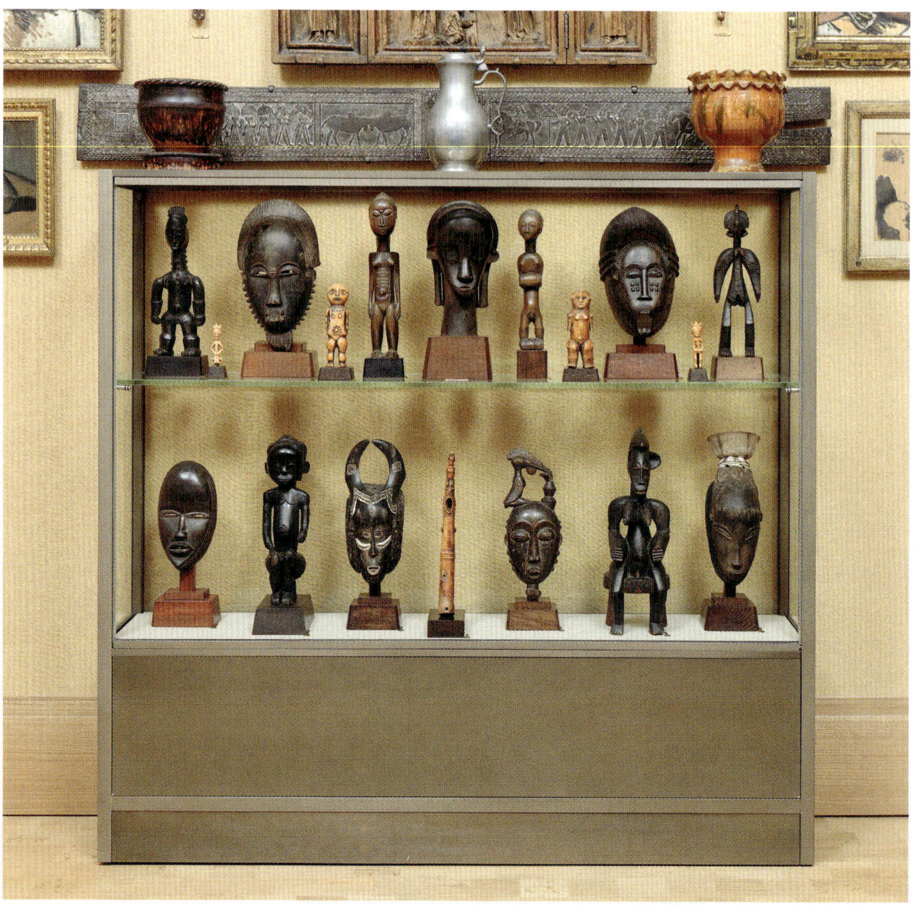

Figure 4:
Barnes Foundation, ensemble view, Room 22, south wall, Philadelphia, 2012.

Dario Gamboni has argued that 'material existence is a necessary but not a sufficient condition of visibility [...] even access is not enough, for visibility and invisibility are not inherent and stable properties but the multiple and changing expressions of relationships with viewers [...] standing on a pedestal in a square does not prevent works from slipping into invisibility, and neither does hanging on a museum wall.'[34] Continual engagement, interpretation, and inscription in broader cultural narratives are key to heritage preservation. For better or for worse, the Barnes ensembles replicated, reconstructed and repeated, paradoxically ensure the visibility of the lost original.

34 Gamboni, 'Preservation and Destruction,' 2005, pp. 165–166.

Bibliography

J. Aynsley, 'The Modern Period Room—a Contradiction in Terms?' in P. Sparke, B. Martin and T. Keeble (eds.), *The Modern Period Room: The Construction of the Exhibited Interior 1870 to 1950* (Routledge, 2006), pp. 8–30.

Barnes Foundation, *Philadelphia Opening Media Report* (The Barnes Foundation, 2012).

A. Barthel, 'The Paris Studio of Constantin Brancusi: A Critique of the Modern Period Room,' *Future Anterior*, 3/2 (Winter 2006), pp. 33–43.

F. Bernstein, 'For the New Barnes, Everything Old Is New Again,' *New York Times* (March 14, 2012).

J. Bryant, 'Museum Period Rooms for the Twenty-First Century: Salvaging Ambition,' *Museum Management and Curatorship*, 24/1 (2009), pp. 73–84.

B. G. Chang, 'Deleuze, Monet, and Being Repetitive,' *Cultural Critique*, 41 (1999), pp. 184–217.

S. Costa, D. Poulot and M. Volait (eds.), *The Period Rooms: Allestimenti storici tra arte, collezionismo e museologia* (Bononia University Press, 2016).

G. Deleuze, *Difference and Repetition*, trans. by P. Patton (Columbia University Press, 1994).

J. F. Dolkart, 'To See As the Artist Sees: Albert C. Barnes and the Experiment in Education,' in J. F. Dolkart and M. Lucy, *The Barnes Foundation: Masterworks* (Skira Rizzoli, 2013), pp. 9–29.

G. Feigenbaum with F. Freddolini (eds.), *Display of Art in the Roman Palace, 1550–1750* (Getty Research Institute, 2014).

D. Gamboni, 'Déplacer égale détruire? Notes historiques sur un argument théorique,' *Annales d'Historie de l'Art et d'Archéologie de l'Université de Bruxelles*, 17 (1997), pp. 33–46.

D. Gamboni, 'The Museum As a Work of Art: Site Specificity and Extended Agency,' *Kritische Berichte*, 33/3 (2005), pp. 16–27.

D. Gamboni, 'Preservation and Destruction, Oblivion and Memory' in A. McClanan and J. Johnson (eds.), *Negating the Image: Case Studies in Iconoclasm* (Ashgate, 2005), pp. 163–177.

I. Gaskell, 'Costume, Period Rooms, and Donors: Dangerous Liaisons in the Art Museum,' *The Antioch Review*, 62/4 (2004), pp. 615–623.

E. Gibson, 'Saving Dr. Barnes's Vision,' *Wall Street Journal* (May 24, 2012).

P. Goldberger, 'The New Barnes Foundation Building: Soulful, Self-Assured, and Soaked with Light,' *Vanity Fair* (May 4, 2012).

C. Hawthorne, 'Barnes Storm,' *Architectural Record* (June 2012).

A. L. Huxtable, 'The New Barnes Shouldn't Work—But Does,' *The Wall Street Journal* (May 24, 2012).

A. R. Lawrence, 'Preservation through Replication: The Barnes Foundation,' *Future Anterior*, 12/1 (2015), pp. 1–15.

T. Loos, 'Vogue's First Look: Exclusive Images of the New Barnes Foundation Museum in Philadelphia,' *Vogue* (May 7, 2012).

D. J. Meijers, 'The Museum and the "Ahistorical" Exhibition: The Latest Gimmick by the Arbiters of Taste, or an Important Cultural Phenomenon?' in R. Greenberg, B. W. Ferguson and S. Nairne (eds.), *Thinking About Exhibitions* (Routledge, 1996), pp. 7–20.

V. Newhouse, *Art and the Power of Placement* (Monacelli Press, 2005).

Philadelphia Museum of Art (ed.), 'Period Room Architecture in American Art Museums,' Special Issue of *Winterthur Portfolio*, 46/2–3 (Summer/Autumn 2012).

D. Poulot, 'The Cosmopolitanism of Masterpieces' in A.-C. Quatremère de Quincy, *Letters to Miranda and Canova on the Abduction of Antiquities from Rome and Athens*, trans. by C. Miller and D. Gilks (Getty Research Institute, 2012 [1796, 1836]), pp. 1–91.

A.-C. Quatremère de Quincy, *Letters to Miranda and Canova on the Abduction of Antiquities from Rome and Athens*, trans. by C. Miller and D. Gilks (Getty Research Institute, 2012 [1796, 1836]).

I. Saffron, 'The Barnes: A Ravishing Building, but Cut Off from the City,' *The Philadelphia Inquirer* (May 5, 2012).

R. Smith, 'A Museum, Reborn, Remains True to Its Old Self, Only Better,' *New York Times* (May 18, 2012).

E. J. Sozanski, 'Review: Galleries Shine at the New Barnes,' *The Philadelphia Inquirer* (May 4, 2012).

P. Sparke, B. Martin and T. Keeble (eds.), *The Modern Period Room: The Construction of the Exhibited Interior 1870 to 1950* (Routledge, 2006).

T. Stuth, 'Continuity, Criticality, and Change,' *Journal of Architectural Education*, 63/2 (2010), pp. 112–127.

B. Vere, 'Authentic the Second Time Around? Eduardo Paolozzi and Reconstructed Studios in a Museum Environment,' in M. Aldrich and J. Hackforth-Jones (eds.), *Art and Authenticity* (Lund Humphries in association with Sotheby's Institute of Art, 2012), pp. 88–97.

R. J. Wattenmaker, *American Paintings and Works on Paper in the Barnes Foundation* (Yale University Press in association with the Barnes Foundation, 2010).

Websites:

http://www.architectmagazine.com/design/buildings/the-burden-of-history_o?o=o.

http://articles.latimes.com/2012/may/18/entertainment/la-et-barnes-art-review-20120518.

https://www.gwarlingo.com/2012/re-branding-the-barnes.

https://www.huffingtonpost.com/lee-rosenbaum/bogus-barnes-foundation-f_b_1531230.html.

https://newrepublic.com/article/106435/barnes-foundation-move-philadelphia-tod-williams-billie-tsien.

http://www.philly.com/philly/entertainment/arts/20120520_Barnes_move_to_Parkway_is_progress__but_a_quirky_something_has_been_lost.html#ixzz1vQnKEIaF.

https://www.thedailybeast.com/philadelphias-reopened-barnes-foundation-puts-its-masterpieces-in-a-better-light.

2. Parergonal Operations

DARIO GAMBONI

Ready-Made Eye-Opener: Models, Functions and Meanings of the Ironwork in Albert C. Barnes's Displays

The Barnes Foundation is both famous and infamous for the way in which it displays the works of art collected by Albert C. Barnes. The displays were designed by Barnes himself and for some commentators, they express the collector's idiosyncrasy and amount to great art being held hostage to a rich man's whims.[1] For others and especially for Barnes's collaborators, his disciples, and the students of the Foundation, they are the instruments of a veritable school of seeing.[2] Another controversy surrounding the Barnes Foundation concerns its location. When it decided to move from suburban Merion, where Barnes had established it, to downtown Philadelphia, opposition resulted in the courts authorizing the move only on condition that the displays be recreated in the new building, which itself replicates the dimensions and disposition of the rooms. A positive outcome of this turn of events is that a greater amount of scholarly and public attention has since been devoted to the displays as such. *Masterworks*, the catalogue written by Judith F. Dolkart and Martha Lucy for the reopening of the Foundation in 2012, and the didactic apparatus included in the new presentation explicitly discuss Barnes's ensembles, the mural compositions that he arranged and rearranged until 1951, when his death and his testament made them final.[3]

Signs on the Wall

A particularly odd aspect of Barnes's displays is the inclusion of ironwork on the walls alongside the paintings. It never fails to strike visitors but remained unstudied until very recently.[4] Yet in relation to the question of display and the agency of objects, this aspect

1 See for example: Greenfeld, *The Devil and Dr. Barnes*, 1987; Anderson, *Art Held Hostage*, 2003. **2** See: Meyers, *Art, Education, & African-American Culture*, 2004. **3** See: Dolkart and Lucy, *The Barnes Foundation, Masterworks*, 2012. **4** See: Wattenmaker, 'In the Light of New Material,' 2015. In her preface to this catalogue, Judith Dolkart estimates the number of objects concerned at 'nearly nine hundred' and lists them as 'hinges and hasps, locks and keys, door knockers and latches, dough cutters and surgical saws' (Cathelineau and Dolkart (eds.), *Strength and Splendor*, 2015, p. 7). Wattenmaker considers that it is 'one

is of particular interest, since it raises the issue of what the ironwork does to the paintings, what they do together to the spectators that the paintings alone could not do, and whether the wrought iron pieces are *parerga* to the paintings, or *erga* in their own right, or play roles that are mutable and exchangeable. The oddity lies in the disregard that their combination manifests toward taxonomy and hierarchy, mixing as it does paintings by the likes of Cézanne and Matisse with anonymous appliances, fine art of the greatest symbolic and financial value with specimens of the so-called decorative and applied arts, which may be beautifully crafted but are much less prized. How should one account for this unusual yet intentional feature of display?

An answer came to me during my first visit to the Foundation in Merion, on 30 January 2009, by way of observations I made and photographs I took, in response to the question itself.[5] What dawned upon me after a while and became a crucial element in the experience of my visit was that there exist meaningful and consistent relations between the paintings and the ironwork, relations that one could call resemblances, analogies or (metaphorically) rhymes, and that the pieces of wrought iron point to characteristics of the paintings. The iron fittings placed on top of Charles Demuth's *Masts* and of Henri Matisse's *Reclining Nude* in Room 18 (Fig. 1), for example, parallel the respectively vertical and horizontal formats of the two pictures and emphasize their contrasted compositional structure: the geometric, almost orthogonal skeleton provided by the mast and yards in Demuth's painting is further abstracted by a hinge topped with a keyhole escutcheon; the same process is applied by a serpentine hinge to the sensuous arabesque of Matisse's odalisque, while the centrality of the nude's belly is wittily underscored by a sixteenth-century *repoussé* plaque in the shape of three intertwined crescents.

Such analogies, once their possibility has entered into one's consciousness, prove to be too systematic to be accidental. Their existence also finds a confirmation and an expansion in echoes of the same kind noticeable among the various paintings as well as between the paintings and other objects, such as pieces of early American furniture or ceramics, the presence of which also tends to confuse visitors used to the purist aesthetics of the white-box displays of modern art. In Room 23, for example, a chromatic, formal and directional analogy connects the nude boy carrying a vase on his head in Pablo Picasso's *Young Girl with Goat* (1906), the red tower of an eponymous painting by Giorgio De Chirico (1913) and an oversized candle, placed side by side.[6]

There is a special quality in the experience of noticing such relations oneself, without being alerted to their existence, and of being at first unsure of discovering or inventing

of the outstanding collections of wrought iron objects in the United States,' with works coming 'mainly from America, France, and Germany, but also [...] by Spanish, Italian, Netherlandish, and English smiths,' while 'the origins, nomenclature, and dates of fabrication often remain imprecise' (Wattenmaker, 'In the Light of New Material,' 2015, p. 26). **5** My thanks to Martha Lucy for welcoming me at the Foundation and authorizing me to take and reproduce photographs of the displays. **6** Reproduced in Gamboni, '"Musées d'auteur",' 2011, p. 199.

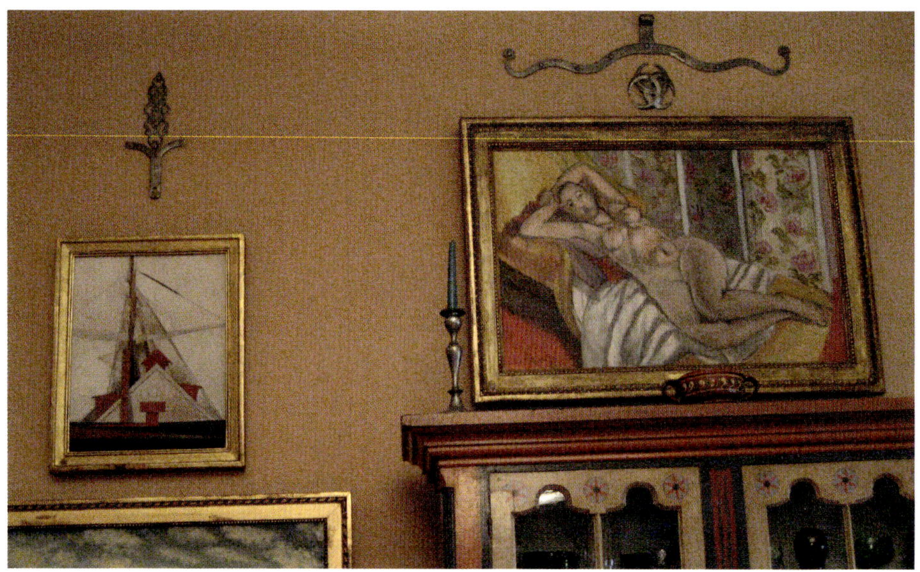

Figure 1:
Barnes Foundation, Room 18, detail from the East wall: *Masts* (1919) by Charles Demuth and *Reclining Nude* (1923–1924) by Henri Matisse, topped by ironwork.

them. Writing about the Musée Gustave Moreau in Paris, André Breton thus spoke in 1960 of the 'intersigns fluttering' between two paintings, and of dreaming to 'intercept' them, 'exactly half-way between the external eye and the white-hot inner eye.'[7] Nonetheless, I was thrilled to find quoted in *Masterworks* an unpublished letter from Barnes to the American painter Stuart Davis in which, on 1 April 1942, the collector explained the inclusion of ironwork in his displays:

'First—the motives, such as arabesques, patterns, etc., discernible in a picture have their analogue, sometimes a very close one, in the iron work. Second—we regard the creators of antique wrought iron, just as authentic an artist as a Titian, Renoir, or Cézanne. This is not to say that what they express is of equal importance or magnitude, but that they do express something of their own experience.'[8]

Since then, Richard J. Wattenmaker quoted two other letters in which Barnes gave similar explanations: on 29 December 1936, Barnes wrote to Kenneth Clark, then director of the National Gallery in London, that he was on his way to show 'that there is no essential esthetic difference between the forms of the great painters or sculptors, and those of the iron-workers of several hundred years who made such commonplace objects as

7 Breton, 'Gustave Moreau [1960],' 2002, p. 363. **8** Quoted after Dolkart, 'To See As the Artist Sees,' 2012, p. 26. The letter is quoted more extensively in Wattenmaker, 'In the Light of New Material,' 2015, p. 33. **9** Quoted in Wattenmaker, 'In the Light of New Material,' 2015, pp. 30 and 25. **10** Dewey, 'The Educational Function of a Museum of Decorative Arts,' 1937, p. 98. **11** Dewey, 'The Educational Function of a Museum

hinges, door handles, locks, etc.'; and on 5 March 1948, he wrote to the antiques dealer and scholar Charles F. Montgomery that he intended to prove his case that 'the great artists of all time' included 'workers in the so-called useful arts like wrought iron, pewter, glass, pottery, etc.' by 'putting pieces of wrought iron next to some of the best paintings covering the period from the 13th to the 20th centuries.'[9]

The disregard of taxonomies, therefore, corresponded to Barnes's anti-hierarchic attitude, also expressed—not without contradictions and unintended results—in his way of granting or refusing access to the collection, which privileged workers and black Americans at the expense of collectors and art historians. Barnes was not alone in his convictions and a 1937 article by his close collaborator the philosopher John Dewey, entitled 'The Educational Function of a Museum of Decorative Arts,' called for 'the breaking down of the walls that so long divided what were called the fine arts from applied and industrial arts,' and hailed the Cooper Union Museum for the Arts of Decoration in New York for arranging its objects 'on the basis of community of design rather than by historic periods,' since 'for the purpose of learning to see the design in virtue of which an object has esthetic form, grouping together a chair, a rug, a ceramic object and a piece of iron work may be much more effective.'[10] This purpose fitted the fact that 'artist-designers' occupied a central place in the public of such museums and of the schools associated with them: 'To learn to see for artistic purposes is to learn to detect organizing design, whether the object seen be a statue, a picture, a tapestry, a pitcher or a roll of wall-paper.'[11]

This aim corresponded to the first reason given by Barnes in his letter to Davis, in which he employed the notion of 'motif' in a formal rather than iconographical sense, as the examples of 'arabesques, patterns, etc.' make clear. Dewey spoke of 'plastic design' and indeed, we can consider that Barnes prioritized the 'plastic sign' over the 'iconic sign'—using the semiotic distinction proposed by the Belgian Groupe µ—without defining them as mutually exclusive.[12] This could suit the art of Stuart Davis, who included iconic references but abstracted elements such as buildings, trees, boats, windows, etc. to the point where they composed a vocabulary of quasi-pictograms, combinable in colourful patterns. There are no works by Davis in the Barnes Foundation, but many objects attest to the collector's preference for abstracted shapes and some of them are very similar to the silhouettes of the ironwork on the walls, for example a bronze statuette in an orant position labelled 'Persian / 8th century B.C.' and animal figures painted on Native American earthenware containers.[13]

Barnes did not collect 'non-objective' art, and the kind of abstraction he enjoyed was indebted to the post-impressionist, 'decorative' ideal of a depiction emancipated from the 'servile imitation of nature.'[14] His explanation to Davis can thus be compared to Maurice

of Decorative Arts,' 1937, p. 98. **12** See: Groupe µ, *Traité du signe visuel*, 1992. **13** See: Dolkart and Lucy, *The Barnes Foundation, Masterworks*, 2012, pp. 344–345. **14** Gauguin, 'Notes sur l'art à l'Exposition Universelle,' 1889, p. 86. See: Gamboni, *Paul Gauguin*, 2014, pp. 33–40.

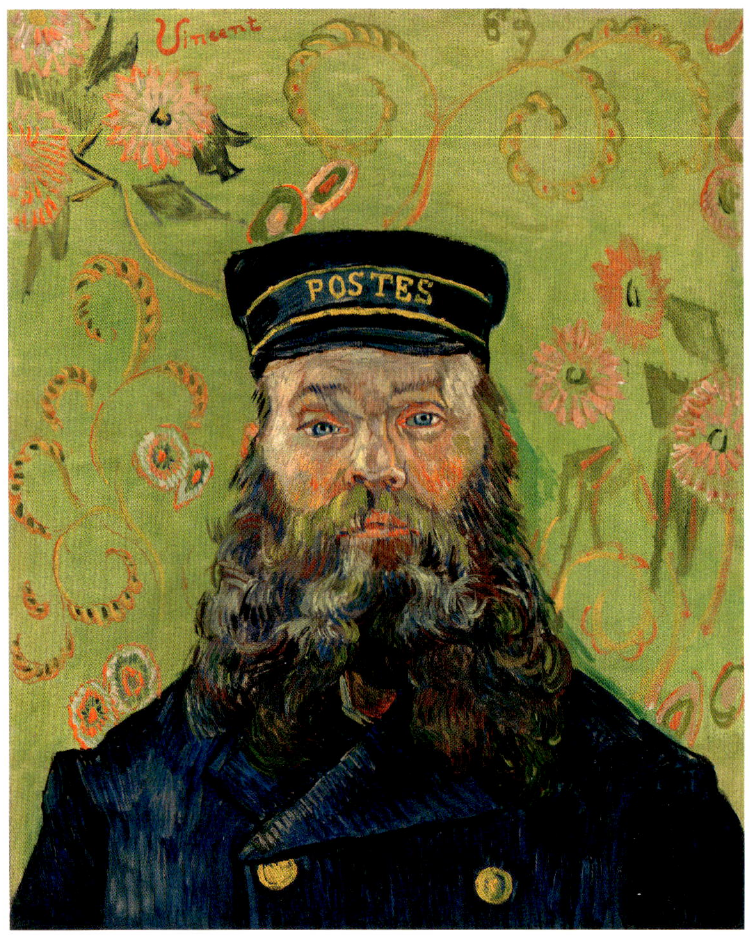

Figure 2:
Vincent van Gogh, *The Postman (Joseph-Étienne Roulin)*, 1889,
oil on canvas, 65.7 × 55.2 cm, inv. BF37. Philadelphia, Barnes Foundation.

Denis's famous dictum that 'a picture—before being a warhorse, a nude woman or telling some other story—is essentially a flat surface covered with colours arranged in a particular pattern.'[15] Another expression of the same ideal in Barnes's collection is Vincent van Gogh's portrait of *The Postman Joseph-Étienne Roulin* (Fig. 2), in which the model's bust is shown in front of an ornamental imaginary wallpaper. The arabesques of the vegetable motif echo those of the postman's bifurcated beard, and Barnes, who could not but notice such a device, may have been inspired by this fictional wall to provide his real ones with metal ornaments—he did not dress the walls of his galleries in patterned fabric or paper, as did the collectors and museum founders of the Gilded Age, nor did he paint them white, like the modernists, but he used jute cloth, a choice consonant with the primitivism of a Gauguin and a Van Gogh. The further abstracted forms of a later generation, for instance those of Georges Braque and Joan Miró, brought the analogies between picture and neighbouring ironwork close to an identity of outline, as if picture and ironwork coincided midway between figuration and ornament.

Antecedents, Models and Parallels

Barnes's inclusion of ironwork was exceptional in the context of art displays, but not in the broader one of collections and museums at large, where precedents and possible models can be found in the realms of the decorative and applied arts and of ethnography. A local antecedent is the Mercer Museum, a vast collection of early American tools and everyday artefacts assembled by Henry Chapman Mercer, an archaeologist close to the American Arts and Crafts Movement, and displayed on a grand scale in a 1908–1910 concrete building in his native Doylestown, Pennsylvania, 27 miles north of Philadelphia.[16] Further away, but internationally famous, was the Musée Le Secq des Tournelles in Rouen. Devoted to all objects made of iron, from Gallo-Roman antiquity to the present (Fig. 3), collected by the painter and photographer Jean-Louis Henri Le Secq Destournelles and his son Henri, it was installed in 1921 in a disused medieval church after partial presentations at the 1900 Universal Exposition and the Musée des Arts Décoratifs in Paris.[17]

Barnes started collecting ironwork in the spring of 1936, after visiting the Victoria and Albert Museum in London and the Musée Le Secq des Tournelles.[18] His interest in such collections may seem surprising, since the focus of his own collecting activity until then had been modern painting, but it was connected to his social origins and concerns.[19] Although he had become extremely wealthy, Albert Coombs Barnes was born in Kensington, a working-class neighbourhood to the north of Philadelphia. His father was a butcher, probably of Quaker origins, and his Methodist mother was descended from the German immigrants who had colonized a large part of the State. Barnes also collected Pennsylvania German furniture and utensils; their presence is relatively discrete in the galleries of the Foundation but they occupy pride of place in his country house Ker-Feal, a 1775 stone farmhouse in Chester County which he purchased in 1940 and arranged as a small museum of popular art.[20] In the realm of wrought iron, Barnes demonstrated a preference for simple, straightforward objects of everyday use, whereas Le Secq had searched for complex masterpieces.[21]

15 Louis [Denis], 'Definition of Neo-Traditionism,' 1890, pp. 540–542. It may be worth noting that Barnes, being born in 1872, belonged to the generation that Denis (born in 1870) called 'of 1890' and which comprised his fellow Nabis. **16** See: *The Mercer Museum Guide*, 1957. **17** See: Cathelineau, 'The Musée Le Secq des Tournelles,' 2015, pp. 11–24. **18** See: Cathelineau, 'The Musée Le Secq des Tournelles,' 2015, pp. 25 and 30. **19** See: Meyers, *Art, Education, & African-American Culture*, 2004. It must be added that Barnes did not only include ironwork in his displays but also, as Wattenmaker summarizes, 'works as diverse as African masks, examples of Chinese painting and calligraphy, New Mexican retablos, and dazzling Navajo rugs' (Wattenmaker, 'In the Light of New Material,' 2015, p. 25). **20** See: Dolkart and Lucy, *The Barnes Foundation, Masterworks*, 2012, pp. 23–25. **21** See: Wattenmaker, 'In the Light of New Material,' 2015, pp. 25 and 38.

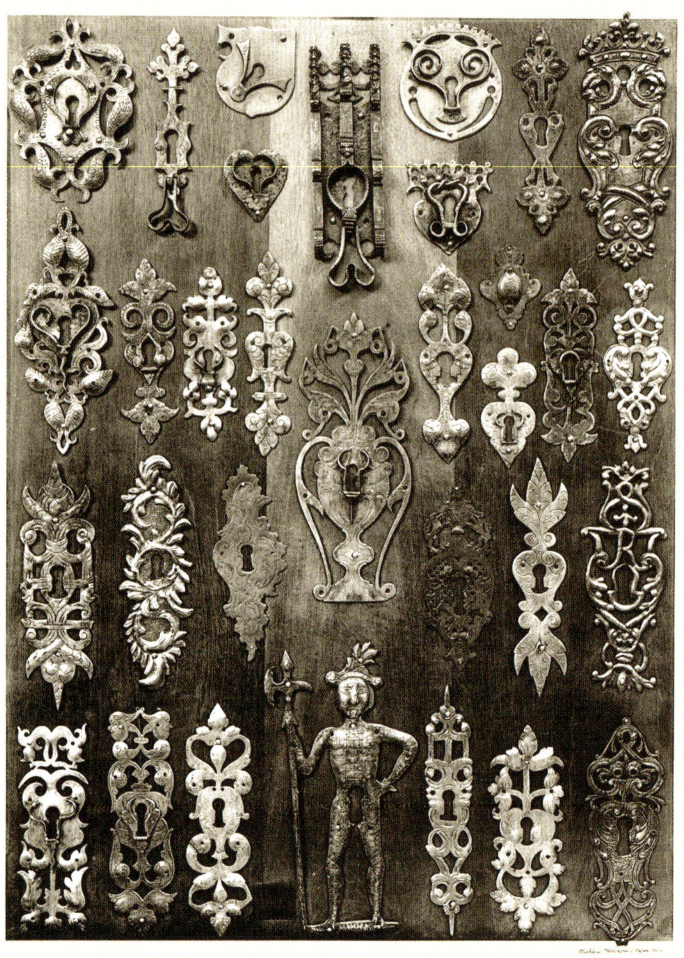

Figure 3:
Seventeenth and eighteenth-century keyhole escutcheons, plate CIV of Henri René d'Allemagne, *Musée Le Secq des Tournelles. Ferronnerie ancienne*, part I (J. Schémit, 1924).

A parallel to Barnes's use of ironwork for pointing out the formal traits of paintings can be found in his method of pairing reproductions of pictures in his publications, regardless of their periods and iconography, in order to emphasize their similarities of shape and composition. An example among many from his major book *The Art in Painting*, first published in 1925, is the vertical juxtaposition of Titian's *Entombment of Christ* with Cézanne's *Curtain, Jug and Fruit Bowl* (Fig. 4), justified by Barnes on the grounds that the design of the two pictures is 'very similar in structure and expressive content.'[22] At first sight, the comparison can seem absurd, given the worlds separating a Renaissance religious history painting from a late nineteenth-century still life; and there is no doubt that

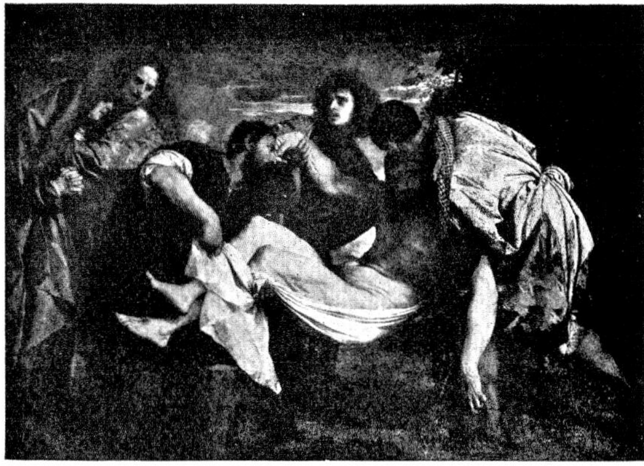

Titian (392)

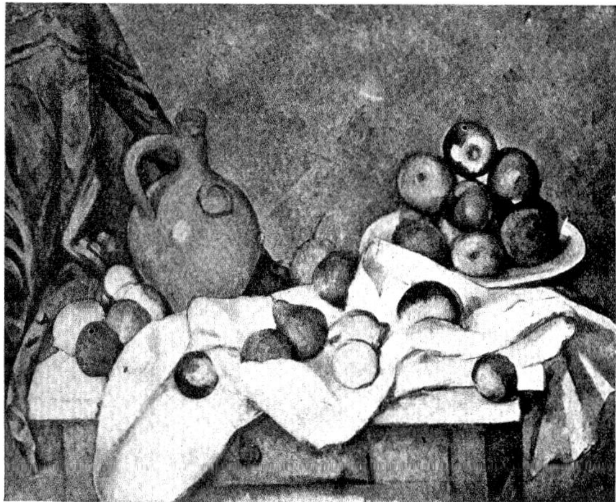

Cézanne (178)

Figure 4:
Albert C. Barnes, *The Art in Painting* (Barnes Foundation Press, 1925), reproductions from *The Entombment of Christ* by Titian (c. 1520, Paris, Musée du Louvre) and *Curtain, Jug and Fruit Bowl* by Cézanne (1893–1894, private collection).

such a comparison could not be made without the equalizing power of the black-and-white photographic reproduction of the two paintings, deprived of their frames and reduced to an identical scale.[23] If one accepts the rules of this game, however, it must be admitted that the comparison is based on objective formal and compositional resemblances and that it is capable of illuminating aspects of Cézanne's still life, such as its peculiar instability and its monumentalizing ambition.

22 Barnes, *The Art in Painting*, 1925, p. 77. **23** On the creative dimension of photographic reproduction and the semiotic challenge of the assemblage of images, see: Ullrich, *Raffinierte Kunst*, 2009 and Thürlemann, *Mehr als ein Bild*, 2013.

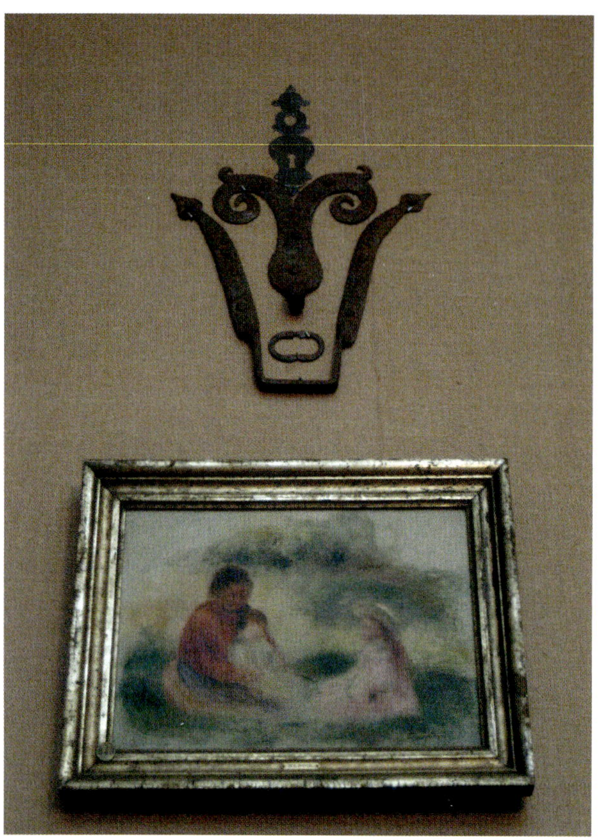

Figure 5:
Barnes Foundation, Room 14, detail from the West wall:
assemblage of wrought iron objects above Pierre-Auguste Renoir's *Young Family* (c. 1902–1903, oil on canvas, inv. BF543).

A broader parallel, which also suggests an element of genealogy, can be made with attempts at revealing the compositional structure of paintings by means of (more or less) diagrammatic drawings.[24] These go back to the eighteenth century but were especially popular in the early twentieth century, when the aesthetics of 'pure visibility,' *Gestalt* psychology and various brands of formalism—including those of Roger Fry and Clive Bell, particularly important for Barnes—concurred to emphasize, analyze and formalize 'plastic' values. Certain formal reductions tended to geometric abstraction, for instance

24 On compositional diagrams, see: Rosenberg, 'Le schéma de composition,' 2008. **25** Itten, 'Analysen alter Meister,' 1921. **26** Benton, 'The Mechanics of Form Organization,' 1926–1927. **27** The arboretum had been created by a veteran of the Civil War, Joseph Lapsley Wilson, and was taken care of by Laura Leggett Barnes, the collector's wife, who organized the courses in collaboration with the University of Pennsylvania. See: Watson, 'The Barnes Foundation. Part I,' 1923, p. 13; Dolkart, 'To See As the Artist Sees,'

the 'analysis' of a late medieval devotional picture, the *Adoration of the Magi* by Master Francke (1426, Kunsthalle Hamburg) drawn around 1920 by Johannes Itten, who was then teaching the 'preliminary course' at the Bauhaus.[25] But other drawings gave more value to the dynamics and complexities of organic form, for instance the diagrams illustrating Thomas Hart Benton's 'The Mechanics of Form Organization,' published in 1926–1927 in *Arts Magazine* and meant as a step toward figural scenes, which must have been known to Barnes.[26]

Barnes's scientific training played a role in this and his approach could be called morphological rather than formalist. An often neglected aspect of his project—which the Foundation's move to downtown Philadelphia marginalized even further—is the parallel he established between the study of artworks and that of plants, by building his museum on the site of an arboretum and organizing courses in horticulture, arboriculture and sylviculture as well as in art appreciation.[27] In his letter to Davis, Barnes expressed a view of the ironwork informed by the biological theory of evolution: 'Another point is that we can show how the objects of each pattern are direct descendants of what has gone before, but modified by new environment.'[28] In the 'so-called useful arts,' such a continuity was a matter of function, material and technique, and Barnes boasted of having 'the best collection that shows the continuity of the traditions from the earliest times until creation stopped in America about 1830.'[29] But he saw and intended to demonstrate—in the face of widespread resistance against European modernism among the cultural elite of the United States—a similar continuity in the fine arts, adding to Davis that 'that is just what we do with the paintings—that is, show how the modern painters are legitimate successors of the old masters.'[30]

Blind Men v. Artists

In contrast to hand-drawn analyses, the 'diagrams' that Barnes used to illuminate the paintings were found ready-made. The implicit reference of such an observation to Marcel Duchamp is intentional: the ready-mades, with which Duchamp started experimenting in 1913, implied a transfer of agency from maker to viewer, since in order to 'make' one, the artist was content with selecting (and at times modifying slightly) an already existing object, and since promoting the result to the aesthetic status required the beholders' assent and participation. During the affair surrounding Duchamp's pseudonymous submission of *Fountain* to the jury of the Society of Independent Artists in 1917, his closest allies pointed to the analogics that the ceramic urinal, presented on the side, suggested to them with the shape of a Madonna or a Buddha.[31] When Alfred Stieglitz photographed the object for

2012, p. 18. **28** Quoted after Wattenmaker, 'In the Light of New Material,' 2015, p. 33. **29** A. C. Barnes to Ch. F. Montgomery, 5 March 1948. Quoted after Wattenmaker, 'In the Light of New Material,' 2015, p. 25. **30** Quotes after Wattenmaker, 'In the Light of New Material,' 2015, p. 33. **31** See: Camfield, *Marcel Duchamp*, 1989.

Duchamp, he took pains to choose the setting and lighting so as to emphasize such associations: he created a shadow suggesting a veil and used as background a painting by Marsden Harley that redoubled the stupa-like shape and reinforced its connotations.[32]

On the lawn in front of the main entrance to his galleries, Barnes installed a twentieth-century fire gong that Wattenmaker compares to David Smith's steel sculptures, and Duchamp's ready-mades include many everyday utensils, such as the *Bottle Dryer* (1914) and the snow shovel of *In Advance of the Broken Arm* (1915).[33] A significant difference between the wrought iron pieces collected and displayed by Barnes and Duchamp's ready-mades concerns the relative importance of craft: when he wrote 'until creation stopped in America about 1830,' Barnes limited the 'expression of experience' to manual work, whereas Duchamp focused on mass-produced items in which he found—as his posthumous notes revealed—an 'infra-thin' difference between objects 'stamped by the same mold.'[34] At a more generic level of intention, however, Barnes's and Duchamp's aims are related. The short-lived publication in which Duchamp's friends defended the cause of *Fountain* and of the ready-made was entitled *The Blind Man*, and the cover of its first issue showed a nude figure in a painting thumbing a nose at a passer-by led by a dog and holding a cane.[35] In accordance with Dewey, Barnes's main objective as a collector and a teacher was to overcome 'blindness' and to open people's eyes, help them 'to see as the artist sees.'[36] It can hardly be irrelevant in this context that Barnes owed his fortune to the discovery and marketing of Argyrol, an antiseptic made of mild silver protein compounds used to prevent blindness in the newborn.[37]

The maieutic function of Barnes's displays probably accounts for the fact that, although he explained his intentions regarding the inclusion of ironwork in a few private letters, he never advertised them or made them explicit for the visitors. As Wattenmaker summarizes, 'the wall ensembles elicited mixed reactions, ranging from scathing disapproval to mere perplexity to enthusiastic acceptance of the displays as works of art in their own right.'[38] The reactions depended to some extent on the degree to which their authors were apprised of Barnes's intentions, which was the case for instance of Owen J. Roberts, the attorney who had drawn up the Barnes Foundation indenture, when he wrote in advance of a visit: 'I join you in marveling that nobody has thought of integrating this work with other artistic and craft work because, as you say, the principles of art are the same no matter in what field they are exhibited.'[39]

32 Camfield, *Marcel Duchamp*, 1989, pp. 33, 35–36 and 83. The painting is *Musical Theme (Oriental Symphony)* (1912–1913, Waltham, MA, Brandeis University, Rose Art Museum). **33** See: Wattenmaker, 'In the Light of New Material,' 2015, p. 30. **34** See: Duchamp, *Notes*, 1980, n° 35 (29 July 1937). **35** Roché (ed.), *The Blind Man*, 1917, cover. **36** See: Barnes, *The Art in Painting*, 1925, pp. 5, 7 and 46. **37** See: Schack, *Art and Argyrol*, 1966. **38** Wattenmaker, 'In the Light of New Material,' 2015, pp. 33–35. **39** O. J. Roberts to A. C. Barnes, 4 March 1937. Quoted after Wattenmaker, 'In the Light of New Material,' 2015, p. 30. **40** Barnes, *The Art in Painting*, 1925, p. 7. **41** A. C. Barnes to J. Dewey, 29 and 30 March 1934, John Dewey Papers.

In his 1937 article, Dewey pleaded for arrangements based on 'community of design' in museums of decorative arts because they were meant for 'artist-designers,' who had to 'learn to see for artistic purposes;' in his preface to Barnes's *The Art in Painting*, however, he wrote that there is 'no essential difference in kind between the experience of the artist and that of the observer of his work.'[40] In a letter of 1934 to Dewey, Barnes mentioned a 'Picasso' that he had seen opposite his office, formed by snow on a stretch of roof, and concluded that there was 'no difference in the essence of the aesthetic response in the two cases,' one of them produced by 'an artist of flesh and blood'—the real Picasso—and the other by God or 'the combination of the forces of nature.'[41] This is again close to Duchamp's dictum that 'it is the beholders who make the pictures' and it must be observed that the ironwork displayed by Barnes, like the majority of Duchamp's ready-mades, is not entirely 'ready-made' but was manipulated to produce the desired effect.[42] Not only had many of these objects been separated—presumably by dealers and antiquaries rather than Barnes himself—from the pieces of furniture or architecture to which they had been attached, but they were also stripped of their colour—partly by Barnes—and often combined with each other. We saw that the metal analogon of Demuth's *Masts* (Fig. 1) is formed by a hinge topped with a keyhole escutcheon; the element surmounting the centre of the West wall in Room 14, just above a small painting by Renoir (Fig. 5), is an assemblage combining (from top to bottom) a keyhole escutcheon, a hinge, a ring and a brace. The result cannot fail to be perceived as a mask or the image of a face and may be compared to Picasso's *Bull's Head* of 1942, assembled from the seat and handlebars of a bicycle.[43] In many cases, the relation between painting and ironwork has an element of playfulness and humour: on the West wall of Room 18, for example, a particularly 'thorny' ram's-horn hinge looms above Renoir's picture of *Roses* (c. 1912).[44]

As is often the case with common names, the expression 'ram's-horn hinge' attests to the existence of a collective, enduring iconic perception of the object. A close look at the pieces of wrought iron included by Barnes in his displays shows that he did not only discover in them echoes of paintings from his collection, but was also sensitive to iconic suggestions inherent in them, so that his juxtapositions may throw a light on both elements, the ironwork and the painting. A plate from Henri René d'Allemagne's catalogue of the Musée Le Secq des Tournelles (Fig. 3) shows various degrees of anthropomorphic suggestion in keyhole escutcheons, including (at the centre of the bottom row) a touch of

Quoted after Meyers, *Art, Education, & African-American Culture*, 2004, pp. 187–188. **42** Schuster, 'Marcel Duchamp, vite,' 1957, pp. 143–145. Quoted after Duchamp, *Duchamp du signe*, 1975, pp. 247–248. **43** See: Gamboni, *Potential Images*, 2002, pp. 214–218. **44** Judith Dolkart notes correctly that 'Barnes sometimes combined two or more disparate objects to create new silhouettes, to strengthen the formal connections between objects, and even to make jokes—some obvious, some subtle.' (Cathelineau and Dolkart (eds.), *Strength and Splendor*, 2015, p. 7).

ribald humour with a nude halberdier rendered ithyphallic by the keyhole. Barnes would have noted such a visual pun, all the more as he had been interested in psychiatry since his medical studies and had criticized the Philadelphia psychiatrists, who tried to explain modern art as 'degeneration,' for ignoring 'the monumental work done by Freud, Jung and Adler.'[45] His formalism was not opposed to semantics and an element of symbolism may be involved in his predilection for keys, keyholes and hinges, referring in cognitive as well as sexual terms to processes of encoding, decoding and connecting. The latter corresponds to display, which consists of modifying the perception and hence the meaning of objects by combining them in specific ways. It is telling that hinges also play an important role in collectors' and artists' museums such as the John Soane Museum in London and the Musée Gustave Moreau in Paris, where they help to increase the combinatorial density of the arrangements.[46] Like Soane and Moreau, Barnes became increasingly involved in such combinatorics, and the inclusion of ironwork and other craft objects corresponded to an interest in what he called the 'transfer of values' from one object to the next.[47]

Wattenmaker points to the inspiration that Barnes derived from the writings on aesthetics of Paul Valéry, whom the collector tried to bring to the United States for a series of lectures.[48] A case in point is Valéry's 1934 essay 'On the Pre-eminent Dignity of the Arts of Fire,' in which he praised wrought iron for the close connection between material, technique and form, as well as for the 'noble uncertainty' resulting from the agency of fire.[49] Another inspiring text may have been the marginal comments that Valéry added in 1930 to his 1894 'Introduction to the Method of Leonardo da Vinci,' which defined the 'usefulness of artists' as the 'preservation of sensory subtlety and instability' and argued that 'a work of art should always teach us that we had not seen what we are seeing.'[50] This is clearly the function that Barnes attributed to his ensembles and although he never

45 See: Meyers, *Art, Education, & African-American Culture*, 2004, pp. 61–63 and 69–73; Braddock, *Collecting as Modernist Practice*, 2012, pp. 105–155 and 254–265. **46** See: Gamboni, '"Musées d'auteur",' 2011, pp. 193–194, and Gamboni, *The Museum As Experience: Artists' and Collectors' Museums, a Dialogue* (forthcoming). **47** Barnes, *The Art in Painting*, 1925, p. 6. On 'transferred values,' see: Bahr, 'Transferring Values,' unpublished Ph.D. thesis, University of Texas at Austin (1998); Johnson, 'John Dewey's Socially Instrumental Practice at the Barnes Foundation,' 2012. **48** See: Wattenmaker, 'In the Light of New Material,' 2015, pp. 28–29. **49** Valéry, 'De l'éminente dignité des arts du feu,' 1934, pp. 7–12. **50** Valéry, *Introduction à la méthode de Léonard de Vinci*, 1957, pp. 25 and 26. See: Dario Gamboni, 'For a Science of the "Preservation of Sensory Subtlety and Instability",' 2008. **51** Ducasse, *Art, the Critics, and You*, 1944, p. 63. Quoted after Wattenmaker, 'In the Light of New Material,' 2015, p. 35. Ducasse was specialized in the philosophy of mind and aesthetics, and a review of this book, which argued for the value of the public's insights, saw it as a 'championship of the general consumer' (Gilbert, '*Art, the Critics, and You.* By Curt J. Ducasse,' 1945, p. 612). **52** See: Naumann and Obalk (eds.), *Affectionately, Marcel*, 2000, p. 179; Craig Adcock, '"Falcon" or "Perroquet"? A Note on Duchamp's *Morceaux choisis d'après Courbet*,' *tout-fait*, 1/1 (Dec. 1999), www.toutfait.com/issues/issue_1/Notes/Faucon.html (last accessed 20 April 2018). **53** MacAgy (ed.), *The Western Round Table on Modern Art*, 1949, p. 66.

claimed to be an artist, one commentator—the philosopher Curt J. Ducasse—wrote in 1944 that 'the works of decorative art these arrangements themselves constitute may well be ranked in aesthetic merit with some of the objects out of which they are composed.'[51] To that extent, one can say that in Barnes's displays and thanks to his promotion of the heuristic agency of objects, *ergon* became a shifting quality susceptible to scale and to exchanging positions with that of *parergon*.

Duchamp visited the Barnes Foundation on 3 December 1933, before the inclusion of ironwork, and he did not comment on what he had seen there, although his posthumous work *Given: 1. The Waterfall, 2. The Illuminating Gas* (1946–1966, Philadelphia Museum of Art) is clearly indebted to Courbet's *Woman in White Stockings* (1864) hanging in Room 7.[52] He may well have thought of Barnes, however, when he made, sixteen years later, a statement about the 'real collector,' whom he contrasted with the speculator: 'he is, in my opinion, an artist—*au carré*. He selects paintings and puts them on his wall; in other words, "he paints himself a collection".'[53]

Bibliography

J. Anderson, *Art Held Hostage: The Story of the Barnes Collection* (W.W. Norton & Company, 2003).

M. G. Bahr, 'Transferring Values: Albert C. Barnes, Work and the Work of Art,' unpublished Ph.D. thesis, University of Texas at Austin (1998).

A. C. Barnes, *The Art in Painting* (Barnes Foundation Press, 1925).

Th. H. Benton, 'The Mechanics of Form Organization,' *Arts Magazine*, 1 (Nov. 1926), pp. 285–289; 2 (Dec. 1926), pp. 340–342; 3 (Jan. 1927), pp. 43–44; 4 (Feb. 1927), pp. 95–96; 5 (March 1927), pp. 145–148.

J. Braddock, *Collecting as Modernist Practice* (Johns Hopkins University Press, 2012).

A. Breton, 'Gustave Moreau [1960]' in A. Breton, *Surrealism and Painting*, trans. Simon Watson Taylor (Museum of Fine Arts Publications, 2002), pp. 363–366.

W. A. Camfield, *Marcel Duchamp: Fountain* (The Menil Collection, 1989).

A.-C. Cathelineau, 'The Musée Le Secq des Tournelles: History of a Passion' in A.-C. Cathelineau and J. F. Dolkart (eds.), *Strength and Splendor: Wrought Iron from the Musée le Secq des Tournelles, Rouen* (Barnes Foundation, 2015), pp. 11–24.

A.-C. Cathelineau and J. F. Dolkart (eds.), *Strength and Splendor: Wrought Iron from the Musée le Secq des Tournelles, Rouen* (Barnes Foundation, 2015).

J. Dewey, 'The Educational Function of a Museum of Decorative Arts,' *Chronicle for the Arts of Decoration of Cooper Union*, 1/3 (April 1937), pp. 93–99.

J. F. Dolkart and M. Lucy [with contributions by D. Gillman], *The Barnes Foundation, Masterworks* (Skira Rizzoli, 2012).

J. F. Dolkart, 'To See As the Artist Sees' in J. F. Dolkart and M. Lucy [with contributions by D. Gillman], *The Barnes Foundation, Masterworks* (Skira Rizzoli, 2012), pp. 9–29.

C. J. Ducasse, *Art, the Critics, and You* (O. Piest, 1944).

M. Duchamp, *Duchamp du signe. Écrits*, ed. M. Sanouillet with E. Peterson (Flammarion, 1975).

M. Duchamp, *Notes*, ed. Paul Matisse (Centre national d'art et de culture Georges Pompidou, 1980).

D. Gamboni, *Potential Images: Ambiguity and Indeterminacy in Modern Art* (Reaktion Books, 2002).

D. Gamboni, 'For a Science of the "Preservation of Sensory Subtlety and Instability"' in O. Bätschmann, J. Gelshorn, N. Gramaccini, B. Nicolai and P. J. Schneemann (eds.), *Art History on Demand? Dienstleistung Kunstgeschichte? 100 Jahre Institut für Kunstgeschichte Universität Bern* (Imorde, 2008), vol. 2, pp. 81–91 and 137–139.

D. Gamboni, '"Musées d'auteur": les musées d'artistes et de collectionneurs comme œuvres d'art totales' in G. Mina and S. Wuhrmann (eds.), *Tra universo privato e spazio pubblico: Case di artisti adibite a museo / Zwischen privatem Kosmos und öffentlichem Raum: Künstlerhaus-Museen* (Office fédéral de la Culture, 2011), pp. 189–206.

D. Gamboni, *Paul Gauguin: The Mysterious Centre of Thought*, trans. Chris Miller (Reaktion Books, 2014).

D. Gamboni, *The Museum As Experience: Artists' and Collectors' Museums, a Dialogue* (forthcoming).

P. Gauguin, 'Notes sur l'art à l'Exposition Universelle,' *Le Moderniste Illustré*, 11 (4 July 1889), pp. 84–86.

K. E. Gilbert, '*Art, the Critics, and You*. By Curt J. Ducasse,' *The Philosophical Review*, 54/6 (1945), pp. 612–614.

H. Greenfeld, *The Devil and Dr. Barnes: Portrait of an American Collector* (Viking, 1987).

Groupe µ (F. Edeline, J. Klinkenberg and Ph. Minguet), *Traité du signe visuel. Pour une rhétorique de l'image* (Seuil, 1992).

J. Itten, 'Analysen alter Meister: *Anbetung* von Meister Francke' in B. Adler (ed.), *Utopia. Dokumente der Wirklichkeit, I–II* (Utopia, 1921), unpaginated.

M. H. Johnson, 'John Dewey's Socially Instrumental Practice at the Barnes Foundation and the Role of "Transferred Values" in Aesthetic Experience,' *Journal of Aesthetic Education*, 46/2 (2012), pp. 43–57.
P. Louis [M. Denis], 'Definition of Neo-Traditionism,' *Art et Critique*, 65 (23 August 1890), pp. 540–543.
D. MacAgy (ed.), *The Western Round Table on Modern Art: Abstract of Proceedings* (San Francisco Art Association, 1949).
M. A. Meyers, *Art, Education, & African-American Culture: Albert C. Barnes and the Science of Philanthropy* (Transaction, 2004).
F. Naumann and H. Obalk (eds.), *Affectionately, Marcel: The Selected Correspondence of Marcel Duchamp* (Ludion Press, 2000).
W. Schack, *Art and Argyrol: The Life and Career of Dr. Albert C. Barnes* (T. Yoseloff, 1966).
J. Schuster, 'Marcel Duchamp, vite,' *Le Surréalisme, même*, 2 (Spring 1957), p. 148.
H.-P. Roché (ed.), *The Blind Man*, 1 (April 1917).
R. Rosenberg, 'Le schéma de composition, outil et symptôme de la perception du tableau' in C. Barbillon, F.-R. Martin, R. Recht and Ph. Sénéchal (eds.), *Histoire de l'histoire de l'art en France au XIXe siècle* (Documentation Française, 2008), pp. 419–432 and 523–525.
Mercer Museum of the Bucks County Historical Society (ed.), *The Mercer Museum Guide: The History of Our Country from the Point of View of the Work of Human Hands* (Bucks County Historical Society, 1957).
F. Thürlemann, *Mehr als ein Bild: für eine Kunstgeschichte des hyperimage* (Wilhem Fink, 2013).
W. Ullrich, *Raffinierte Kunst. Übung von Reproduktionen* (Wagenbach, 2009).
P. Valéry, 'De l'éminente dignité des arts du feu' in P. Valéry, *Pièces sur l'art* (Gallimard, 1934), pp. 8–9.
P. Valéry, *Introduction à la méthode de Léonard de Vinci* (Gallimard, 1957).
F. Watson, 'The Barnes Foundation. Part I,' *The Arts*, 3/1 (Jan. 1923), pp. 9–24.
R. J. Wattenmaker, 'In the Light of New Material: The Place of Antique Wrought Iron in the Collection and School of the Barnes Foundation' in A.-C. Cathelineau and J. F. Dolkart (eds.), *Strength and Splendor: Wrought Iron from the Musée le Secq des Tournelles, Rouen* (Barnes Foundation, 2015), pp. 25–39.

Website:
www.toutfait.com/issues/issue_1/Notes/Faucon.html.

PETER SCHADE

The Reframing of Lazarus[1]

The frame as a construct of agency establishes a boundary relationship between the work of art and itself.[2] With respect to the work of art, the frame determines the object of art in-itself (its limits) and the object of art for-itself (its boundary). Establishing the object-of art in-and-for-itself.[3] With respect to the frame, it is on the boundary—the co-determinate demarcation (geometric and material) between the work of art and the frame—that the frame as *parergon* is realized.[4]

It is, moreover, on the boundary that the rhetorical device of the frame is most intimately and directly efficacious. The frame is a rhetorical device that directly (discreetly and/or indiscreetly) affects the viewers' relationship with and experience of the work of art, in that it presents conditions (perceptual, conceptual, aesthetic, historic, economic and ideological) that influence, indeed help shape and direct, the viewers' eidetic perception (both retentive and protentive) of the work of art.[5] The effect can range from subtle to radical; from profoundly positive to its opposite. It is, thus, clear that curatorial decisions regarding frames and the framing of works of art are hugely important.

Sebastiano del Piombo's great altarpiece *The Raising of Lazarus,* so iconic for the National Gallery in that its accession number is NG1, lasted 200 years in its original setting, and since then has been displayed until recently in an inappropriate selection of frames.

It was commissioned in December 1516, completed in 1519, and shipped soon after that to Narbonne, where it stayed in the spectacular but unfinished cathedral until 1722, when the duc d'Orléans, Regent for the infant Louis XV, managed to acquire it from the cathedral authorities in exchange for a grant for repairs, a copy by Carl Van Loo, and a new and fashionable frame for that copy.[6]

1 Based in part on a collaboration with Lynn Roberts for *The Frame Blog*. **2** See also: Duro (ed.), *The Rhetoric of the Frame*, 1996, pp. 1–10. **3** The origin of this concept of boundary relationship—so essential to phenomenology and hermeneutics—can be traced to Hegel's *The Phenomenology of Spirit* and his *Science of Logic*. **4** A secondary boundary relationship is, of course, also established, namely between the framed work of art and the space wherein it is exhibited. But it is not within the scope nor interest of this article to consider the nature of this boundary relationship. **5** On eidetic perception, see: Husserl, *Cartesian Meditations*, 1999. **6** See: Dunkerton and Howard, 'Sebastiano del Piombo's *Raising of Lazarus*,' 2009, p. 45, note 4.

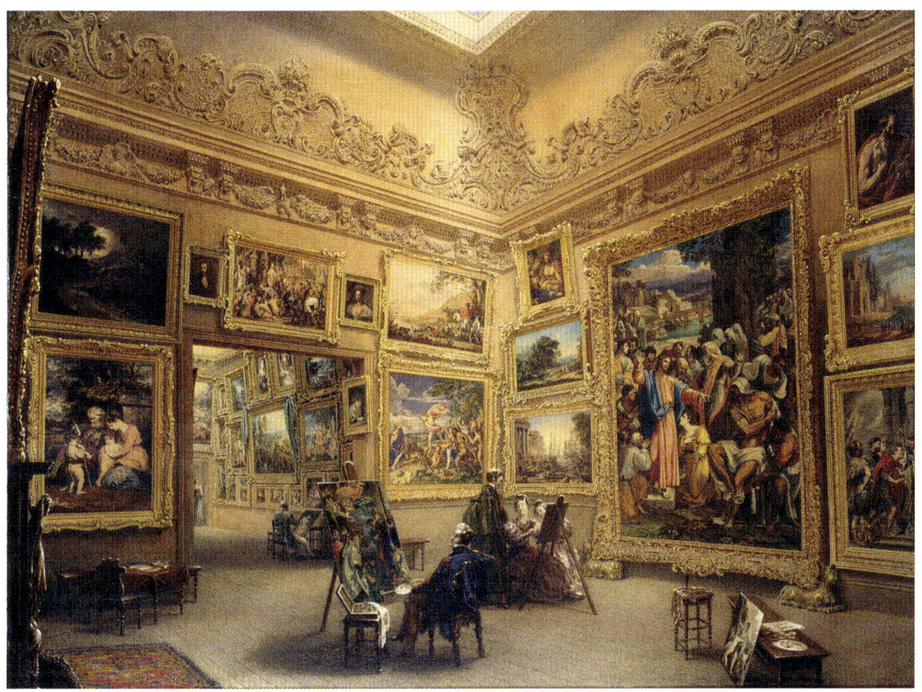

Figure 1:
Frederick Mackenzie, *The National Gallery when at Mr J. J. Angerstein's House, Pall Mall*, watercolour, 1824–1834. London, Victoria and Albert Museum.

The real Sebastiano was installed in the Palais-Royal until it was sold during the French Revolution, and purchased by John Julius Angerstein. With thirty-seven other paintings, it went on to form the core of the nascent National Gallery in the early nineteenth century, continuing to be displayed in Angerstein's house in Pall Mall until a suitable gallery was built. At that point it was still in the frame, which seems to have been commissioned for it by the duc d'Orléans—a massive and opulently-carved and gilded Régence frame—which would have integrated it into his collection but was extraordinarily unsuitable for a Renaissance altarpiece (Fig. 1).

When the new National Gallery opened in 1838, a gradual programme of reframing began. In 1861 the *Illustrated London News* published an image of a *New Room at the National Gallery*, a detail of which shows *Lazarus* in a hollow frame lined with moulded composition acanthus leaves, very similar to the kind of frame that Joseph Mallord William Turner had chosen for his work at the turn of the century (Fig. 2). This pattern was also used for other frames in the Gallery.

The National Gallery was the first institution of its kind to have a programme for reframing its large Renaissance altarpieces in copies of architectural frames. About thirty paintings were framed in this way between the 1860s and 1910. Many of these have survived, but *The Raising of Lazarus* was left in its Neo-Classical setting.

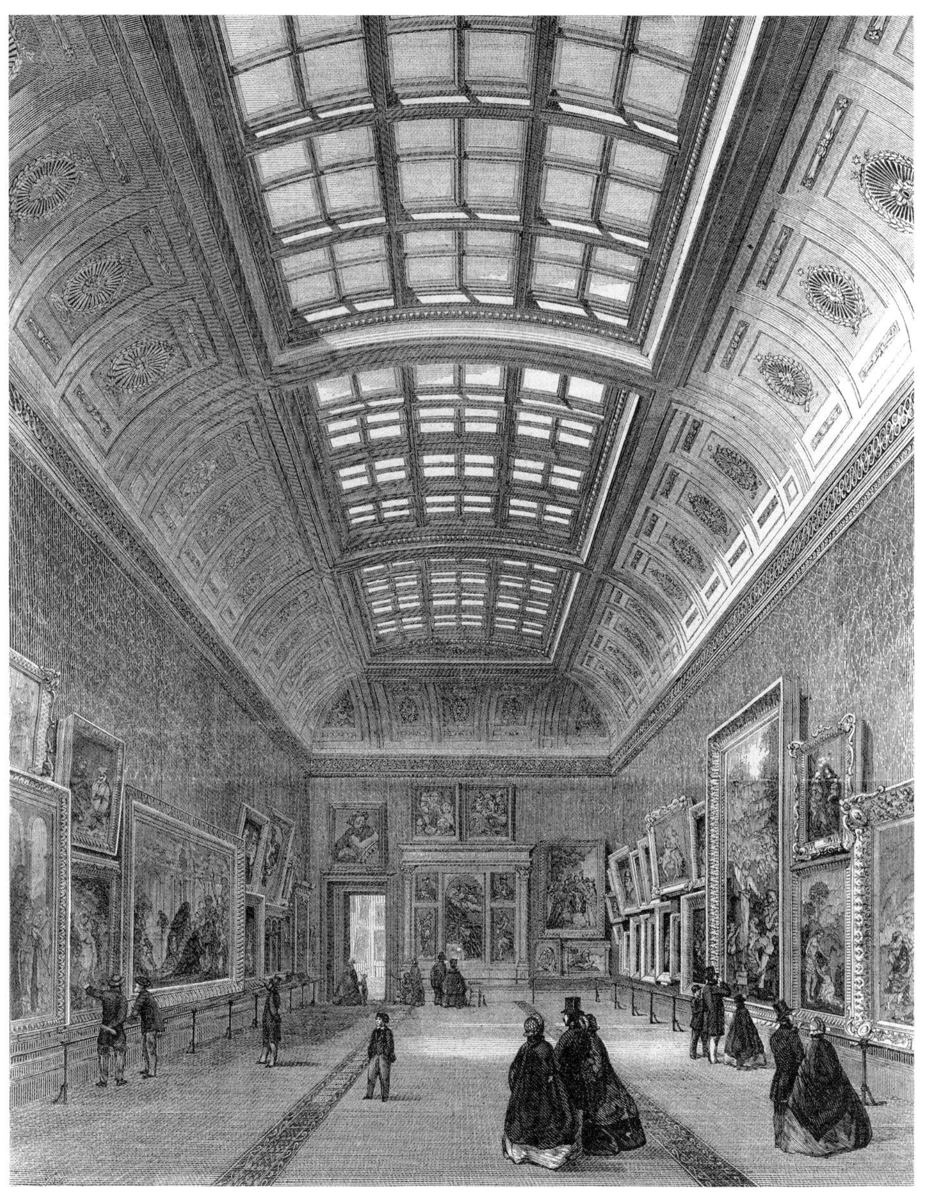

Figure 2:
New Room at the National Gallery, in *The Illustrated London News,* 6 June 1861.

After 1945, NG1 was kept in conservation and in 1967 *Lazarus* was reframed again, under the auspices of Philip Hendy. He had apparently bought some architectural wooden elements in Italy, described as sixteenth- to eighteenth-century ceiling mouldings, and these were made into a frame for the painting. It made a gesture towards a Mannerist walnut frame, but is barely adequate, being far too narrow and spindly to contain such a monumental work; and so it sat uncomfortably on the wall for half a century, looking partly like the inside of a much bigger frame and partly like a zip fastener (Fig. 3).

Meanwhile, back in the cathedral of Narbonne, the art historian Christa Gardner von Teuffel had discovered that the predella panel from the original frame carved for the *Lazarus* had been incorporated into the eighteenth-century frame made for the Van Loo copy. In 1984 she published this discovery in the *Burlington Magazine*, along with the measurements of the panel (which corresponded with those of the painting), and also with an image of the top of the carved moulding.[7] This showed that it had been cut across diagonally on both sides at the time that it was made, revealing that it had been tailored to fit between two projecting architectural elements: the pedestals of the original framing columns. The predella is carved with a scrolled leatherwork cartouche in the centre, from which are strung two swags of bay leaves centred with a band of pomegranates (the pomegranate is a motif—probably symbolizing rebirth—associated with the Medici.)[8] Above each swag is the *impresa* of the Medici family—a diamond ring and three differently-coloured feathers, with the motto 'SEMPER' on the scrolling banner between them. All these features mark the frame and its original contents as a Medici commission; and the size of the predella, along with the opulence of the carving and polychromy, compared with the size of most donor shields on altarpiece frames, indicate that the whole object must have been extremely splendid.

Early in 1515 Giulio de' Medici had been appointed Archbishop of Narbonne, where it was the custom on nomination to donate a sacred work of art. Cardinal Giulio de' Medici, later Pope Clement VII, was the client who had commissioned Sebastiano in 1516 to paint *The Raising of Lazarus*, and had also commissioned Raphael to paint a panel with *The Transfiguration*.[9] The cathedral was thought to possess relics of Lazarus. Apocryphally, Lazarus, his sister Martha and Mary Magdalene were all supposed to have settled in Provence, performing miracles, and finally being buried near Narbonne. This set the programme the two paintings, of which Sebastiano's includes all three saints, and Raphael's includes Mary Magdalene in the center foreground.

In 2009, an architectural element on a grand scale came up for auction in Genoa, and was acquired by the National Gallery framing department. The entablature measured 3.5 metres across, with ornament highly reminiscent of the vocabulary used in Raphael's *Stanze* in the Vatican. The small morphing figures at each side were very like—for example—

7 Gardner von Teuffel, 'Sebastiano del Piombo, Raphael and Narbonne,' 1984, pp. 764–766. **8** See: Reiss, *Cardinal Giulio de' Medici*, 1992, p. 251, note 141. See also p. 235. **9** Raphael's commission seems to have been prior to Sebastiano's, see: Barbieri, 'The Competition Between Raphael & Michelangelo,' 2005, p. 160.

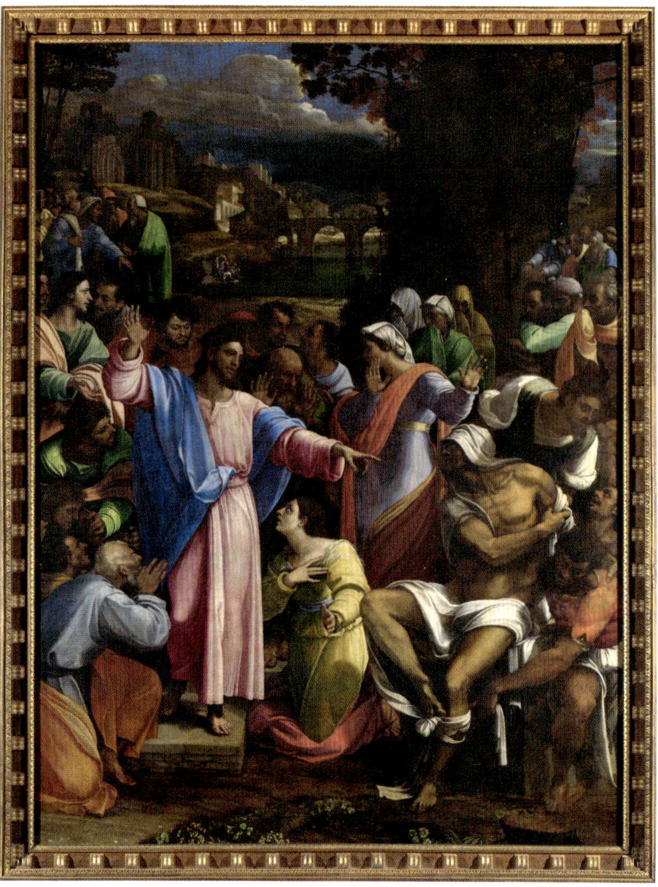

Figure 3:
Sebastiano del Piombo, *The Raising of Lazarus*, frame used between 1967–2016.

the figures on a window shutter and also on a stone chimneypiece in the *Stanze*. Completely contemporary with the two Narbonne altarpieces, and bound up with the Medicean decoration of the Vatican rooms, this was a fortuitously happy discovery for the project to reframe *The Raising of Lazarus*. The swagged bay leaves on the frieze also echoed those on the predella panel in Narbonne.

Universal agreement to proceed with the making of a large architectural frame could not be reached in 2009, but it was agreed to copy the Narbonne predella as a first step. It was not until early 2016 that it was decided to proceed with making the entire frame initially only to be shown during the *Michelangelo & Sebastiano* exhibition held at the National Gallery in 2017 (Fig. 4).[10]

10 *The Credit Suisse Exhibition: Michelangelo & Sebastiano*, The National Gallery, March–June 2017. See: Wivel with Joannides and Barbieri, *Michelangelo & Sebastiano*, 2017.

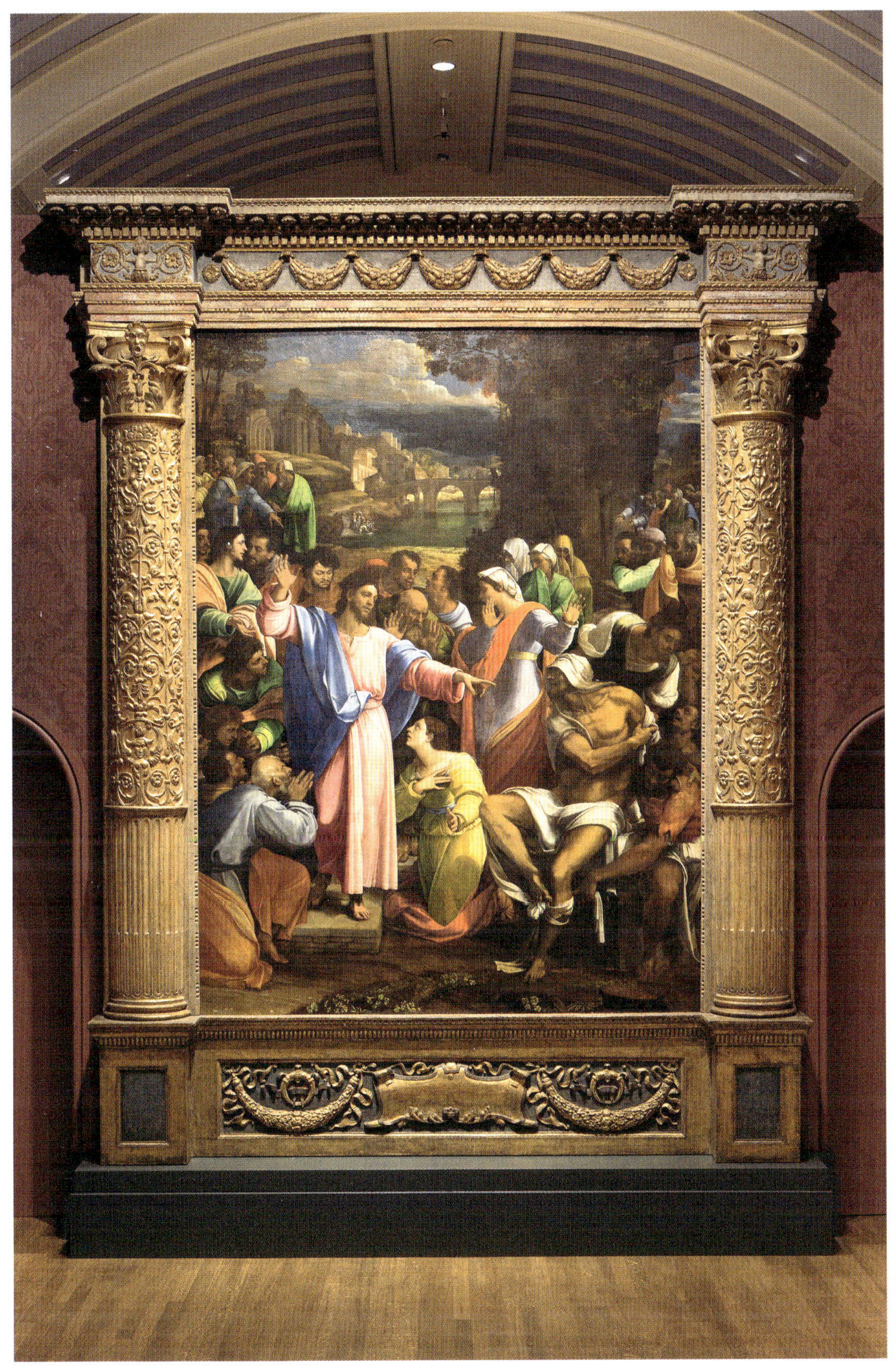

Figure 4:
The Raising of Lazarus reframed for the *Michelangelo & Sebastiano* exhibition, 2017.

The width of the entablature, which was bought in 2009, although original, was very narrow for its depth, which meant that it could be widened to fit the Sebastiano by adding three more swags of leaves. This work was undertaken first, before the design of the sides of the frame was finalized. The initial montage used images of two antique pilasters, which were part of an original sixteenth-century altarpiece reconstructed earlier for Leonardo's *The Virgin of the Rocks* in the National Gallery.

It became apparent that flat pilasters would be insufficient to support the projecting corners of the entablature. We were fortunate to have a pair of antique columns in the National Gallery's frame store. They are of the right period, and fortuitously also use the same vocabulary of motifs as the carvings in Raphael's *Stanze*. They had been acquired in the 1980s from the frame maker and restorer Paul Levi; and although they were too small and fully round, they provided an excellent pattern for two half-round columns and capitals.

A large part of the harmony between the various architectural sections is dependent on the ornamental coherence between them. This has been influenced to a great extent by the decoration of the *Domus Aurea*, which was familiar to Raphael and all his peers, and had had an extraordinarily great effect on the ornamental style of the period since its discovery in 1480. Although it has degraded catastrophically since then, the series of plates published by Lodovico Mirri in the late eighteenth century give a clear impression of the detail and colour of the various rooms in the palace.[11] Influence of the decoration in the *Domus Aurea* can be seen in, for instance, the capitals used as models for the *Lazarus* frame: for example, the mask with open mouth, crimped petal-like hair and curling locks like mustachios, surrounded by delicate pierced scrolls and leaf fronds. The *Domus Aurea* was, of course, central to the decorative schemes executed by Raphael and his colleagues, notably by Giovanni da Udine, in the *Stanze* of the Vatican, and also influenced the carved stone and woodwork installed there. Entwined with this ornamental programme was the stamp of the two Medicean popes who commissioned it—Leo X, and Clement VII, who, as Cardinal Giulio de' Medici, also commissioned the altarpieces of the *Transfiguration* and the *Lazarus*.

The process of making the frame was carried out using very similar methods to the original, and all decorative elements were hand carved in Lombard poplar. The chalk and glue used for the *gesso*, the bole colours and the gold leaf are all traditional materials, which have not changed over the centuries. Constant revision and critical analyses of already completed parts was a very important component of the making of this frame; for instance the entire predella was, after it had already been gilded and painted, stripped back to the wood because the *gesso* which was applied in 2011 was too thick and did not correspond to the images we had of the Narbonne piece.

11 Carloni, *Vestigia delle Terme di Tito*, 1776–1778; for example, plates 5 and 56. **12** Sebastiano del Piombo to Michelangelo, 2nd July 1518. Quoted by Gardner von Teuffel, 'Sebastiano del Piombo, Raphael and Narbonne,' 1984, p. 765.

Possibly the most important art employed in the making of convincing reproduction frames is the creation of surfaces which emulate that of well-preserved originals. In this case we had the original surface of the entablature as guidance. Much of the eventual design of the frame was informed by the original substance of the entablature, the columns, which we were able to copy, and the surviving predella (Narbonne). As a project, it evolved during the making and it was crucial that we did not follow an exact blueprint.

The Renaissance-style tabernacle frames, which were made for the National Gallery in the nineteenth century, were at the time thought to be faithful reproductions. The first questions about them were raised in a report on behalf of the Trustees in the early twentieth century, when the ornament and, especially, the quality of the gilding were criticized. These frames look entirely nineteenth century to us now, and no experienced observer would mistake them for anything else. The frame of the *Lazarus* appears harmonious with the painting to us now, and similar to authentic carved and gilded ornament of the early sixteenth century. Whether we have completely managed to keep the look of the early twenty-first century out of this frame will only become apparent over time.

For now, we can assert that it is a visual resurrection of *The Raising of Lazarus*. The painting will reclaim the status it has, both because of the story of its creation and as the very first painting catalogued in our collection. The frame makes many of the qualities of the painting more legible, and we can experience at first-hand Sebastiano's remark in a letter to Michelangelo: '[M]y work will have more grace when clothed [with its frame] than if naked.'[12]

Bibliography

C. Barbieri, 'The Competition Between Raphael & Michelangelo, and Sebastiano's Role in it' in M. B. Hall (ed.), *The Cambridge Companion to Raphael* (Cambridge University Press, 2005), pp. 141–164.
M. Carloni, *Vestigia delle Terme di Tito* (L. Mirri, 1776–1778).
J. Dunkerton and H. Howard, 'Sebastiano del Piombo's *Raising of Lazarus*: A History of Change,' *National Gallery Technical Bulletin* (2009), pp. 26–51.
P. Duro (ed.), *The Rhetoric of the Frame. Essays on the Boundaries of the Artwork* (Cambridge University Press, 1996).
C. Gardner von Teuffel, 'Sebastiano del Piombo, Raphael and Narbonne: New Evidence,' *Burlington Magazine* (December 1984), pp. 764–766.
E. Husserl, *Cartesian Meditations: An Introduction to Phenomenology* (Kluwer Academic Publishers, 1999).
S. Reiss, 'Cardinal Giulio de' Medici as a Patron of Art, 1513–1523,' unpublished Ph.D. thesis, Princeton University (1992).
M. Wivel with P. Joannides and C. Barbieri, *Michelangelo & Sebastiano* (The National Gallery, 2017).

DIANA STÖRT

Displaying Knowledge:
Goethe's Cabinets as Epistemic Furniture

When he visited Weimar in 1821, Carl Gustav Carus was impressed by the wealth of displayed artwork at the home of Johann Wolfgang Goethe:

'When I was left alone in the room for a short time, the arrangements and embellishments were remarkable to me. Except for a repository with huge folders for copperplate engravings in their historical sequence, I was interested in a cabinet furnished with drawers for the storage of a coin collection. The essence of this was, under glass, a considerable quantity of images of ancient gods, larvae, faunas, etc., among which a very small golden Napoleon, placed in the bell-shaped end of a barometer tube, looked strangely enough. Yet, many more things were still to be observed.'[1]

Johann Wolfgang Goethe, unquestionably one of the last great universal collectors of the nineteenth century, was apparently fond of presenting his collections. He possessed both fine art and scientific objects and regarded his collections as a scientific ensemble whose components were mutually complementary.[2] In figures, he collected about 27,000 objects of fine art: approximately 450 sculptures and reliefs, over 8,000 gems and gem imprints, about 4,000 medals, coins, and casts of coins and medals, 100 majolicas, 9,100 prints, 2,500 drawings, 2,000 drawings done by Goethe himself, and 1,200 silhouettes. This is complemented with his natural science collection, which consisted of 23,000 objects on mineralogy, botany, zoology, and physics. Of course, he also had a library with about 7,500 volumes. Each of these items had to be housed.

1 Carus, 'Lebenserinnerungen und Denkwürdigkeiten,' 1998 [1817–1825], p. 263. Translated by the author. German original: 'Merkwürdig waren mir, als ich jetzt kurze Zeit im Zimmer allein blieb, die Anordnungen und Ausschmückungen desselben. Außer einem hohen Gestelle mit gewaltigen Mappen für Kupferstiche in ihrer geschichtlichen Folge, interessirte mich ein, mit Schubkästen behufs der Aufbewahrung einer Münzsammlung versehener Schrank. Der Aufsatz desselben trug nämlich unter Glas eine ansehnliche Menge antiker Götterbildchen, Larven, Faunen u.s.w., unter welchen ein ganz kleiner goldener Napoleon, in das glockenförmig verschlossene Ende einer Barometerröhre gestellt, sich sonderbar genug ausnahm. Auch sonst aber wollte noch manches beachtet sein.' **2** On Goethe as collector see: Grave, 'Goethes Kunstsammlungen,' 2011, pp. 46–83 and Trunz, 'Goethe als Sammler,' 1972, pp. 13–61. Trunz records many occasions, when Goethe proudly showed off his collections.

Goethe's own cabinets for his collections are today one of the most important elements of the Goethe National Museum furnishings, as they give an authentic impression of how the public intellectual lived and worked. Preserving more than 50,000 artificial and natural objects, the cabinets were originally kept for their storage capacity only. From the named groups of objects result six sets of collection furniture in Goethe's residence: coin cabinets, medal cabinets, mineral cabinets, majolica cabinets, folder cabinets and artistic cabinets.[3] However, at present they are largely empty, as most collection items are kept in modern storage facilities.[4] This accident of history provides two silver linings: not only does the Goethe Residence in Weimar have originals in the exibition, but science also has the chance to explore an ensemble of approximately sixty pieces of collection furniture from the 1800s. This is such a rarity because objects of utility, in particular from private collections, often fall victim to being claimed by heirs or removed due to a change in concept from a museum.

But why should it be relevant in which repositories Goethe kept his collections? In general, we focus on the items, not the container. Is there anything that these cabinets can tell us about Goethe's collecting practices or how he presented his objects? The furniture of utility is indeed likely to show the aesthetic and scientific requirements of the time. As the quote above demonstrates, the obvious character of the furniture as object of use has a direct effect on the viewer. Carus recognizes Goethe immediately as a connoisseur. At the same time, he notices intended techniques of display and the epistemic function of the furniture ('storage of a coin collection'), although he cannot see the objects inside.[5] To illustrate what we can gain from an examination of such epistemically shaped furniture, I will give a brief insight into my studies.

Cabinets as Parerga

Let me begin with a general claim: an accumulation of a multitude of objects can only be constituted as a systematic collection with the aid of a clearly perceptible border. For example: if you saw a pile of stones lying in a room, you would not automatically identify them as a valuable geological collection. Even if those stones were neatly numbered on small labels, they would be lacking a form of organized, recognizable structure from the seemingly random pile. Accordingly, in order to be defined as a collection, minerals should be kept in a cabinet or at least a box or a drawer, or—to give another example—books should be put in shelves or bookcases to be perceived as a library. A repository provides for the handling, organization, and perspective of the objects: a collection is not a collection if the objects are not kept in a certain way that, on the one hand, clearly separates it from its surroundings, and, on the other hand, shapes it into something whole.

3 Excluded at this point are the numerous shelves, which Goethe also had in large numbers. **4** Only the mineral cabinets still shelter their objects as in Goethe's days. **5** The questions characterize the research issue of my study *Goethes Schränke. Epistemische Möbel um 1800* (forthcoming, 2018). The study is developed within the context of the BMBF project *Parerga and Paratexts—How Things Enter Language. Practices and Forms of Presentation in Goethe's Collections.*

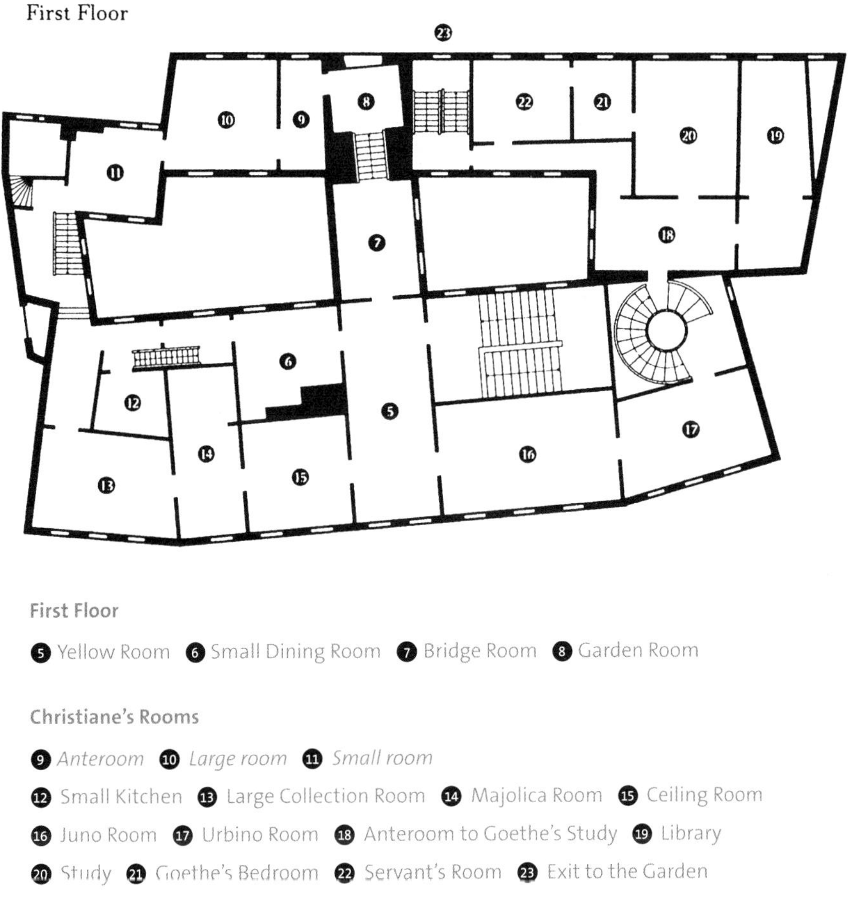

Figures 1:
The floorplan of Goethe's residence with the conditions and names of the rooms from 1832.

These properties transform the repository—in my work the cabinet—into a so-called '*parergon*'. It is an 'accessory' that helps to distinguish between what matters and what does not. According to Jacques Derrida, the function of a *parergon* is to make the main thing—in this case the collection—isolatable and recognizable. In fact, *parergon* and *ergon* are inextricably linked: 'A parergon comes against, beside, and in addition to the *ergon*, the work done [*fait*], the fact [*le fait*], the work, but it does not fall to one side, it touches and cooperates within the operation, from a certain outside. Neither simply outside nor simply inside. Like an accessory that one is obliged to welcome on the border, on board [*au bord, à bord*]. It is first of all the on (the) bo(a)rd(er) [*Il est d'abord l'à-bord*].'[6] Hence, each *parergon* adds only to a certain 'lack' of the *ergon*: 'And this lack would be constitutive of the very unity of the *ergon*. Without this lack, the *ergon* would have no need of a *parergon*. The *ergons* lack is the lack of the *parergon* [...].'[7]

When transfered to the field of collection practice it means this: only the framing *parergon* can give a collection a recognizable form as a self-contained system or as an *ergon*. Indeed, an empty cabinet with twenty-four drawers does not make much sense, either. When thinking about the arrangement of the items, it is of relevance if the cabinet had six, twelve, or twenty-four drawers. For the presentation, it is not insignificant whether a cabinet is fully glazed, partially glazed, or perhaps not glazed at all. And it is also not insignificant which material the repository was made of, or whether it was built to a high quality or not. Collection furniture is used to present objects and create appreciation for these objects. It is not only used to preserve the collections, but to deal with them, to explore them, or to at least show them. In this sense, cabinets can not only be defined as *parerga*, but they can also be called 'epistemic furniture.'[8] This term relates to collection practices—meaning at this point less the classical questions of classification systems of certain disciplines such as taxonomies or schools, but rather the material arrangement of the objects and the concrete work situations of the collectors and scientists. In order to define such situations and thus the aesthetic and epistemic functions of collection cabinets as *parerga*, the following questions are interesting: how is such furniture designed and arranged? And what traces can be read today of how they were actually used? We can examine the functions the cabinet has to offer, open its doors, pull out the drawers, etc., but it can be assumed that these capabilities have been changed over time. Instead of relying solely on the materiality of the object, other sources like archive material must—of course—be included in order to reconstruct such 'affordance' in different contexts of use.[9]

Goethe's cabinets are not ready-made furniture, but handmade, and most were prepared according to the terms and conditions of the collector, precisely for a specific kind of object. In Goethe's time, the beginnings of uniform modules of cabinets for modern museums were established. The growing number of collections of all kinds intensified the demand for such furniture, while the increasing professionalization and specialization of the collections forced certain requirements on the repositories of the objects, which developed accordingly. Instructions for collectors provide a clear picture of these needs. Thanks to the tiniest details on design and dimension specifications, or color and surface finishes, not only is furniture introduced as a special issue in the guideline literature, but at the

6 Derrida, *The Truth in Painting*, 1987, p. 54. **7** Derrida, *The Truth in Painting*, 1987, p. 59 ff. **8** I use the term 'epistemic' following the concept of 'epistemic objects' by G. Abel: he defines them as phenomena, on which we focus our knowledge-oriented attention. Epistemic objects are objects of sensual, vivid and intellectual perception. In this sense collections (and therefore collection furniture) can be seen as epistemic objects and raise issues such as: which cognitive, aesthetic and pragmatic functions do they have?

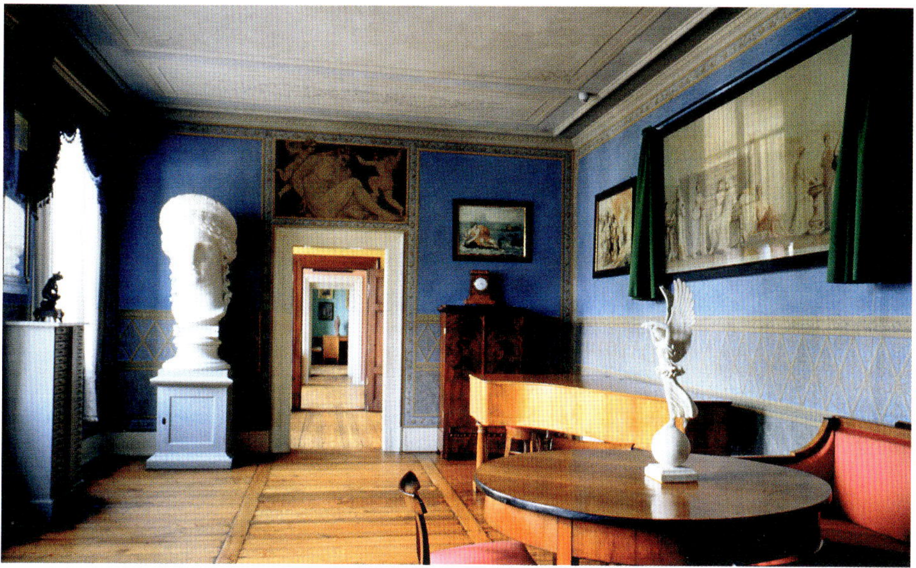

Figure 2:
The Juno Room with the Aldobrandian Wedding,
Goethe Residence. Weimar, Goethe-Nationalmuseum.

same time the seemingly self-evident collection practices—namely the direct handling of the objects—become part of the discourse. The consistency of the relevant literature in Goethe's library and the precise object positioning show that Goethe as a collector was familiar with the most recent standards and, therefore, his practice can be regarded as representative of common practice at that time.[10]

Interior Design, Display and Storage

For Goethe, the furniture he used for his collections was an important part of his interior living arrangement (Fig. 1). Almost all the rooms where Goethe resided had cabinets for his collections. That is to say, he lived together with his collections and always had them at his disposal in his daily living environment. As one can see from the floorplan of Goethe's residence, he set up his workplace in the back building (n° 20), establishing a secluded area that was only accessible to his family and co-workers (rooms n° 18–22). Besides the library, there were various desks in his study and some mineral cabinets in his anteroom (n° 18), which were particularly important to him. From here Goethe would

What makes them valuable in an epistemic and epistemolocical way? See: Abel, 'Knowledge-Research,' 2012 and Abel, 'Sammlungen als epistemische Objekte,' 2014. **9** On the concept of affordance as it is employed in this study see: Hodder, *Entangled*, 2002. **10** For instance: Thon, *Handbuch für Naturaliensammler*, 1827. Goethe owned this book, which gives instructions on how to arrange natural collections.

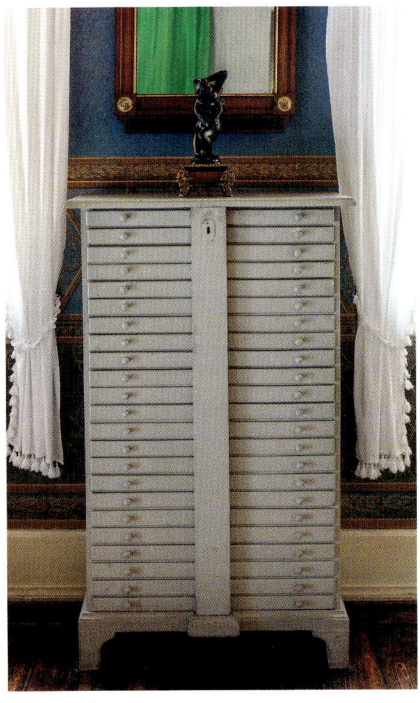

Figure 3:
One of Goethe's medal cabinets in the Juno Room, coated with grey-white paint, Goethe Residence. Weimar, Goethe-Nationalmuseum.

enter the social rooms in the front house. Those were the foyer, the so-called Yellow Room (n° 5), which at the same time served as the reception and dining room, and five different shared rooms: the Garden Room (n° 8), the Bridge Room (n° 7), the Ceiling Room (n° 15), and a kind of salon with a sliding door that separated two rooms, the Juno Room (n° 16) and the Urbino Room (n° 17). They were all used in the entertaining of his guests.[11] One of Goethe's visitors, Carus, cited above, gives us a brief impression of these rooms:

'The foyer itself was adorned with copper engravings and busts, and opened towards the rear of the house by a second corridor of busts, onto the strangely entwined balcony and a staircase leading to the garden. Taken to another room, I saw myself surrounded again by works of art and antiquities: beautifully polished shells of chalcedony stood around marble tables; above the sofa, partially covered by green curtains, a large replica of the old wall painting known under the name of the Aldobrandian Wedding was hanging (Fig. 2), while the works of art exhibited under glass and frameworks, mostly reproducing objects of ancient history, also demanded careful examination.'[12]

11 For details of the individual names and social functions of the rooms, see: Knebel and Holler (eds.), *The Goethe Residence*, 2016 and Trunz, 'Das Haus am Frauenplan in Goethes Alter,' 1990 [1980]. On social arrangements in these rooms, see: Holm, 'Olymp und Malepartus,' 2015. **12** Carus, 'Lebenserinnerungen und Denkwürdigkeiten,' 1998 [1817–1825], p. 263. German original: 'Der Vorsaal selbst war mit Kupferstichen und Büsten auf das Reichste verziert und öffnete sich gegen die Rückseite des Hauses durch eine zweite Büstenhalle auf den lustig umrankten Altan und auf die zum Garten hinabführende Treppe. In

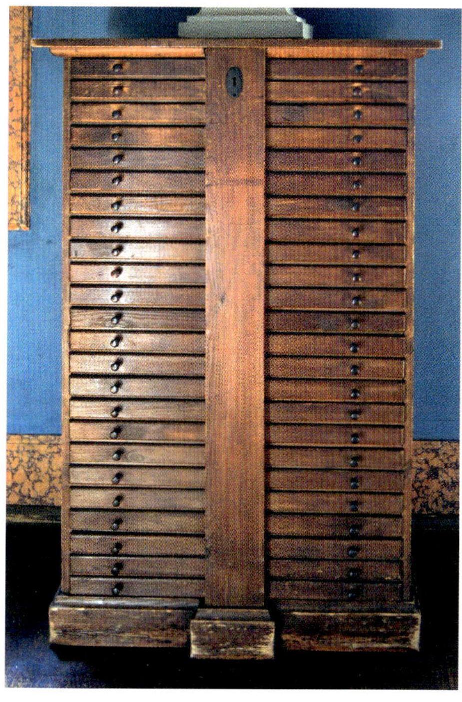

Figure 4:
One of Goethe's medal cabinets in the Bridge Room, not overcoated, Goethe Residence. Weimar, Goethe-Nationalmuseum.

Spread throughout the common rooms, according to sources, we find the coin and medal cabinets, two mineral cabinets, a majolica cabinet, a cabinet with gems and gem imprints, as well as a large prints cabinet (folder cabinet). All the furniture in these rooms was included in the social program, thus making the living room a 'representative art space.'[13]

In the eastern part of the front house—from 1816, after the death of his wife, and with a growing collection—Goethe arranged two more rooms for the art collections, which in turn were exclusively accessible to him, his closest collaborators, and his son. It is because of the abundance of objects that—according to old inventories—were kept in these rooms, that we are now able to talk about his art storage.

However, the bulk of his geoscientific collection Goethe sheltered in the two garden houses in his backyard. Inside, the mineral cabinets stood tightly together side by side—again as if in storage, but for stones. Here, too, we know that only selected experts, such as befriended natural scientists, were allowed access. It remains to be noted that Goethe kept parts of his collection distinctly perceptible in sociable spaces, while other parts were shown only to a chosen circle.

ein anderes Zimmer geführt, sah ich mich auf's Neue von Kunstwerken und Alterthümern umgeben: schön geschliffene Schalen von Chalcedon standen auf Marmortischen umher; über dem Sopha verdeckten halb und halb grüne Vorhänge eine große Nachbildung des unter dem Namen der Aldobrandinischen Hochzeit bekannten alten Wandgemäldes, und außerdem forderte die Wahl der unter Glas und Rahmen bewahrten Kunstwerke, meistens Gegenstände alter Geschichte nachbildend, zu aufmerksamer Betrachtung auf.' **13** Holm, 'Olymp und Malepartus,' 2015, p. 161. Translated by the author.

In the research on Goethe's interior design it has been found that Goethe cared about the organisation of fertile perceptions, communication and knowledge in his surroundings.[14] Goethe did not envision his collection as an 'exhibition' in the modern sense, but regarded it as part of his life, as a material basis for his numerous studies, yet also as an occasion for socializing, proudly showing his collections like any passionate collector would do. To quote further from the memory of the physician and natural scientist Carus:

'Then he had his portfolio of comparative anatomy brought over and showed his earlier work. Later we came upon the most significant in the form of rocks and mountains for determining the nature of the rock, indeed, for the whole formation of the surface of the earth; and even in these ideas he was entirely profound; indeed, he had collected for it, as a second well-filled portfolio with rock drawings from the Harz and other places clearly exhibited.'[15]

It can be assumed that Goethe was aware of the effect his displayed collections had, indeed he placed them in his rooms with careful deliberation. The aspects of presenting and concealing which he practices in presenting his collections continue in the design of the furniture. One can clearly distinguish the types of furniture from their functions: the drawer and folder cabinets for coins, medals, minerals or copperplate engravings hide their objects and afford a phased view of them. The glass cabinets for majolica and other works of art, but also the glass attachments of the medal and mineral cabinets, are designed for the sensual effect at a glance. I would like to draw on two examples.

Goethe had two medal cabinets, which had a glass attachment on top to exhibit small bronzes, both standing in the Juno Room between the windows and under mirrors. During the day they were well lit by natural light, at night the effect of the bronzes was strengthened by chandeliers placed next to the mirrors. The actual function of the cabinet itself—sheltering the medals—seems to be sublimated (Figs. 3–4) in favour of the benefit of the sensual impression.[16] The cabinet holds a double function as *parergon*: on the one hand, it is an elegant pedestal for the bronzes. On the other hand, it provides storage and

14 See: Holm, 'Olymp und Malepartus,' 2015; Trunz, 'Goethe als Sammler,' 1972 and Trunz, 'Das Haus am Frauenplan in Goethes Alter,' 1990 [1980]. **15** Carus, 'Lebenserinnerungen und Denkwürdigkeiten,' 1998 [1817–1825], p. 263. German original: 'Dann ließ er sein Portefeuille über vergleichende Anatomie bringen und zeigte seine frühern Arbeiten. Späterhin kamen wir auf das Bedeutungsvolle in der Form der Felsen und Gebirge für Bestimmung der Art des Gesteins, ja, für die gesammte Bildung der Erdoberfläche; und auch in diesen Ideen war er völlig einheimisch, ja, er hatte dafür gesammelt, wie eine zweite wohlgefüllte Mappe mit Felsenzeichnungen vom Harz und andern Orten deutlich bewies.' **16** But we know from different sources that Goethe was very fond of showing objects from these cabinets. And when we look at the cabinet more closely, the special handling of the cabinet becomes clearer. Like the medal cabinets, most of Goethe's cabinets are locked or have a bolting bar. Of course, Goethe as the head of the household had the keys. The special feature of the cabinets is emphasized by the act of unlocking. Goethe would have pulled out one of the drawers to present it on a table, or have had individual medals on display to show to guests. Unfortunately, we do not know with absolute certainty how he actually kept

display for the medal collection. It was the host only who could make the hidden visible. Only Goethe possessed the keys of the cabinets and decided what to show.

To intensify the atmosphere of a representative art space, the outward impression of the furniture was important. Most of Goethe's collection cabinets are presented today finished with a classic grey-white paint—a curatorial decision from the previous century. In Goethe's time, the original cabinet surfaces in the residence were mainly made of mahogany or varnished in a mahogany color. Our restoration research within the project on Goethe's cabinets revealed that, under the overcoating of most of the coin and medal cabinets, the majolica cabinets, and artistic cabinets, was a red lacquer finish.[17] It is evident from the choice of materials that the lacquer surfaces of the cabinets had a clear glossy finish. In Stöckel's *Praktisches Handbuch für Künstler, Lackirliebhaber und Oehlfarben-Anstreicher* (Handbook for Artists, Connoisseurs of Lacquer, and Oil Painters), there is a description of this kind of 'magnificent and still quite secret lacquer, which is quite similar in color to mahogany,'[18] which Goethe used for some of his cabinets. It was rather important to Goethe that the cabinets left an impression of high quality even though they were largely made from timber. The craftmanship of the cabinets was of a high standard, while the imitation of mahogany was a common trend in furniture-making during the 1800s. The idea that Goethe, as was often described, did not place any importance on his furniture and only chose simple repositories to display his objects, can simply no longer be justified.[19] The fact is, however, that his cabinets cannot be compared with the rather lavish furniture that we can find in courtly sphere. Goethe's furniture collection, in its original form, fitted with the image of a well-off bourgeois household.

In the design of cabinets for collections, Goethe also had a pragmatic approach to the objects, as I would like to demonstrate in the second example of showing and concealing by furniture. In a controversy over the furnishing of the Jena mineral collection, for which he was responsible as minister,[20] Goethe made some negative remarks about the presentation of rocks in glass cases, since in most of the compartments of such full-glazed cabinets, the stones could hardly be seen as a system, and many beautiful rear pieces were concealed by

the medals in the cabinets. All of the original trays for coins and medals have been lost, but it is conceivable that the medals were similarly preserved like most collections of the time. We know from letters and historical narratives like the one by Carus that Goethe used to present his medals and coins, thereby assuming a communicative role. See also: Trunz, 'Goethe als Sammler,' 1972. **17** See: Skwierawski, *Untersuchungsbericht zu den Schränken aus dem Majolika-Zimmer im Goethe-Haus zu Weimar*, 2017; Skwierawski, *Untersuchungsbericht zu Schränken aus dem Majolika-Zimmer, dem großen Sammlungszimmer und dem Durchgangszimmer*, 2017. See also: Holm, 'Schreib- und Sammlungsmöbel in Goethes Haus am Frauenplan,' 2012, p. 29. **18** Stöckel, *Praktisches Handbuch für Künstler*, 1799, p. 81, §85. Translated by the author. German original: 'Eine herrliche und noch ganz geheime Lackierung, welche an Farbe dem Mahagoniholz ganz ähnlich ist.' **19** See for instance: Trunz, 'Das Haus am Frauenplan in Goethes Alter,' 1990 [1980], p. 50. **20** Since his duties were the superintendence of the institutions for the arts and sciences of the duchy.

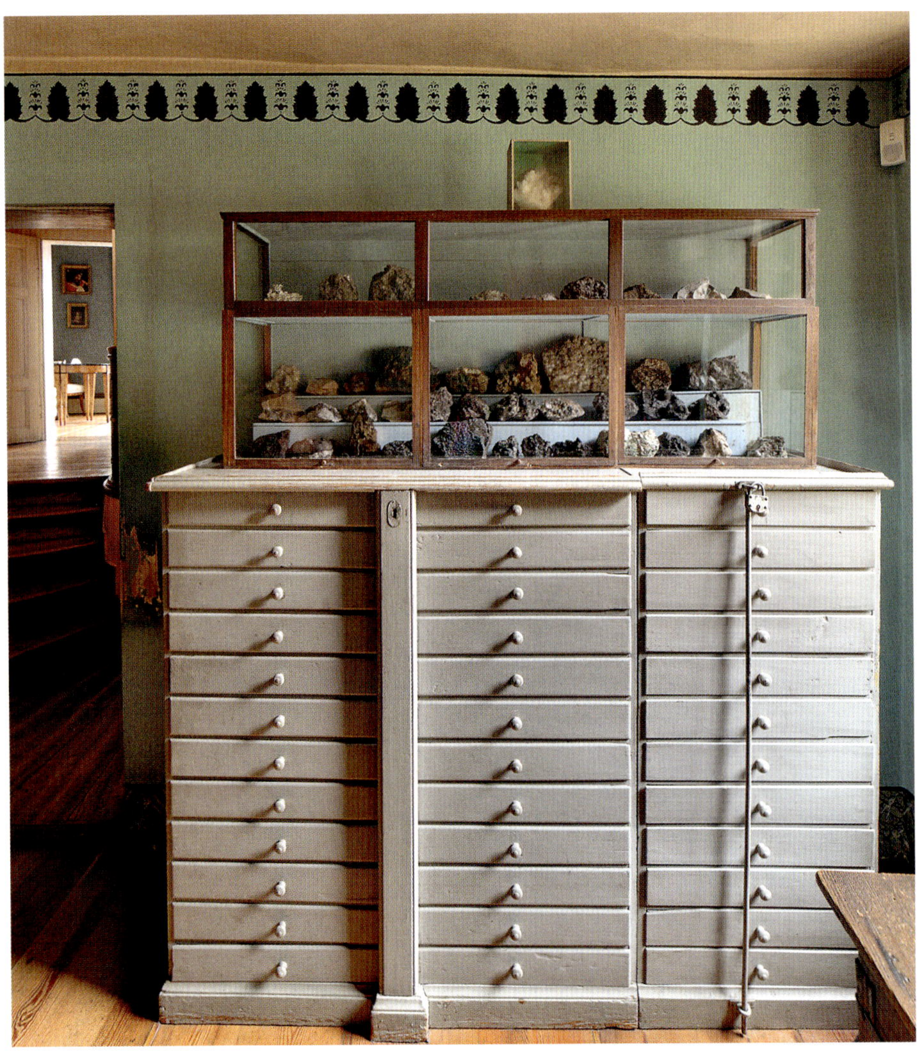

Figure 5:
One example of a mineral cabinet in Goethe's residence, anteroom to Goethe's study, Goethe Residence. Weimar, Goethe-Nationalmuseum.

the ones in front: 'The most magnificent pieces are often placed in the dark, because they are arranged according to the system, [...]. The rest of the third is, of course, splendid and imposing enough, and so always sufficient material for the gawking crowd to be fooled [...].'[21]

Goethe was aware of the fact that different perceptions of objects are evoked depending on the mode of presentation. Glass showcases, for example, seemed to give a better view of collections. As shown above, Goethe himself purposefully manipulated the forms of presentation to direct the perception of the viewer in his own house. Astonishingly, he resolutely opposed presenting objects behind glass as a natural scientist. He writes to his collegue at the Jena University: 'But if you really want to use the cabinet, then the trouble begins, as I had just encountered during my recent stay.' He tells of his efforts, where he had to carefully select the rocks from the cabinet one by one, and after examining them, put them back in the right order without any drawers for practical organization. The kneeling, craning, reaching and searching involved in using a collection stored this way was clearly problematic for Goethe. Moreover, the comparative view of the systematic series of rocks in such an arrangement in showcases would not be possible in his eyes: 'It is a mere delusion that one imagines that one can take a look at such a series with the naked eye and follow it [...] especially in a single moment, which expresses the volatility and inadequacy of such an exhibition.' The large number of rocks overwhelmed the human eye, according to Goethe, and he notes: 'so I remain of faith that every series of this kind should not be watched with the eyes of the body, but of the spirit.'[22]

At the same time, he provides the reasons why drawer cabinets are more suitable, and how they can be used profitably: 'This is actually what the catalog is for, I have read it through and know exactly what categories I will make first. You start with taking out the drawers, which are already numbered and must refer to the catalog. If there are several to be looked at, the racks and panels are ready, which are placed in the best light, and so, if desired, the whole sequence can be observed most conveniently [...].'[23]

The selective, concentrated view of individual rows, which can be compared with one another, is the best method of display for a scientist, according to Goethe. This practice is also better known as the so-called 'comparative view.'[24] The scientist places the items in a row, where they can be looked at as a whole and their transitions can be mentally captured. This practice is reflected quite self-evidently in Goethe's own cabinets.

21 Johann Wolfgang Goethe to Christian Gottlob Voigt, 13.7.1816 in Goethe, *Goethes Werke*, 1887–1919, vol. 4:27, pp. 87–93. Translated by the author. German original: 'So liegen nun oft im Dunkeln, weil sie nach dem System gereiht sind, die prächtigste Stücke [...] Freilich ist das übrige Drittel noch prächtig und imposant genug und also für die gaffende Menge, der man vorgaukeln will, immer hinreichender Stoff [...]' See also: Holm, 'Goethes Gewohnheiten,' 2012, especially p. 121. **22** Johann Wolfgang Goethe to Christian Gottlob Voigt, 13.7.1816. German original: 'Will man aber das Kabinett wirklich benutzen, dann geht erst die Noth an, wie ich sie noch erst bei meinem neulichen Aufenthalte erfahren habe. [...] Es ist ein bloßer Wahn, dass man sich einbildet, eine solche Reihe mit dem leiblichen Auge übersehen und ihr folgen zu können...und noch sogar in einem Augenblick, welches gerade das Flüchtige und Unzulängliche solchen Ausstellens ausspricht. [...] so bleib ich doch des Glaubens, daß eine jede Folge dieser Art nicht mit den Augen des Leibes sondern des Geistes beschaut werden müsse.' **23** Johann Wolfgang Goethe to Christian Gottlob Voigt, 13.7.1816. German original: 'Dazu ist eigentlich der Catalog, ich hab ihn durchgelesen und weiß genau welche Rubriken ich zuerst vornehmen werde. Man zieht alsdann die Schubladen heraus, die ohnehin numeriert sind und sich auf den Catalog beziehen müssem. Sind es mehrere die man zu übersehen wünscht, so sind Gestelle und Tafeln bereit, welche man in's beste Licht setzt, und so kann man, wenn man will, die ganze Folge auf's bequemste betrachten.' **24** See the different articles on this topic by Grave and Maatsch: Maatsch, 'Ideen mit den Augen sehen,' 2012; Grave, 'Schule des Sehens,' 2012; Grave and Maatsch, 'Das Allgemeine im Anschaulichen,' 2014.

The mineral cabinets have a rather simple appearance and are oil-painted in grey (Fig. 5). But this was not done without a pragmatic reason, as a glance at Stöckel's handbook shows: 'The advantage to using this paint is this: it is not damaged by moist and wet conditions, and can be cleaned with cold and warm water without being harmed in the least.'[25] Since the cabinets were mostly located outside the residence in the garden houses, this paint served as a protection for them. The mineral cabinets were exclusively intended for a more technical use, and only other collectors and natural scientists could see them.

As mentioned above, the storage character of the cabinets is predominant. The drawers and their interior are at least equally as important as the exterior in terms of innovative design solutions. In the case of the cabinets, it is, above all, easier to handle the objects when they are displayed in drawers. Each cabinet had a label for the given collection, and in some cases even the drawers had labels. What were these labels for? They gave reference to a certain point in a catalog, so with the catalog in hand, one could easily find the right drawer. The drawer then had to be carefully taken out and set down, because they would be so heavy that they could possibly fall out, as there were no restraints.

In his scientific practice, Goethe preferred to look at matching suites in drawers side by side. Here is a quote taken from one of his letters:

'Moreover, it was a delightful coincidence that your thought-provoking letter reached me when I was about to arrange the wealth of Nordic minerals, and to label them according to the collection; every single specimen had already been carefully marked, but now they are all grouped together, ordered, in six adjacently placed drawers which can be seen all at once, and, to the delight of native and visiting natural scientists, are now to be placed into the cabinets, stored for the present as well as the future.'[26]

This 'drawer method' stands in contrast to the new trend of the fully-glazed cabinets, as for example the paper from the famous minerologist Trebra in 1795 shows. Trebra formulates it, merely *en passant*, in his writing that objects could be viewed in the glazed cabinets: 'Even without difficulty, I was able to learn about it in fleeting conversations with my friends, without ever opening the doors of the cabinets.'[27] Goethe, on the other hand,

25 Stöckel, *Praktisches Handbuch für Künstler*, 1799, p. 85, §87. German original: 'Der Vorzug eines solchen Anstriches ist folgender: es schadet ihm keine Feuchtigkeit und Nässe, und man kann ihn mit kaltem und warmen Wasser reinigen, ohne daß es ihm nur im geringsten etwas schadet.' **26** Johann Wolfgang Goethe to Karl Friedrich Reinhard, 18.6.1829 in Goethe, *Goethes Werke*, vol. IV.45, 1887–1919, p. 294. Translated by the author. German original: 'Ferner war es denn doch ein erfreuliches Zusammentreffen, daß ihr inhaltsschwerer Brief mich so eben über der Beschäftigung traf, den Reichtum nordischer Mineralien abschließlich zu ordnen und der Sammlung gemäß zu etikettieren; jedes einzelne Exemplar war schon dorten sorgfältig bezeichnet nun aber liegen sie alle gehörig beisammen, geordnet, in sechs neben

explicitly rejects fully-glazed cabinets for scientific collections because it makes the handling of the objects more difficult, and it is impossible to look at and grasp everything at once. Both viewing habits existed side by side during this period. For Goethe, looking at items should always be limited to a certain grouping of objects, to a manageable number. In Goethe's practice of tacit knowledge, it is not possible to comprehensively grasp a multitude of objects in a glass cabinet.

But how, then, are we to account for the glass attachments in Goethe's cabinets, which we find in the case of the mineral cabinets as well as the medal cabinets? This looks like a contradiction between saying and doing. These covers are not about viewing the entire collection in detail, but are rather intended to display special pieces. As in the case of the mineral cabinets, they would show especially beautiful or large pieces, and in the case of the medal cabinets, they would show curious or outstanding works of art. Here, the 'solitary' is emphasized, and not the systematic row. The (temporary) display behind glass affords another complementary sensual perspective on (scientific) objects.

Let us conclude with a summary comparison of the two examples of Goethe's cabinets treated here. The two cases keep completely different objects: medals as artifacts on the one hand, and natural history objects on the other. But both types of collection furniture are faced with a similar task: to organize an enormous number of objects that, at first sight, look the same. Their functional similarities are: The storage part of the cabinet is predominant. There are locking parts that prevent any unauthorized access. Glass covers can be used in order to present special pieces. By integrating the cabinets into the living space, they foster communication in a social situation.

In the construction of Goethe's cabinets for his collections, an emphasis on the pragmatic and epistemic elements of their design could be detected, but it is still connected with the desire for presentation and its effects for interior decoration. Thinking about the agency of display, especially concerning the display of scientific objects, I want to point out that it is worth not only to consider the—in a wider sense—aesthetic but also the pragmatic decisions and effects, and how these decisions and effects get entangled together. As we have seen in Goethe's example, it is not only the showing of objects, but also their handling, preservation and protection, which shapes the agency of display.

einander gestellten und auf einmal übersehbaren Schubladen, und sollen nun, zu freudigem Anteil einheimischer und besuchender Naturforscher, in Schränke geschoben und für die Gegenwart sowohl als für die Zukunft aufbewahrt werden.' **27** Trebra, *Mineraliencabinett*, 1795, p. 5. Translated by the author. German original: 'Ich konnte mich auch ohne alle Schwierigkeit in flüchtigen Unterhaltungen mit meinen Freunden darüber lehrreich vernehmen, ohne nur einmal die Thüren der Schränke zu öffnen.' On the changes of furnishing collections of natural history in the 18th century see the fundamental article by Anke te Heesen, who also refers to Trebra and his mineral cabinet: 'Geschlossene und transparente Ordnungen,' 2011 [2001].

Bibliography

G. Abel, 'Knowledge-Research: Extending and Revising Epistemology' in G. Abel and J. Conant (eds.), *Rethinking Epistemology* (De Gruyter, 2012), pp. 1–52.

G. Abel, 'Sammlungen als epistemische Objekte und Manifestationen von Ordnungen des Wissens' in U. Hassler and T. Meyer, *Kategorien des Wissens. Die Sammlung als epistemisches Objekt* (vdf Hochschulverlag AG an der ETH Zürich, 2014), pp. 109–132.

S. Böhmer, Ch. Holm, V. Spinner and T. Valk (eds.), *Weimarer Klassik. Kultur des Sinnlichen* (Deutscher Kunstverlag, 2012).

C. G. Carus, 'Lebenserinnerungen und Denkwürdigkeiten' in W. Herwig (ed.), *Goethes Gespräche. Biedermannsche Ausgabe* (Deutscher Taschenbuchverlag, 1998 [1817–1825]), vol. 3.1.

J. Derrida, *The Truth in Painting*, trans. by G. Bennington and I. McLeod (The University of Chicago Press, 1987).

J. W. von Goethe, *Goethes Werke [Weimarer Ausgabe]*. Ed. by S. von Sachsen (Böhlau, 1887–1919).

J. Grave, 'Goethes Kunstsammlungen und die künstlerische Ausstattung des Goethehauses' in A. Beyer and E. Osterkamp (eds.), *Goethe Handbuch. Suppl. Bd. 3: Kunst* (Metzler Verlag, 2011), pp. 46–83.

J. Grave, 'Schule des Sehens. Formen der Kunstbetrachtung bei Goethe' in S. Böhmer, Ch. Holm, V. Spinner and T. Valk (eds.), *Weimarer Klassik. Kultur des Sinnlichen* (Deutscher Kunstverlag, 2012), pp. 96–105.

J. Grave and J. Maatsch, 'Das Allgemeine im Anschaulichen. Morphologische Reihen in Goethes Sammlungen' in T. Valk (ed.), *Heikle Balancen. Die Weimarer Klassik im Prozess der Moderne* (Wallstein Verlag, 2014), pp. 287–310.

A. te Heesen, 'Geschlossene und transparente Ordnungen. Sammlungsmöbel und ihre Wahrnehmung in der Aufklärungszeit' in S. Hackenschmidt und K. Engelhorn (eds.), *Möbel als Medien. Beiträge zu einer Kulturgeschichte der Dinge* (transcript Verlag 2011 [2001]), pp. 85–102.

I. Hodder, *Entangled. An Archaelogy of the Relationships between Human and Things* (Wiley-Blackwell, 2002).

Ch. Holm, 'Goethes Gewohnheiten. Konstruktion und Gebrauch der Schreib- und Sammlungsmöbel im Weimarer Wohnhaus' in S. Böhmer, Ch. Holm, V. Spinner and T. Valk (eds.), *Weimarer Klassik. Kultur des Sinnlichen* (Deutscher Kunstverlag, 2012), pp. 116–125.

Ch. Holm, 'Schreib- und Sammlungsmöbel in Goethes Haus am Frauenplan. Expertisen von Katharina Popov-Sellinat (Möbel),' unpublished examination report, Klassik Stiftung Weimar (2012).

Ch. Holm, 'Olymp und Malepartus. Goethes gesellige Einrichtungen in seinem Weimarer Wohnhaus' in G. Oesterle and T. Valk (eds.), *Riskante Geselligkeit. Spielarten des Sozialen* (Königshausen und Neumann, 2015), pp. 141–165.

K. Knebel and W. Holler (eds.), *The Goethe Residence* (Klassik Stiftung Weimar, 2016).

J. Maatsch, 'Ideen mit den Augen sehen. Anschauliche Erkenntnis bei Goethe' in S. Böhmer, Ch. Holm, V. Spinner and T. Valk (eds.), *Weimarer Klassik. Kultur des Sinnlichen* (Deutscher Kunstverlag, 2012), pp. 66–75.

F. W. H. von Trebra, *Mineraliencabinett* (n.n., 1795).

T. Thon, *Handbuch für Naturaliensammler oder gründliche Anweisung die Naturkörper aller drei Reiche zu sammeln, im Naturalienkabinet aufzustellen und aufzubewahren, namentlich Thiere aller Arten, Säugethiere, Vögel, Reptilien, Fische, Conchylien, Crustaceen, Insekten, Zoophyten und Eingeweidewürmer auszustopfen, zuzubereiten, zu versenden, so wie Pflanzen zu trocknen, Herbarien, Fruchtkabinette, Holzbibliotheken und Mineraliensammlungen anzulegen, einzurichten und in vollkommener Schönheit zu erhalten. Frei nach dem Französischen bearbeitet und vervollständigt von Theodor Thon, Mitglied und Bibliothekar der mineralog. Societät zu Jena, Mitgl. d. Wetterauischen Gesellsch. für Naturkunde u. der Societät für Natur- u. Jagdkunde zu Dreißigacker. Mit acht und dreissig Figuren* (Voigt, 1827).

E. Trunz, 'Goethe als Sammler,' *Goethe Jahrbuch*, 89 (1972), pp. 13–61.
E. Trunz, 'Das Haus am Frauenplan in Goethes Alter' in E. Trunz, *Ein Tag aus Goethes Leben. Acht Studien zu Leben und Werk* (Beck, 1990 [1980]), pp. 42–71.
H. F. A. Stöckel, *Praktisches Handbuch für Künstler, Lackirliebhaber und Oehlfarben-Anstreicher* (Stein, 1799).
K. Skwierawski, *Untersuchungsbericht zu den Schränken aus dem Majolika-Zimmer im Goethe-Haus zu Weimar. Technologische und naturwissenschaftliche vergleichende Untersuchungen an vier Schränken*, unpublished examination report, Klassik Stiftung Weimar (2017).
K. Skwierawski, *Untersuchungsbericht zu Schränken aus dem Majolika-Zimmer, dem großen Sammlungszimmer und dem Durchgangszimmer im Goethe-Haus zu Weimar*, unpublished examination report, Klassik Stiftung Weimar (2017).

ANGELA MATYSSEK

Death by/Life by Wall Label[1]

In *The Truth in Painting*, Jacques Derrida reflected on the relationship between what he called '*ergon*' and '*parergon*.' While the former term refers to the work itself, the latter describes its accompaniments, which are neither part of nor distinct from the work. Within this category, he placed such details as clothes in pictures, or columns in architecture, but also picture frames. Following a long art-theoretical and philosophical tradition, he studied their interconnectedness as well as the ways in which they struggle for the viewer's attention. This breakout from the domain of the work and the outreaches of the *parerga* to neighbouring structures such as frames or museum walls, and thus the shifting conflict between 'work' and 'accompaniments,' have also drawn the attention of other scholars, such as Gérard Genette in literature and Joseph Grigely in art exhibitions.[2] The particular *parerga* of interest in this volume are precisely those whose exhibitory purpose is to mediate artworks in museums for their viewers. This includes material elements such as frames, pedestals, vitrines, and presentational aspects of gallery setup such as lighting, and informational accompaniments such as catalogues and pedagogical resources. A number of these powerful means for staging artworks have repeatedly been the subject of debates around the question of displaying art for the past thirty years. Among these, the wall label in its most reduced form, i.e. as a pure object label—on which I focus here—seems hardly spectacular, and appears to be nothing more than a mere bureaucratic, and in most cases very inconspicuous, addendum. This seemingly 'pure facticity' might be a reason why, in contrast to what we observe with their larger, pedagogically motivated, relatives (i.e. fully-fledged explanatory or interpretation-guiding wall texts), object labels have thus far not drawn much scholarly attention.[3]

In most cases, object labels consist of only a few lines, giving such factual information as the name of artist, the title of object, the date, and—definitely—the owner. Occasionally, there is additional information on the material, size, and remarks on the work's

1 Many thanks to Regine Ehleiter, Mario Kramer, Marc Naroska, Jeffrey Saletnik, Barbara Segelken, for hints, comments, a text, a photograph from a US-american museum display, and an interview; to the participants of the workshop *Collections, Displays and the Agency of Objects* (Cambridge, UK, 20–23.9.2017); and to Ruben Bieker for his translation. **2** Genette, *Paratexts*, 1997; Grigely, *Exhibition Prosthetics*, 2010. **3** Art history as well as museum studies and interest in museum didactics has thus far addressed only the pedagogical/elaborate version of wall texts and labels. The only work from which

provenance. And yet, in museum and exhibition practices, their status is quite ambivalent. On the one hand, an object label can be seen, as Derrida put it, as an element whose 'traditional determination [is] not that it stands out but that it disappears, buries itself, effaces itself, melts away at the moment it deploys its greatest energy.'[4] On the other hand, the *added* effect the label bestows on the artwork obviously 'is threatening' in two senses.[5] Firstly, it disrupts viewers' aesthetic experience of the artwork, and secondly, it jeopardizes the survival of the artwork through its potential to undermine its status as perceived from various angles: objects, viewers, and curators.

With regard to their epistemic status, wall labels in art galleries can be compared to labels for plants such as those found in herbals.[6] Both are among the 'material constants' of their disciplines;[7] both provide information in a condensed form (the plant labels only include name, location, and date); and both primarily serve as a means of identification. Moreover, as is the case with systematic organization in botany, art displays, too, are dedicated to designating the presented objects accurately. Indeed, correctly identifying objects is the foundation of practically all areas of art history. Despite these commonalities, there is some difference in the value traditionally attributed to either form of identification with regard to their relationship to the actual object. While the botanist who headed for the fields with pencil, paper, and vasculum was 'scoffed at'[8] in the nineteenth century, art history, on the other hand, has, for the last two hundred years, caricatured the museumgoer who ignores the artwork in favour of thoroughly studying the label or the catalogue.[9] Isaac Robert and George Cruikshank's etching *A Shilling Well Laid Out* is one example of this kind of mockery (Fig. 1). The picture shows an exhibition room of the early nineteenth century crowded with visitors who are all busying themselves with sophisticated chit-chat or at best glancing at the catalogue, but no-one actually engages with a painting. This is highlighted even more as an absurdity by the fact that many of the works are portraits. It seems that these visitors are quite ignorant of the proper behaviour in the presence of art as they absurdly overestimate the significance of the accompanying written material. This illustrates the precarious status of exhibition catalogues, collection guides and labels throughout their history.

And yet, their function as the identifying markers of art objects turns out to be perennial. Not only are objects without labelling just as confusing in a museum as wall labels next to empty showcases. The value of the minimal version of the wall label also remained undisputed during the heated debate that took place in Germany in the 1970s about the question of the museum as 'Lernort contra Musentempel' (place of study versus temple

the present essay was able to take some examples is Voss, *Hinter weißen Wänden*, 2015, pp. 17–27. **4** Derrida, *The Truth in Painting*, 1987 [1978], p. 82. **5** Derrida, *The Truth in Painting*, 1987 [1978], p. 56. **6** On labels in herbals see: te Heesen, 'Beschriftungsszenen,' 2008, pp. 106–115. **7** te Heesen, 'Beschriftungsszenen,' 2008, p. 108. **8** te Heesen, 'Beschriftungsszenen,' 2008, p. 114. **9** Voss, *Hinter weißen Wänden*, 2015, pp. 18–19, see also for the following example.

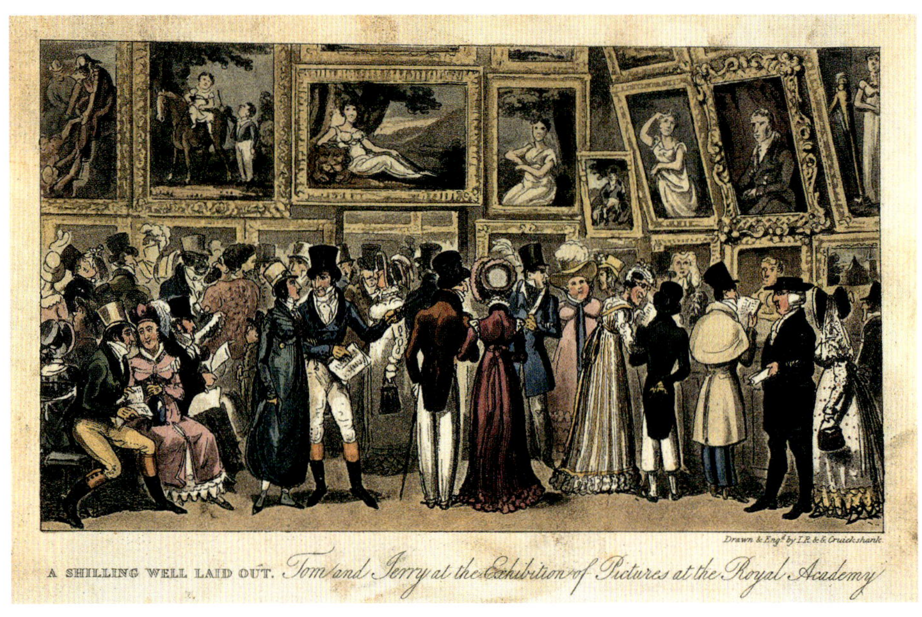

Figure 1:
Isaac Robert and George Cruikshank, *A Shilling Well Laid Out*, 1821, hand-coloured etching and aquatint, 15 × 23.6 cm.

of muses).[10] Interestingly, it was precisely the disagreements about wall labels that sparked the debate. There were voices such as Erich Steingräber's—then director of Germanisches Nationalmuseum in Nuremberg—who at the annual conference of the Association of German Museums 1974 called wall label a 'destruction of art.'[11] However, such positions were primarily directed at the interpretive object explanations, and did not intend to question the validity of the bare label. Beyond the polar opposition of information and explanation versus aesthetic experience, the question of how a museum understands its pedagogical duty is still subject to negotiation. The worry that the *parergon* might override the *ergon* is still present among those concerned even with object labels.

10 See the volume Spickernagel and Walbe (eds.), *Das Museum: Lernort contra Musentempel*, 1976. **11** Quoted in Steen, 'Ausstellung und Text,' 1995, pp. 46–62, especially p. 47. **12** Grigely, *Exhibition Prosthetics*, 2010, p. 7: 'I use the critical term "exhibition prosthetics" to describe an array of these conventions, particularly (but not exclusively) in relation to exhibition practices. Perhaps out of habit, we seem decidedly inured to the experience of conventions like these. They are a part of the machinery of exhibiting—we read titles, labels, and catalogues because their authority establishes for the artwork a sense of place. In this respect, moving closer to the artwork involves moving away from the artwork—to look closer at fringes and margins and representations, and ask what seems to me a very fundamental question: to what extent are these various exhibition conventions actually part of the art—and not merely

Labels make a contribution to the myth of the 'pure' artwork since they are instructive about what significance is to be attributed to the work (a Picasso? a copy?), and in doing so they suggest certainty. They seem to be so closely interlinked with artworks that they can be included in what Joseph Grigely described as 'exhibition prosthetics.'[12] Grigely, an artist and a theoretician, wrote, 'a prosthesis remediates—it fills, it extends, it supplements. But it does not do this without also becoming a part of, not a part from, the body that it fills, extends, and supplements.'[13] '[W]e read titles, labels, and catalogues because their authority establishes for the artwork a sense of place,' Grigely states.[14] Empirical observations of museumgoer behaviour have shown that 85.1 percent of the visitors observed actually read museum texts.[15] It can be assumed that many more read labels. After looking briefly at the object, viewers—as has also been observed by another author—turn to the object label to cross-check the visual against the linguistic information.[16]

Because of their often temporary materializations as well as their replaceability, labels are ephemera by nature. Detached from the object, they are placed not only in the above-mentioned tension between information and aesthetics, but also in a tension between 'fact' and form. In what follows, I am going to investigate further the power and the association of object labels as well as the tensions and conflicts which characterize them.

'Death by Wall Label'

In his 2008 essay, 'Death by Wall Label,' the artist and media-art curator Jon Ippolito polemicized against the dominant norms of object labels' content.[17] Ippolito was opposed to the practice of ascribing a single artist's name, title, date, or definite specifics on material and media or dimensions to a piece of media art, and thus fixing it in a way which is in most cases impossible to preserve. To his mind, media art crucially depends on its variability, i.e. the possibility of modifying most of these features if necessary. The wall label, for him, was the symbolic representation of the obsolete urge for an original:

'The gravest threat to the cultural survival of new media art may very well be its wall label. Few manacles on creativity have been as ubiquitous [...]. [T]he reductionism of the wall label [...] threatens to obliterate digital culture. For new media art can survive only by multiplying and mutating. From computer-based installations to video multicasts, digital collaborations are the rule rather than the exception, and a work often undergoes

an extension of it?' **13** Grigely, *Exhibition Prosthetics*, 2010, p. 8. **14** Grigely, *Exhibition Prosthetics*, 2010, p. 7. **15** McManus, 'Oh, Yes, They Do,' 1989, pp. 174–189. **16** Tyradellis, *Müde Museen*, 2014, pp. 117–118: '90% of all visitors first look at the exhibit, then look at the wall label. It is a cultural reflex of ours that sensory experience immediately strives to be cancelled out conceptually, which in everyday life takes care of itself (in that we attribute the correct terms to everyday objects without much prior thinking), which is achieved, though, in the artificial context of the museum through the textual authority of the standard items author and title. Both indications represent knowledge which helps deprive the object of its disquieting strangeness.' **17** Ippolito, 'Death by Wall Label,' 2008, pp. 106–132.

changes in personnel, equipment, and scale as it diffuses across new media festivals, exhibitions, and Web sites. Like a shark, a new media artwork must keep moving to survive.'[18]

In the subsequent passages, Ippolito examines each of the constituent data of object labels in turn. I shall describe here only a few examples. Firstly, re-creators who may be obliged to adapt software or re-install works in exhibition spaces and thus make consequential decisions, are often not named at all. Secondly, in the development of media art works throughout successive festivals and exhibitions, changes are often made to titles, but objects' biographies are not traceable because older titles are normally not included in the information on labels. Thirdly, given the phenomenon of media obsolescence, it is impossible to fix the material and media of a piece to one specification.[19] In short, Ippolito saw in the wall label the model and the metaphor of a static attitude and a reductionism which is in dire need of reform, because of its falsifying nature. To go even further, he claims that his observations are applicable not only to media art, but to installation art in general and at least in part also to pieces of performance and process art. Moreover, in museum jargon, the exhibit label is commonly referred to as 'tombstone.' While Ippolito does not address this peculiarity, it seems that in his view, the label can be said to accomplish its task.

The extent to which alterations to object labels are representative of a status loss is seen most distinctly in adjustments of ascriptions that are discovered to be incorrect. This kind of 'death by wall label' is perhaps the most feared in museums—the object is not what it pretends to be. It is an imposter that has sneakily intruded on our attention and deceived us into granting it our admiration. In other words, the experts have failed us with an incorrect statement—the Emperor is not wearing any clothes!—and the authorities are exposed along with the object.

One example of a long-postponed label adjustment is the bust of *Flora* kept in Berlin, which Wilhelm Bode attributed to Leonardo. Indeed, soon after Bode purchased the sculpture in 1909 for the Kaiser-Friedrich Museum in Berlin (today the Bode-Museum) as a hitherto undiscovered masterpiece, some claimed that the piece was in fact not a Leonardo, but a work by the British nineteenth-century sculptor Richard Cockle Lucas. However, against all critical voices, Bode stood by his initial ascription, claiming that the bust had been heavily restored in the nineteenth century and thus made the conflict one of the most long-lasting ascription and dating debates in art history.[20] Indeed, the provenance and age of the piece remained contested long after this initial challenge partly because of

18 Ippolito, 'Death by Wall Label,' 2008, p. 106. **19** As additional possibilities to be considered in the case of media art, he names the year of conception, of the first implementation, of a refabrication, or later variations. See: Ippolito, 'Death by Wall Label,' 2008, p. 114. **20** Up until the mid-1930s alone, more than 700 articles on the subject had been published. The entire history is thoroughly traced in Wolff-Thomsen, *Die Wachsbüste einer Flora*, 2006. See: Kobi (ed.), *The Limits of Connoisseurship*, 2017. **21** I thank Dario Gamboni for pointing this out. **22** Geimer, 'Das falsche Original,' 2010, pp. 23–39, here p. 23. **23** Van de Wetering, *A Corpus of Rembrandt Paintings VI*, 2014. **24** See Geimer, 'Das falsche Original,' 2010, p. 36.

Bode's influence and his power to suppress doubts and opposing evidence, and partly because scientific studies on the material produced ambiguous results. Until the late 1990s, the bust was displayed as a piece from the Renaissance, albeit without the direct ascription to Leonardo.

In a similar way, our perception of *Man with Golden Helmet* in the Berlin Gemäldegalerie might be altered given that, since 1986, the painting has no longer been considered 'a Rembrandt' but a work of his studio or 'circle' (Umkreis), as its object label indicates. Put forth as a prime example of depreciation through re-attribution, the piece is shown as a framed painting hanging on a museum wall on the title page of an exhibition catalogue entitled 'Wertwechsel: Zum Wert des Kunstwerks' (Value Changes: On the Value of the Artwork). The catalogue was published by the Cologne Museum für Angewandte Kunst to accompany the 2001 exhibition of the same name. The painting also played an important role in the exhibition, with the curators allegedly having added a wall label to say that they would have neither requested, nor received this loan piece if it was still considered a Rembrandt.[21] Looking at the evolution of the research on Rembrandt, we find what may be the most remarkable, and certainly the most well-known fluctuations in the recognized scope of an œuvre: as Peter Geimer reminds us, Wilhelm Bode had originally identified 595 paintings as 'Rembrandts'. In 1909, Valentiner counted only 558 pieces, while Abraham Bredius, in 1935, extended the scope to 630 pieces, of which 56 were removed again by Horst Gerson in 1969.[22] In 1968, at the beginning of the Rembrandt Research Project, many more pieces were discounted; however, in the resulting 2014 publication, Ernst van de Wetering re-evaluated the question of what would have to be considered a 'Rembrandt' under the conditions of the artist's workshop practices in the seventeenth century (336 paintings).[23] Just like expert statements, the work directories resulting from research efforts represent an authority that object labels more or less willingly follow along with. Consensus cannot always be reached, with owners sometimes refusing to accept that their masterpiece is in fact a forgery.[24]

Object labels suggest certainty—or at least they represent the received expert view, which sometimes is verified by the results of latest scientific studies on the objects. Thus, they are a kind of certificate of identity as, for example, official accreditations. The trust in the processes of authentication and in the museum system is considerably damaged when labels are changed. However, it is of course also the case that incomplete or ambiguous labels point to unresolved art historical problems and the porousness of expertise.[25]

25 Two examples are a casket and a trestle table at Berlin Kunstgewerbemuseum, labeled 'Italy, 16th and 19th century' and '16th and 19th century' respectively. It is uncertain whether these objects are sixteenth-century pieces heavily renovated, amended, or copied in the nineteenth century, or whether they were made in the nineteenth century with sixteenth-century materials—we are instantly reminded of the problem of the *Flora*. Art trade in the nineteenth century, for lack of originals, brought forth a large number of such compounds.

This function, which makes the label the place where identification and, in the case of an incorrect ascription, changed value manifest themselves, distinguishes object labels from any other type of *parerga* in the visual arts.

It is worth pointing out that both in the case of Ippolito's 'Death by Wall Label' and in the case of the status loss manifested in the replacement of the labels of the *Flora* bust and the 'ex-Rembrandt' painting, what was at issue were formal, factual mismatches between label and work. In contrast, the line in wall labels that, in the last few decades, has caused more public anger than most, is the very last line, which specifies the owner of the piece. This line is particularly contentious in the case of stolen artworks, such as those looted by the Nazis. Provenance researchers indicated, for example, on the labels in the exhibition of Cornelius Gurlitt's art collection in Bonn in 2017, that works were 'currently not suspected to be Nazi looted art.'[26] Anger has also been expressed against exhibitions that were composed almost exclusively of pieces belonging to the same private collector, such as the 2012 Bonn retrospective of Anselm Kiefer, which drew on the works in the possession of the controversial collector Hans Grothe. Grothe had been known to use the museum as a value-adding temporary residence for his art before it was auctioned.[27] Another peculiar example is the exhibition of works by Carolee Schneemann, which in the summer of 2017 travelled from Museum der Moderne in Salzburg to Museum für Moderne Kunst in Frankfurt am Main (MMK). It consisted largely of works whose credit line read 'Courtesy Carolee Schneemann and P.P.O.W. Gallery New York.' A likely conclusion drawn by the art historian and critic Julia Voss is that, in such cases where curating is obviously not involved, 'the only contribution made by the museum is to open the doors.'[28] Reading wall labels thus obviously also has a discrediting power—here, too, it alters our perception of the objects and leads to a disappointment in the apparent utilization of the museum. However, these last cases discredit curators and museums, not, like the eighteenth-century etching, visitors.

Life by Wall Label

In contrast to *death* of media art, such as a work's status loss by discount or scandals caused by credit lines, there is the much more common situation in which object labels are the very thing that designates an object as art. This applies primarily, but certainly not exclusively, to the White Cube in which contemporary art is usually shown and which seems to be a space where the practical handling of labels is much more difficult than in galleries of older art. I will return to this below.

In his seminal essays *Inside the White Cube* from 1976/1986, the artist and author Brian O'Doherty put forward the concept of the White Cube as a new exhibition aesthetics

26 Thanks to Christiane Holm for drawing my attention to this example. **27** See Voss, *Hinter weißen Wänden*, 2015, p. 25. Voss refers to another example, the presentation 'Andy Warhol. Zeichnungen der 1950er Jahre' shown in 2013 by Staatliche Graphische Sammlung at Pinakothek der Moderne in Munich, which relied almost exclusively on the gallerist Daniel Blau's possessions which were for sale, as well as

established in the twentieth century. In his view, the gallery space designed in this way becomes a place of transformation, because objects appear as art simply as a result of being presented in it. In one of the most well-known passages, O'Doherty notes:

'In this context [the White Cube, A. M.] a standing ashtray becomes almost a sacred object, just as the firehose in a modern museum looks not like a firehose but an aesthetic conundrum. Modernism's transposition of perception from life to formal value is complete.'[29]

Apart from everyday objects in contemporary art, which O'Doherty here alludes to, Tino Sehgal's *constructed situations* are an excellent example of the persistence of wall labels, even where their deployment is impossible due to the nature of the work. In such cases, they obviously must be given a new form. Sehgal, whose choreographies only exist in the moment and are performed by amateur actors, avoids any form of written or visual records of his artworks. There are neither contracts nor scripts for the performance-like *constructed situations*, nor are there authorized photographs, films or wall labels. Instead, the performers verbalize a bare minimum of basic information: name of artist, title, and date. It is these verbalizations that reassure visitors that the *constructed situations* are to be regarded as art. This can become quite amusing when, for example, a couple lying on the floor kissing makes efforts to articulate in as clear a way as possible the words 'Tino Sehgal,' 'Kiss,' and '2002.'

However, it was the Columbus Museum of Art in Columbus, Ohio that provided what was probably the clearest confirmation of both O'Doherty's claim that gallery space and its design and aesthetic function are creators of art, and my assertion that the wall label plays a key role among the 'exhibition prosthetics.' In the summer of 2017, the museum had put up a note to visitors which read, 'Not sure if something is art?,' and the solution which was added was to '[l]ook for a label like this one. If you see a label near an object, it's a work of art' (Fig. 2). This note was obviously necessary because the museum has devoted the ground floor of its original building to a very innovative education centre in which works from the collection mingled with 'works' made by classes or students. Object labels can thus mark the distinction between art and non-art.

Artists have continually been working with and against this power of the object label since the Institutional Critique of the 1970s. This seems to be so, for example, in the case of Gregor Schneider's 1994 *Schwarzes Quadrat in Wand* (Black Square in the Wall) at the Museum für Moderne Kunst Frankfurt am Main (MMK). In 2002, according to the wall label, Schneider had arranged for a square-shaped area in one of the museum's walls to remain filled with black plaster cement for the next fifty years. Since the intervention did not leave any traces, the wall label is the only visible clue of Schneider's artwork. The piece

on the possessions of his collectors. In this Munich exhibition, there were no wall labels; the information was provided on handouts. See: Voss, *Hinter weißen Wänden*, 2015, p. 24. **28** Voss, *Hinter weißen Wänden*, 2015, p. 25. **29** O'Doherty, *Inside the White Cube*, 1986, p. 15.

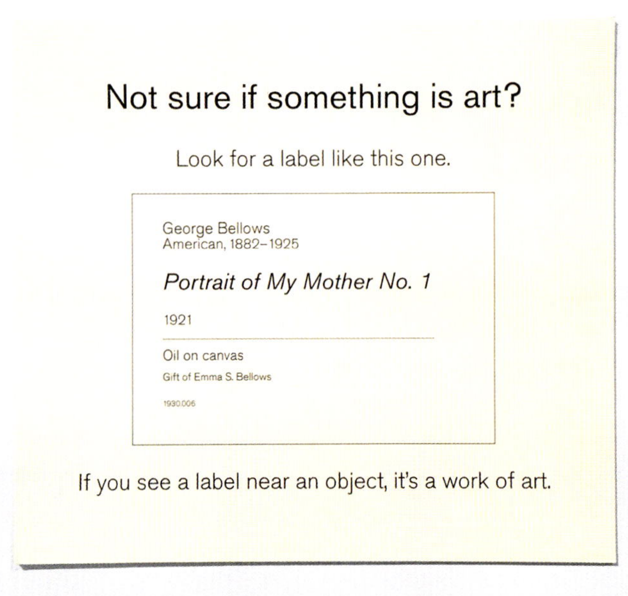

Figure 2:
Note on a wall of the Columbus Museum of Art, Columbus, Ohio, US, July 2017.

is a reference to Kazimir Malevich's 1915 piece *Black Square*, a key work of the avant-garde, through which Schneider plays with the notion of the 'Museum für Moderne Kunst' and at the same time puts the label to the test—since the intervention he describes is not traceable.

Forms of substitution or reversal—the wall label either stands for or overrides the piece of art—are often found among what Grigely called 'prosthetic art.'[30] One example of this is Hans Hollein's reversal of size and position of wall labels and the actual paintings which he practiced at Documenta 8 in 1987, and with which he forced visitors to make contortions to see the small reproductions of works of art. Other examples are 'flickering labels' used for example by Philippe Parreno.[31] Quite a few artists also (allegedly) steal object labels from museums and display them, such as Maria Anwander, who has been running her collection *My Most Favourite Art* as an open project since 2004.

While these are examples of a substitution of labels for artworks, one of the old masters of 'prosthetic art,' Marcel Broodthaers, was among those who employed the strategy

30 Grigely, *Exhibition Prosthetics*, 2010, p. 21. **31** Grigely, *Exhibition Prosthetics*, 2010, p. 51 (Joseph Grigely in conversation with Hans Ulrich Obrist and Zak Kyes, Architectural Association, 18 February 2009). **32** On Broodthaers see: König and Broodthaers, *Musée d'Art Moderne*, 2012, in particular pp. 26–28 and pp. 38–44. **33** Pauli, 'Die Kunsthalle zu Bremen,' 1905, pp. 139–149, especially pp. 148–149. **34** See: Back,

of using a label to deprive the artwork of its status. His 1972 exhibition piece *The Eagle from the Oligocene Until Today*, part of his *Musée d'Art Moderne, Département des Aigles*, questioned wall labels as status markers.[32] To each exhibit of his randomly-displayed eagle collection consisting of objects from art, popular culture, natural history, military, and politics, he added a small plastic label bearing the catalogue number of the piece along with the sentence, 'This is not a work of art.' Regardless of whether one reads the labels as referring to the objects or to themselves, this is an instance of a central status marker serving to withdraw status. And yet, ultimately, the vast abundance of the labels, all of them the same, and all of them attempting to void the status of the object, in the end does nothing so much as highlight their power.

Marginalizations of Wall Labels

Looking around in museums and exhibitions, there seems to be an antagonism between the power of labels and the way curators and institutions work with them. Fragments of the history of wall labels suggest as much. Since labels took their place on the picture frame in the nineteenth century and then moved to walls in the beginning of the twentieth century, curating has time and again sought to marginalize them because of their ambivalent nature of being indispensable 'prostheses' which give crucial information, but at the same time disturbing the experience of the art and the aesthetics of hanging. Since pictures no longer served a purely representative purpose, but were now meant to edify and educate the visitor, labelling them was a necessity.

'The labelling of the art works may be awful since it does not add anything to their beauty, but in a public collection it is simply indispensable. It must unite clarity with inconspicuousness and provide the visitor with the essential details on the creator and the subject of the picture, that is 1. catalogue number, 2. name and life dates of the artist, 3. subject of the picture, 4. date of acquisition, if applicable, details on the donor.'[33]

In keeping with this spirit, labels are today still kept as discrete as possible, for example by giving them the same colour as the wall so that they can blend into the background (a strategy also endorsed by Pauli's compatriots)[34] or, alternatively, by printing the text on transparent foil. It is striking that there is such a large number of photographs of exhibition halls in which no labels at all can be made out. Indeed, in order to reduce the wall label to an absolute minimum, it was common practice until the beginning of the twentieth century to number the pieces and provide the information in pocket guides.[35]

In the research on the history of labelling artworks in museums and exhibitions to date, not even rough sketches can be found of the evolution that has taken place since the eighteenth century from catalogues, small pocket guides or simple lists to provide orienting

'Die Einrichtung der Kunst- und Historischen Sammlungen des Großherzoglichen Landesmuseums in Darmstadt,' 1909, pp. 63–82, especially p. 80. See also: Richter, 'Das neue Stadtmuseum in Dresden,' 1911, pp. 61–66, especially p. 65. **35** See: Voss, *Hinter weißen Wänden*, 2015, p. 19.

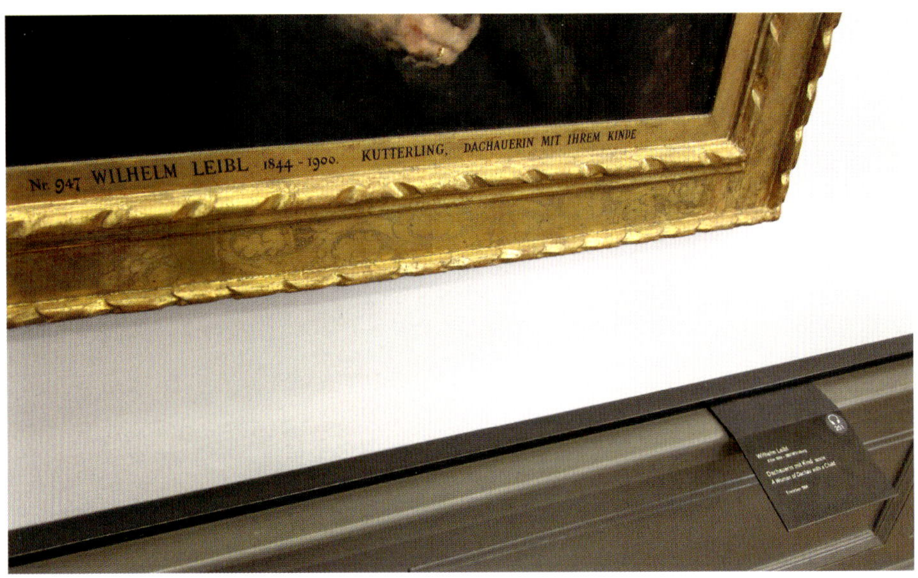

Figure 3:
Details of the labelling of the Alte Nationalgalerie, Berlin, February 2018.

information, to labels placed directly on the picture frame.[36] The preferred style for those labels with museum directors in Germany in the early twentieth century was black leather or cardboard with golden letters printed on or—in case of golden frames—as gilded platelets with black letters.[37] During these years, as hangings became sparser, labels migrated from the frames to the walls and the panneling.[38] In present-day galleries of older masters, there is often an old and a new label, with the latter not only affirming that the information on the former is still valid, but also making the collection as a whole appear homogeneous (Fig. 3). It can also be observed at museums like Alte Nationalgalerie in Berlin that in the small cabinets, labels are directly attached to the frames. However, apart from that, the tendency to attach them to panneling—sometimes leaning towards the viewer—seems to prevail. Adding longer object descriptions apparently was not established as an option until the 1970s, despite the fact that some scholars had begun to promote the idea as early as the 1930s, leading at this early point to a direct opposition between proponents of the museum as an 'educational institution' (Lehranstalt), and those who believed that the museum was a place of undisturbed experience of art akin to

36 A practice which specialists such as Beverly Serrell in her volume *Making Exhibit Labels*, 1985, p. 102 condemns: 'Placement. A few basic rules about placement will greatly contribute to the success of your labels and may be summarized briefly. *Don'ts:* Don't stick labels on objects as if they were price tags.' One could argue that in fact labels are a kind of price tag. **37** See: Pauli, 'Die Kunsthalle zu Bremen,' 1905, p. 149; Richter, 'Das neue Stadtmuseum in Dresden,' 1911, p. 65. **38** For a comment in favour of this see: Fuhse, 'Das neue Städtische Museum in Braunschweig,' 1906, pp. 128–139, here p. 139. **39** See: Müller-Wulckow,

a 'concert hall.'[39] It thus becomes apparent that today's customary practices of labelling older art had already been established by the 1910s and have since remained under common consensus.

However, a significant difference can be observed in the practice of labelling between the White Cube of contemporary art and galleries displaying old masters. While the latter is marked by proximity between the object and the label(s), in the White Cube, curators are much more careful to separate art from its identifier. In contemporary-art exhibition labelling, there seems to be much more inhibition and discomfort. This may be, on the one hand, because of the ideology of the 'pure' aesthetics of the white wall and, on the other hand, because critical discourse on museums, display and Institutional Critique as an art practice is far more present.

Consequently, clusterings of labels seem much more abundant in places of contemporary art, perhaps in order to avoid seeming overly didactic by being too explicit about the reference.[40] In contrast to galleries of old masters, most White Cubes obviously suppress the possibility of learning something about art history by reading labels in favour of pure ocular labour. At times, clusters of labels put up on walls become anchoring points for the visitors, but the correspondence between the labels and the pieces is not always self-explanatory. In the Warhol Room at Museum für Moderne Kunst in Frankfurt am Main (MMK), the visitors have to make the effort of walking to the labels, which were coyly put in the corners of the room, far away from the objects. Mario Kramer, who curated the presentation, gives a primarily aesthetic rationale for this decision:

'As a general rule, the view of the work should not be disturbed by a label. The information on the label (name of artist, title, year, provenance, etc.) is important for the museumgoer, but secondary. The artwork is first of all the work of the artist. The label only has a service function and is a tool of the museum.'[41]

But still, crossing the distance to satiate a need for information almost feels embarrassing given the obvious curatorial commitment to the aesthetic experience of the artwork. In doing so, one is inescapably reminded of the eighteenth-century critique of the audience, which scoffed at those who perused the catalogues as ignorant and incapable of the dialogue with the art itself. Moreover, nowhere do viewers have to bow down so deep to labels as in places of contemporary art. The labelling established at C/O Berlin, a space for photography (Fig. 4), for example, takes the skirting as an architectural reference. From the perspective of the designer, but most likely also representative of many practitioners, Marc Naroska describes labelling as a kind of squaring the circle, almost impossible

'Frankfurter Museumsfragen,' 1930, pp. 14–18, especially p. 15 and Freiherr Schenk zu Schweinsberg, 'Die Beschriftung in Kunstsammlungen,' 1934, pp. 92–95. **40** This can lead to situations as for example at Berlin Kunstgewerbemuseum, where visitors are faced with two long chair rows and have to count the chairs as well as the labels in order to identify the object beheld. **41** Kindly communicated to me by email on 18 December 2017.

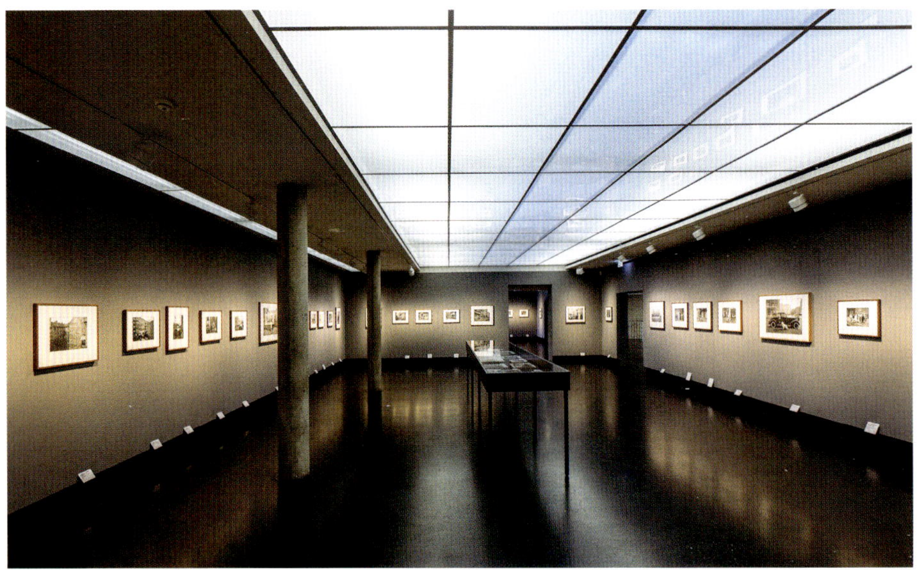

Figure 4:
Exhibition view *Harf Zimmermann*, C/O Berlin, April 2017.

to get right.[42] The label must by no means be a disturbance, but must still be close enough to associate it intuitively with the object. While the sign ought to be as small as possible, the length of the content is often dictated by the artists or the lender; at the same time, the font must be large enough to be easy to read. For Naroska, each new plaque on the wall adds something disruptively pictorial to the situation. However, applying the text to the wall directly is not an option because of the recurring need for correction, and because it is the space the curator needs for the hanging. In any case, aside from design advantages, he sees it—for the time being—as the easiest for all parties involved to place the labels on the skirting and have them blend in with the appearance of the museum. In summary, Naroska's position is that the label is part of the architecture, not of the art. This is possible since he works exclusively on the design of 'exhibition prosthetics.' At the same time, however, this highlights the difference between his conception and Grigely's 'exhibition prosthetics' as well as Derrida's *parerga*. Both Derrida and Grigely start from the premise of what Grigely calls a 'dialogic relationship' between work and 'prosthesis,'

42 Mentioned to me in a conversation in Berlin on 22 December 2017. **43** Grigely, *Exhibition Prosthetics*, 2010, pp. 12–13. **44** Derrida, *The Truth in Painting*, 1987 [1978], p. 64. **45** Expectations of the 1990s for a digital take-over—e.g. David C. Devenish expected 'high tech substitutes' for *real* labels—, have so far not been met (Devenish, *Museum Display Labels*, 1996, p. 32). Marc Naroska presumes that most people seem to hesitate to download data on their own smartphones in exhibition halls—in spite of the fact that everybody constantly sends and receives all kind of data.

'each "informing" the other.'[43] While Grigely's 'prostheses' are conceptualized from the outside, i.e. from the perspective of exhibiting art, Derrida's *parerga* start from the artwork itself in describing its blurred boundaries. Despite this, the question of whether the label and its information is part of the exhibition or of the art remains unanswerable for either of them. At the same time, as can be seen in the spaces of contemporary art, the more effort that is made to neutralize object labels, as it were, and make them disappear by attributing to them a service or architectural nature, the more obtrusive they become. As stressed by Derrida, *parerga* carry out a kind of boundary work, taking a subordinate position. However, this type of boundary work can also cross and reverse the boundaries: 'The deterioration of the *parergon*, the perversion, the adornment, is the attraction of sensory matter.'[44] We do not need to see this as negatively as Derrida did because this also encapsulates their central function and their power.

In assembling these episodic fragments into a history of the object label, we seem, at least to a certain extent, to have come full circle. Spaces of contemporary art are increasingly returning to the eighteenth-century choice of leaving out wall labels as much as possible, instead providing the information on hand-outs or pocket guides (though Naroska sees such paper provision as a waste of material and money).[45] Thus, if there is a history of labels in art museums, it seems to be at least in part a circular one. The different ways of working with labels in art museums and exhibition spaces show their variable forms and numerous approaches from directors, curators, authors, designers and artists to (new) formats and placements, ways of doubling and attempts to marginalize as well as to question and challenge their function and role. Older art is almost systematically granted more and closer labelling—i.e. 'prostheses?'—than younger art. As a materialized form, labels can even disappear in pocket guides for exhibitions. But still, their information remains indispensable—it is about identification, expertise, status and hierarchy, and even about 'death' and 'life.' There has been no attempt to discard them completely.

Bibliography

F. Back, 'Die Einrichtung der Kunst- und Historischen Sammlungen des Großherzoglichen Landesmuseums in Darmstadt,' *Museumskunde*, 5 (1909), pp. 63–82.

J. Derrida, *The Truth in Painting*, trans. by G. Bennington and I. McLeod (University of Chicago Press, 1987 [1978]).

D. C. Devenish, *Museum Display Labels* (ICOM Golden Jubilee Publication, Indian National Committee of ICOM, 1996).

F. Fuhse, 'Das neue Städtische Museum in Braunschweig,' *Museumskunde*, 2 (1906), pp. 128–139.

P. Geimer, 'Das falsche Original. Aufbau und Abbau von Aura' in A. Matyssek (ed.), *Wann stirbt ein Kunstwerk? Konservierungen des Originalen in der Gegenwartskunst* (Verlag Silke Schreiber, 2010), pp. 23–39.

G. Genette, *Paratexts. Thresholds of Interpretation* (Cambridge University Press, 1997).

J. Grigely, *Exhibition Prosthetics* (Bedford Press, 2010).

A. te Heesen, 'Beschriftungsszenen. Über Etiketten und ihre Bedeutung' in A. te Heesen, B. Tschofen and K. Wiegmann (eds.), *Wortschatz. Vom Sammeln und Finden der Wörter* (Stadtmuseum Tübingen, 2008), pp. 106–115.

J. Ippolito, 'Death by Wall Label' in C. Paul (ed.), *New Media in the White Cube and Beyond* (University Press Group Ltd, 2008), pp. 106–132.

V. Kobi (ed.), *The Limits of Connoisseurship. Attribution Issues & Mistakes*, special issue of the *Journal of Art Historiography*, 16 (2017).

S. König and M. Broodthaers, *Musée d'Art Moderne, Département des Aigles* (Reimer, 2012).

P. M. McManus, 'Oh, Yes, They Do: How Museum Visitors Read Labels and Interact with Exhibit Texts,' *Curator*, 32/3 (1989), pp. 174–189.

W. Müller-Wulckow, 'Frankfurter Museumsfragen. Zu Georg Swarzenskis Neugestaltungsplänen,' *Museumskunde*, N. F., 2 (1930), pp. 14–18.

B. O'Doherty, *Inside the White Cube. The Ideology of the Gallery Space* (Lapis Press, 1986).

G. Pauli, 'Die Kunsthalle zu Bremen,' *Museumskunde*, 1 (1905), pp. 139–149.

O. Richter, 'Das neue Stadtmuseum in Dresden,' *Museumskunde*, 7 (1911), pp. 61–66.

E. Freiherr Schenk zu Schweinsberg, 'Die Beschriftung in Kunstsammlungen,' *Museumskunde*, N. F., 6 (1934), pp. 92–95.

B. Serrell, *Making Exhibit Labels. A Step-by-Step Guide* (American Association for State and Local History, 1985).

E. Spickernagel and B. Walbe (eds.), *Das Museum: Lernort contra Musentempel* (Anabas Verlag, 1976).

J. Steen, 'Ausstellung und Text' in G. Fliedl, R. Muttenthaler and H. Posch (eds.), *Wie zu sehen ist. Essays zur Theorie des Ausstellens* (Turia & Kant, 1995), pp. 46–62.

D. Tyradellis, *Müde Museen. Oder: Wie Ausstellungen unser Denken verändern können* (Edition Körber, 2014).

E. van de Wetering, *A Corpus of Rembrandt Paintings VI: Rembrandt's Paintings Revisited. A Complete Survey* (Springer, 2014).

J. Voss, *Hinter weißen Wänden. Behind the White Cube. Zeichnungen von Philipp Deines* (Merve, 2015).

U. Wolff-Thomsen, *Die Wachsbüste einer Flora in der Berliner Skulpturensammlung und das System Wilhelm Bode. Leonardo da Vinci oder Richard Cockle Lucas* (Verlag Ludwig, 2006).

NOÉMIE ÉTIENNE

When Things Do Talk (in Storage). Materiality and Agency between Contact and Conflict Zones

Conservation within ethnographic and anthropological museums raises a number of issues, discussed by conservators and curators since 2000. Commonly used in these debates, the concept of 'cross-cultural conservation' presupposes at least two important networks: a first culture, which produced the things and no longer always legally owns them; and a second culture—mostly European or Euro-American—which controls and conserves the objects. In this context, conservation and restoration bring together differing types of knowledge, experiences and interpretations around a single artefact, which at times leads to dilemmas. I am using here the word artefact in a broad sense, to describe anything constructed by human beings, without discussing its artistic or sacred value. Furthermore, these artefacts were not made to be exhibited in a museum, and are not 'ethnographic' by nature. According to Barbara Kirshenblatt, '[t]hey did not begin their life as ethnographic objects. They became ethnographic through processes of detachment and contextualization.'[1]

This paper examines the conservation of Native American objects in the National Museum of the American Indian (NMAI) in Washington DC and New York City. I will argue that framing is not only an action produced through physical devices in the museum gallery, but also a gesture giving—or denying—the ability to talk to an object in storage or the conservation laboratory. In order to underline how things may actually be talking in a museum, I will focus on an unpublished source. In the beginning of the 1990s, a report on conservation methods pointed out that the elders of certain Native American and First Nations communities claimed that their artefacts possessed agency. They asked museums to preserve the life and power of these material things and to provide them with the

1 A first version of this paper was presented in Leiden, in December 2012, during the annual conference of LUCAS, *Presence and Agency*. I would like to thank Caroline van Eck, Johannes Grave and Valérie Kobi for their feedback. Special thanks to Ivan Gaskell for his help and support. For a similar discussion of notions at the core of this text, such as the lives of things, storage, and touch in the museum world, see: Gaskell, 'The Life of Things,' 2015. Kirshenblatt, *Destination Culture*, 1992, p. 3.

conditions necessary to their survival. This report, titled *The Way of the People* had been commissioned on behalf of the NMAI by Venturi, Scott Brown and Associates, the Philadelphia firm founded by the famous postmodernist architects Robert Venturi and Denise Scott Brown.[2] Indeed, the architects founded a private consulting bureau, where they act as experts in urban planning and architecture.

While focusing on a case study, I will show that the properties of objects may change under the influence of specific gestures and apparatuses within a given context. More precisely, I will argue that conservation is an understudied practice shaping the life and identity of things. Material transformations and uses of the artefact provide it with various identities during its life. Therefore, the goal of this paper is not to discuss whether an object is alive or not, but rather to focus on the practices that activate its qualities. The movement I will trace is circular: on the one hand, the life of an object depends on its reception and the manner in which it is perceived. On the other hand, agency can be activated by practices, and notably by conservation practices. From this perspective, conservation and storage studies are key fields to explore the multiplicity of spaces and gestures taking place in a museum, and the defining of the identity of things.

'I Don't Call It a Museum… It Is Alive'

The NMAI is part of one of the Smithsonian Museums, and includes three sites: the main building in Washington DC, a second building in New York City, and an annex called the Conservation Research Centre in Suitland, Maryland. The NMAI is not the only museum to conserve Native artefacts in New York. The American Museum of Natural History (AMNH), for instance, is an important institution in this respect. Many of the displays in the AMNH and the NMAI differ from each other considerably. The AMNH still use lifelike dioramas, for instance, which is not the case at the NMAI. Other displays do share similar framing devices, in particular the glass boxes used as vitrines. Nevertheless, there are notable, though less immediately visible, differences in how the two institutions approach conservation and storage. Indeed, the main difference between these institutions remains out of the public view and concerns the conservation and storage of artefacts.[3] The NMAI aims to offer an alternative to regular ethnography museums, providing—among other things—new forms of conservation practice and new rules on preservation issues.

The Way of the People, a report commissioned in the early 1990s, includes substantial interviews with Native Americans communities. Two parts of the report are particularly relevant to my investigation: the first is a long series of quotations, presenting Native voices, unfortunately without any clear discursive context; the second is a series of forms,

2 Venturi, Scott Brown and Izenour (eds.), *The Way of the People*, 1991–1993. For their most famous work, see: Venturi, Scott Brown and Izenour, *Learning from Las Vegas*, 1972. **3** Art history is currently taking a growing interest in storage. See for instance: Brusius and Singh, *Museum Storage*, 2017. **4** Venturi, Scott Brown and Izenour (eds.), *The Way of the People*, Phase 2 Final Report, p. 20. Again, many individual names have not been preserved in the report—one of many inconsistencies and difficulties of this source. **5** Hopi Tribal Museum, in Venturi, Scott Brown and Izenour (eds.), *The Way of the People*, Native American Tribal

filled out by Native delegates responding to specific questions about conservation issues. Many precise claims emerged from this documentation. The most important one, and probably the most surprising one, according to western conservation standards, is the will to preserve the life of objects by giving them the opportunity to breathe, eat, drink, move and exercise many other functions pertaining to life. A member of the Lakota tribe described the storage conditions he personally applied to the preservation of his grandfather's pipe: 'The pipe is kept in a frame building without environmental controls—I don't call it a Museum... It is alive.'[4] The privileged environment is without hygrometric control—unlike many museums and storage rooms—and is described as 'alive.' The same report reveals that Hopi people were required to feed the artefacts: 'These materials should be treated only by us, and fed periodically by us.'[5] To be sure, feeding in that context most likely takes a wider sense that it would in a restaurant: feeding encompasses actions that sustain living things with appropriate items—such as corn, tobacco, and sage. Nevertheless, the presence of organic products in storage does not fit western conservation's standards.

The people consulted in this report, in line with the life and power attributed to the objects, encourage these specific methods of conservation. In other words, arguing a specific definition of the artefacts legitimates these wishes: 'The objects have power, have life.'[6] This special quality also implies certain conservation norms in the use of particular materials, as well as in storage methods. Plastic is prohibited, not only because it would be exogenous or have a bad impact on natural materials, but also because it potentially prevents the whole living object from breathing. The scholar Edmund J. Ladd (Zuni) stated, '[i]t is not the fact that the material actually breathes, but the fact that the spiritual content of it, the condition of it, has to breathe through some means of its own not to be hampered by plastic or being constrained by having it in a container.'[7] Similarly, certain artefacts cannot be stored in the same room because of the power they exert over each other. According to Melvin Larocque (Dene), '[t]here are also certain artefacts that should not be mixed with those of another culture. The power and strength of one cultural item can be destroyed by the presence of that from another culture.'[8]

Thus, these objects are alive, and they require space to breathe, eat, and move They also have power, which directly influences other objects and human beings. Indeed, Native people often accuse curators of destroying their artefacts by preventing their use, while the conservators anxiously prevent the proliferation of insects and bacteria—a consequence of the introduction of people, food and liquid into the storage rooms. In *The Way of the People* Jamie Kolker, one of the consultants of Venturi and Brown's Firm, even described a fundamental difference between the two cultures:

Museum and Center Survey on Storage, Care and Access, National Museum of the American Indian: Phase 2, 25 May 1995. **6** Jones quoted in Clavir, *Preserving What Is Valued*, 2002, p. 205. **7** Ladd (Zuni), in Venturi, Scott Brown and Izenour (eds.), *The Way of the People*, National Museum of the American Indian, Master Facilities Program: Suitland vol. 2, 23 April 1993, Traditional Care consultation, VII. p. 442. **8** Larocque (Dene), in Venturi, Scott Brown and Izenour (eds.), *The Way of the People*, Native American Tribal Museum and Center Survey on Storage, Care and Access, National Museum of the American Indian: Phase 2, 25 May 1995.

'Bottomless, according to Kolker, there is a fundamental philosophical incompatibility between western and Non-western perception of material objects, their handling and care. The western obsession for the insurance of an object's physical immortality, including its removal from the contamination of human association, is totally counter to the Native American orientation of "use it or loose it".'[9]

This opposition between two cultures and two visions—one obsessed with the use of objects, and the other one fascinated by their preservation—seems simplistic. First, because not all artefacts are supposed to be used by Native people, nor preserved by western curators. Secondly, human identities are mixed and hybrid, particularly in places underlined by an intense colonial history, as post-colonial scholarship has demonstrated. Indeed, a claim that the first and second cultures are completely aligned or polarized may be misleading. There is no insuperable opposition between a western conservation practice, which engages with objects as passive and dead artefacts, versus a Native one that advocates for their use and fully acknowledges their agency and life. If the cultural context is important, the example of the NMAI shows us that conservators and curators can also take the agency of an object into consideration. Following the results of this report, the storage rooms of the NMAI are indeed now increasingly accessible to people, liquid and smoke, as well as to dance and musical performances.

Living Objects in the West

Considering things as alive is not alien to western world, as scholarship has pointed out since the 1990s. The agency of things has been increasingly taken into account by the humanities and social sciences. First and foremost, the anthropologist Alfred Gell suggested moving from an aesthetical theory of art to an anthropological one.[10] According to him, an anthropological theory of art shall no longer be based on the idea of beauty, as the western aesthetic philosophy has done since the eighteenth century, but rather on the idea of action and efficiency. In this perspective, agency is not a quality of the thing, but a power attributed to it by members of the nexus in which the thing is inserted. More recently, Caroline van Eck has studied the way statues generated feelings and (re)actions (including vandalism, love devotion or erotic desire) in the West, in particular during the seventeenth and eighteenth centuries.[11] Such behaviours belong to earlier time periods,[12] but also to different networks: contemporary collectors of African art, for instance, have been recorded domesticating and exoticizing their belongings while moving them, for instance, to various places in a same apartment.[13]

9 Kolker, in Venturi, Scott Brown and Izenour (eds.), *The Way of the People*, Wendy Jessup Report, Phase 2, Final Report. **10** Gell, *Art and Agency*, 1998. **11** van Eck, 'Living Statues,' 2010. **12** See for instance: Wirth, 'Perfomativité de l'image?,' 2009. **13** Derlon and Jeudi-Ballini, 'Domestification,' 2014. **14** Szymborska, 'Museum,' 1993 [1962]. **15** van Eck, *Art, Agency and Living Presence*, 2015, p. 28.

Artistic texts also often embrace the idea of living objects. In her poem entitled 'Museum,' for instance, the Polish writer Wisława Szymborska beautifully evokes the tension between missing bodies and remaining material culture in such institutions:

> The crown has outlasted the head.
> The hand has lost out to the glove.
> The right shoe has defeated the foot.
>
> As for me, I am still alive, you see.
> The battle with my dress still rages on.
> It struggles, foolish thing, so stubbornly!
> Determined to keep living when I'm gone![14]

In this poem, the dress is fighting to survive her human owner. Once in the museum, clothes, gloves and shoes keep enjoying their triumph.

Obviously, attributing agency to things is a process shared by different people in different places and at different times. This, then, raises a question: is agency a universal given, widely attributed to things by people? Caroline van Eck has studied what she describes as a 'universal human characteristic, making representations and endowing them with life and agency.'[15] Following her analysis, the agency of objects takes different meanings depending on the background and political interests of the people involved: as my case study shows, the leaders interviewed in the report consider the things as alive and powerful by nature. The museum curators and conservators value first their beauty and attractiveness to the visitors. In that regard, we are indeed facing two different conceptions of what agency can be.

In fact, agency signifies different things for different people, and the diversity of these conceptions can lead to confusion in academic writing as well as curating. On the one hand, my example shows a conflict between an emic and etic conception of agency: in other words, between a conception that would be proper to indigenous beliefs, and one representing the outsider view represented by the museum and all its framing devices—physical and conceptual. On the other hand, as we shall see, museums and storages are places where emic and etic conceptions of agency actually get to influence each other. Indeed, the boundary between these groups and their views is more fluid than expected. There will certainly be instances of incompatibility, but they do not predominate. I would like to go beyond the idea of culture that the word 'cross-cultural' suggests, in order to explain conflicts in the field of conservation. Instead, each intervention is a particular negotiation, sometimes political, which potentially modifies the identity of artefacts.

From this perspective, conservation and restoration are practices which increase or decrease the aliveness of things over the course of their existence. What these groups have in common is not only the idea that an object can potentially be alive, or active, but the fact that agency can actually be activated, an idea that seems a powerful bridge to see where the two systems connect. Following Szymborska's input, I argue that the life of things indeed does not stop in storage, but rather is activated through more discrete, yet no less powerful, practices in the museum. Conservation itself is a form of activation that reshapes the identity, authenticity, and agency of things.

Between Contact and Conflict Zones

Indeed, issues related to conservation and museum practices can open up the discussion around the power of objects that exist at the intersection of different worlds, institutions and cultures. In this sense, the material things discussed in this paper exist in a 'contact zone,' to quote the expression coined by Marie Louise Pratt and already applied to museums by James Clifford.[16] However, contact zones are numerous and function on many different levels, ranging from the institution that displays the objects, to the diminutive space of the conservator's hand trying to fix them. Furthermore, the idea of *contact* sounds somehow too neutral, as this case will demonstrate, to convey the complexity and power relation at stake in cross-cultural interaction. Therefore, I would suggest counterbalancing the idea of the contact zone with the idea of conflict zones, coming from the political sciences. As already stated by Kavita Singh about museums: in fact, contacts in asymmetrical contexts are more than often the occasion of unresolved tensions and conflicts.[17]

Furthermore, the objects are themselves the place of these various contacts. From that perspective, human touch carries a specific meaning and holds the power to transform the things.[18] The agency of objects may increase or decrease under the influence of particular practices and framing devices. One of these operations, already addressed by Kirschenblatt and mentioned in the introduction of this paper, is the relocation of the artefacts in the museum gallery. Indeed, fragments are extracted from their original context to be reintroduced in another setting, very often decontextualized from their original surrounding, and exhibited in a glass box or vitrine. Such devices are expected to preserve the object from degradation and physical interactions with the visitors. Furthermore, the building itself works as a frame, re-inscribing the things in another place and narrative. Yet, as with many conservation interventions, reframing tends to a certain invisibility: it is perceived as successful when it erases itself, improving the view of an object without underlining its own existence. It this sense, both conservation intervention and display are additions to an artwork, supporting its presence in the museum space but meant to be unseen. They nonetheless transform seriously what is displayed.

Storage and conversation laboratories have also been conflict and contact zones since their creation. In this regard, it is worth noting that conservation has always been used as a political tool. In France, between the Revolution (1789) and the Restauration (1815),

16 Pratt, 'Arts of the Contact Zone,' 1991; Clifford, 'Museum As Contact Zones,' 1997. **17** On museums (and other places) as conflict zones, see: Singh, *Museums, Heritage, Culture*, 2015. For a discussion about conservation treatment, see, for instance, p. 17. On Native American objects, see pp. 57–60. **18** On

revolutionary and Napoleonic troops took objects from all over Europe and particularly in Italy, in order to re-exhibit them in the newly founded Louvre Museum. Preservation was key, in this context, to legitimate the transport of paintings to France. Indeed, the museum administrators argued that artworks were not well conserved in their former locations, and were invisible to the public in small churches. Preservation and access were the values promoted by the French army to face the criticism they encountered.[19] Consequently, artworks were highly restored when they arrived in France—and often exhibited in a state of pre- and post-conservation—although ironically the transport itself probably contributed to their degradation. A rhetoric of preservation and public good emerged in revolutionary France that still has consequences today in the rhetorical tropes used to legitimate global preservation campaigns.

Ancestors or Pieces of Wood?

The idea of two different cultures of conservation does not seem strong enough to explain the conflicts that arise in museums. Rather, I would like to emphasize that the power of an object is also related to practices—such as conservation and restoration—as well as to individuals—depending, for instance, on which conservator is treating the artefact—all of this inevitably taking place in a political context. The question of the agency of a precise thing is also linked to specific times or places—such as museums and storage rooms.

The definition of conservation—and basically, whether or not manipulation *is* conservation—is directly related to an understanding of the thing. The perception of the object prompts its manipulations and conservation treatments. New Zealand conservator Rose Evans relates her choices of treatment directly to her approach to the artefact: 'When I'm treating a carving, I'm not treating it as a piece of wood. So, that's the first issue—that I'm treating an ancestor—so that's quite a different thing.'[20] From this perspective, restoration is part of a transformation process: almost killed in very cold storage rooms or asphyxiated in boxes for some people, but disinfected in anoxia boxes and respectfully conserved for others, the value and identity of the artefact change according to how it is manipulated. Rosita Worl, a Tlingit anthropologist, underlines that the museum is transforming the exhibited objects: 'How could the NMAI overcome what has been described by others as our "ethnological fate," whereby our sacred objects are treated and exhibited as artefacts?'[21] Thus, restoration and conservation are specific forms of reception, which relate to the singular definition of the object and also modify the curated objects, changing their life and power.

Let us now look at another example taken from a different context, exemplifying ways in which restoration and perception—in a philosophical but also visual sense—are

embodied knowledge, see: Sennett, *The Craftsman*, 2008. **19** See: Étienne, *The Restoration of Paintings in Paris*, 2017, pp. 223–244 as well as Savoy, *Patrimoine annexé*, 2003. **20** Quoted in Clavir, *Preserving What Is Valued*, 2002, p. 233. **21** Clavir, *Preserving What Is Valued*, 2002, p. 59.

connected. In the mid-1990s, exactly when the report for the NMAI was written, a discussion took place in the conservation studio of the Louvre. Former director of the Louvre, Pierre Rosenberg, was surprised by an unidentified shape in a painting of the French seventeenth-century painter Eustache Le Sueur: the presence of a blue/grey form in the image could not be clearly identified. The curator had to decide how to deal with it, and experts were called in to give their opinion regarding the shape. Finally, basing their decision on eighteenth-century prints, they decided that the shape must be a hat.[22]

As such, restoration facilitates the materialization of potential images—not only images that are created in the spectator's mind or perception, as Dario Gamboni has demonstrated[23]—but an actual transformation in the appearance and function of the thing. Depending on the way in which a painting is perceived, the conservators endow it with a specific interpretation, which becomes the object itself. Indeed, some paintings seem to be falsified, lost or 'ruined' according to the language generally used to describe an unsatisfactory intervention. When a restoration is perceived as unsuccessful, the painting may become a 'fake' or even a different painting. In this case, all of its original power is supposed to be lost following the intervention. But another kind of power can also emerge. In this case, restoration may also reveal an artwork and increase its value as well as its prestige, as was stated by Francis Haskell and Nicholas Penny in their study on the rediscovery of antique sculptures in the eighteenth century.[24] In this sense, restoration and conservation are part of a process of reception. However, conservation also happens to be a form of recreation and requalification, with an active effect.

A similar conclusion can be reached for Native objects. Restoration and conservation recreate a potential object by attributing a particular identity and ascribing a certain power, status or agency. From the perspective of a global approach to agency, it would be interesting to ask the same questions of other kinds of artefacts—such as objects used in contemporary art performances.[25] It would also be interesting to explore further the connection between authenticity and agency for western material culture. Indeed, one of the major critiques made of restoration in the context of painting is that it destroys not a painting's agency, but its very authenticity. This is the case, for instance, for the famous repainting of Barnett Newman's *Who Is Afraid of Red, Yellow and Blue II* (1967). Here, the conservation treatment created a famous scandal, decreasing the economical value of the artwork, which was brought back to storage.[26] In opposition, various Christian sacred items (Roman Catholic and Orthodox, mostly) have been restored multiple times, and retain their full authenticity and agency in the mind of the devotees.[27] Again, the ways in which conservation treatments are interpreted varies depending on the nature of the intervention and the way communities perceive them. But in any case, conservation treatments are neither neutral nor without consequences.

22 C2RMF, Versailles, File n° 4532 (June 14, 1991). **23** Gamboni, *Potential Images*, 2002. **24** Haskell and Penny, *Taste and the Antique*, 1981. **25** On residual objects see for instance the exhibition catalog: Schim-

Conservation as Activation

Thus, the agency of a specific object may depend on practices and material life rather than on ontological and definitive qualities. A large part of the scholarship on agency addresses the 'responses' made to artworks, as the subtitle of David Freedberg's book suggests: *The Power of Images. Studies in the History and Theory of Response.* It might also be productive to study further how the artworks themselves are constructed and activated through various gestures and practices. It is indeed useful to shift the question from an ontological interrogation ('is agency a property of the artefact?—essential or accidental?') to a practical and anthropological interrogation ('how is agency created? with which tools, practices and products?'). Agency is never just an essential or accidental property of a thing, but always requires practices—like volt sorcery and rituals—to be established and exerted. Works of art, defined by Gell in performative terms as systems of actions, involve the beholder as much as the creator. I argue that the conservator extends this performance. As the example below suggest, conservation affects the object and modifies its agency as much as touching it for ritual purpose does. Further, one can identify specific treatments and singular methods of curating, which may either preserve the agency of the artefact or destroy this capacity.

The objects—Native American artefacts as well as western paintings—reveal themselves as perpetual works in progress, continually produced and reproduced through a process of transformation and various manipulations. The ancient metaphor—used in the nineteenth century in the writings of John Ruskin among others—describing the existence of artefacts following an anthropomorphic schema, depicting their birth, life and death, may then be reconsidered. The study of restoration invites us to consider the life of an object as the sum of all the states and transformations it endures. Focusing on the material existence of objects in time, this reflection addresses the artwork as a *continuum*, i.e. a material object undergoing perpetual transformations. This focus on continuous modification bridges the distinction between creation and reception of artworks, while acknowledging the constant refashioning of these objects, and the manner in which material transformation impacts on their life and power.[28]

The agency of an object is not only a matter of culture, but of context as well. Conservation and restoration update the object and change what I propose terming its *ways of existing* (modes d'existence), according to the expression of Étienne Souriau—i.e. transforming a grandfather into a pipe or a pipe into a grandfather. This expression has the great advantage of being able to suggest a multiplicity, or even hybridity of identities, successively or simultaneously. The life of an artefact does not stop once it is put into a museum. My case study demonstrates that conservation is a form of activation and, to speak more broadly, of consumption that takes place inside the museum storage room.

mel (ed.), *Out of Action*, 1999. **26** For more on this topic: Étienne and Hénaut, *L'histoire à l'atelier*, 2012. **27** See: Gaskell, 'The Life of Things,' 2015. **28** Appadurai (ed.), *The Social Life of Things*, 1988.

Conservation activates artworks by providing them with a specific agency or authenticity. In this sense, restoration may also be called instauration, following the word used by Souriau to describe the shift that creates a new regime of life.[29] The challenge here is then to determine the processes that instigate new regimes—to the point of blurring the rigid distinctions between object and subject, passive and active.[30]

The contemporary art world also interrogates what reparation does to things and people. In a slide show entitled *Open Your Eyes* (2010), the French-Algerian artist Kader Attia confronts African statues with photographs of soldiers mutilated during the First World War, developing elements of a politic and aesthetic of reparation. Soldiers are brutally mutilated and repaired as objects. They resemble the repaired artefacts while the sculptures seem to come alive in this confrontation. Attia's work aims to present material culture as well as people as a series of shifts that (re)shape, that change their appearance as well as their identity. Thus, it may be productive to connect the power of artefacts to the gestures and thoughts underlying the interconnections between material and symbolic, but also to the political or economic dimensions of things.

Conclusion

Critics have widely commented upon 'Gell's indifference to [...] politics.'[31] Yet my case study underlines the political dimension of such shifts. Nicholas Thomas suggested that even if '*Art and Agency* is largely unconcerned with the political manipulation of art,' yet 'the political may be enriched by an anthropology beyond aesthetics.'[32] Indeed, the study of agency gains value when it is reintegrated into the power structure that shapes gestures and practices. The discussions mentioned above cannot be isolated from a larger set of debates and issues. One must remember that *The Native American Graves Protection and Repatriation Act* (NAGPRA), which requires federal agencies and institutions that receive federal funding to return sensitive Native American cultural items (including human remains), was voted into law in 1990, just a few years before Venturi's report. Additional acts were passed in the late 1980s in the United States. The NMAI is not covered by NAGPRA, for instance, but by a similar act named the National Museum of the American Indian Act from 1989.

The highly asymmetrical power relation in which these gestures (conservation treatments, storage, framing, display) took place, i.e. in a major museum in the capital of the United States, provides a political context that unfolds these practices and debates. In this context, the argument of two cultures definitely opposed to each other sounds very much like recent discussions about the 'clash of civilizations' supposedly occurring between the West and the East.[33] This argument may work well as a pretext for disregarding

29 Souriau, *Les différents modes d'existence*, 1943. **30** See also: Miller, 'Introduction,' 2005, p. 14. **31** See: Chua and Elliott, 'Adventures in the Art Nexus,' 2013, p. 17. **32** Thomas, 'Introduction,' 2001, pp. 9 and 11. **33** For a similar point in a different context, see: Flood, *Objects of Translation*, 2009, pp. 1–14. **34** Said, 'Representing the Colonized,' 1989, p. 225.

indigenous claims to management of their patrimony as fundamentally irrelevant and, ultimately, vandalistic. If we nevertheless want to use the word 'culture' to describe various conventions and preferences in the field of conservation, then it might be productive to use the term as defined by Edward Said:

'[I]f we think of cultures as permeable and, on the whole, defensive boundaries between polities, a more promising situation appears. Thus to see others not as ontologically given but as historically constituted would be to erode the exclusivist biases we so ascribe to culture, our own not least. Cultures may then be represented as zones of control or of abandonment, of recollection and of forgetting, of force or of dependence, of exclusiveness or of sharing, all taking place in the global history that is our element.'[34]

Finally, thinking about the potential agency of an artefact is also an occasion to underline the power balance of people surrounding it. This leads one to consider not only general states but also precise events and moments that determine, and shift, the life of things. In this case study, the agency of things is highly affected by the situation and power relation between the communities at the core of these debates. The ones who have power over the artefacts—in this case, the conservators in the museum—are responsible for a certain number of actions determining the identity of what they are treating. The others are fighting for a variety of claims connected to their ownership of the artefacts, but also more broadly to their access to lands and resources. From this perspective, agency is definitely a topic that grounds art history and conservation studies in a larger cultural and political context. It provides an occasion to underline the power configurations that surround and even produce—or destroy—the agency of things (and people).

Bibliography

A. Appadurai (ed.), *The Social Life of Things: Commodities in Cultural Perspective* (Cambridge University Press, 1988).

M. Brusius and K. Singh (eds.), *Museum Storage and Meaning: Tales from the Crypt* (Routledge, 2017).

L. Chua and M. Elliott, 'Adventures in the Art Nexus' in L. Chua and M. Elliott (eds.), *Distributed Objects. Meaning and Mattering after Alfred Gell* (Berghahn, 2013), pp. 1–24.

M. Clavir, *Preserving What Is Valued. Museums, Conservation and First Nations* (UBC Press, 2002).

J. Clifford, 'Museum As Contact Zones' in J. Clifford, *Routes: Travel and Translation in the Late Twentieth Century* (Harvard University Press, 1997), pp. 188–219.

B. Derlon and M. Jeudi-Ballini, 'Domestification and the Preservation of Wildness. The Self and the Other in Primitive Art Collecting,' *Material Culture Review*, 79 (2014), pp. 92–101.

N. Étienne, *The Restoration of Paintings in Paris, 1750–1815. Practice, Discourse, Materialiy* (Getty Publications, 2017).

N. Étienne and L. Hénaut (eds.), *L'histoire à l'atelier. Restaurer les œuvres d'art* (Presses Universitaires de Lyon, 2012).

F. B. Flood, *Objects of Translation. Material Culture and Medieval 'Hindu-Muslim' Encounter* (Princeton University Press, 2009).

D. Freedberg, *The Power of Images. Studies in the History and Theory of Response* (The University of Chicago Press, 1989).

D. Gamboni, *Potential Images: Ambiguity and Indeterminacy in Modern Art* (University of Chicago Press, 2002).

I. Gaskell, 'The Life of Things' in S. Macdonald and H. Rees Leahy (eds.), *The International Handbook of Museum Studies: Museum Media* (John Wiley, 2015), pp. 167–190.

A. Gell, *Art and Agency. An Anthropological Theory* (Clarendon Press, 1998).

F. Haskell and N. Penny, *Taste and the Antique. The Lure of Classical Sculpture, 1500–1900* (Yale University Press, 1981).

B. Kirshenblatt, *Destination Culture. Tourism, Museums and Heritage* (University of California Press, 1992).

D. Miller, 'Introduction' in D. Miller (ed.), *Materiality* (Duke University Press, 2005), pp. 1–31.

M. L. Pratt, 'Arts of the Contact Zone,' *Profession* (1991), pp. 33–40.

E. Said, 'Representing the Colonized: Anthropology's Interlocutors,' *Critical Inquiry*, 15 (1989), pp. 205–225.

B. Savoy, *Patrimoine annexé. Les biens culturels saisis par la France en Allemagne autour de 1800* (Maison des Sciences de l'Homme, 2003).

P. Schimmel (ed.), *Out of Action. Between Performance and the Object. 1949–1979* (Thames and Hudson, 1999).

R. Sennett, *The Craftsman* (Yale University Press, 2008).

K. Singh, *Museums, Heritage, Culture: Into the Conflict Zone* (Amsterdam University of the Arts, 2015).

É. Souriau, *Les différents modes d'existence* (Presses Universitaires de France, 1943).

W. Szymborska, 'Museum' in S. Baranczak and C. Cavanagh (eds. and trans.), *View with a Grain of Sand: Selected Poems* (Harcourt, 1993 [1962]), pp. 11–12.

N. Thomas, 'Introduction' in C. Pinney and N. Thomas (eds.), *Beyond Aesthetics: Art and the Technologies of Enchantment* (Berg, 2001), pp. 1–20.

C. van Eck, 'Living Statues. Alfred Gell Art and Agency, Living Presence, Response and the Sublime,' *Art History*, 33 (2010), pp. 643–659.

C. van Eck, *Art, Agency and Living Presence: From the Animated Image to the Excessive Object* (Akademie Verlag and Leiden University Press, 2015).

R. Venturi, D. Scott Brown and S. Izenour, *Learning from Las Vegas* (MIT Press, 1972).
J. Wirth, 'Perfomativité de l'image?' in G. Bartholeyns et al. (eds.), *La Performance des images* (Presses Universitaires Bruxelles, 2009), pp. 125–135.

Archive materials:

C2RMF, Versailles, File n° 4532 (June 14, 1991).
R. Venturi, D. Scott Brown and S. Izenour (eds.), *The Way of the People. National Museum of the American Indian* (Venturi, Scott Brown and Associates Inc., 1991–1993).

Contributors
Picture Credits
Imprint

Contributors

Noémie Étienne is SNSF Professor at the Universität Bern and a specialist in early modern art and culture. She is currently leading a research project on exoticism in the Enlightenment. Her first book, *The Restoration of Paintings in Paris (1750–1815)* (Presses Universitaires de Rennes) was published in 2012, and subsequently translated into English and published by Getty Publications in 2017. She recently finished writing her second book on dioramas around 1900 in the USA (forthcoming, the Getty Research Institute Publications). Noémie Étienne also co-founded and directed the project *Eternal Tour* between 2005 and 2011, and is a founding editor of *Journal18*.

Mechthild Fend is Reader in History of Art at University College London. She specialises in eighteenth- and nineteenth-century French art and visual culture. Major research interests are the representation of the body, the historical relations between art and science, and the medical humanities. She is currently working on the pathological image. Her most recent book is *Fleshing Out Surfaces. Skin in French Art and Medicine, 1650–1850* (Manchester University Press, 2017).

Dario Gamboni is Professor of Art History at the Université de Genève. He has been a Fellow at CASVA, the Henry Moore Institute, the Clark Art Institute, the Freie Universität Berlin, the Swiss Institute for Art Research, the Kunsthistorisches Institut in Florenz, the Getty Research Institute, and a guest professor across three continents. He has (co-) curated exhibitions including *Iconoclash* and *Making Things Public* in Karlsruhe (ZKM), and *Une image peut en cacher une autre* in Paris (Grand Palais). His publications include *The Destruction of Art: Iconoclasm and Vandalism Since the French Revolution* (Reaktion Books, 1997), *Potential Images: Ambiguity and Indeterminacy in Modern Art* (Reaktion Books, 2002), *The Brush and The Pen: Odilon Redon and Literature* (University of Chicago Press, 2011 [1989]), and *Paul Gauguin: The Mysterious Centre of Thought* (Reaktion Books, 2013/2014). His forthcoming book is entitled *The Museum As Experience: Artists' and Collectors' Museums, a Dialogue*.

Ivan Gaskell is Professor of Cultural History and Museum Studies at Bard Graduate Center, New York City. His work addresses intersections among history, art history, anthropology, and philosophy. He is the author, co-author, or editor of thirteen books, most recently *Tangible Things: Making History through Objects* (Oxford University Press, 2015). He is a Permanent Senior Fellow of the Institute of Advanced Study, Georg-August-Universität, Göttingen.

Johannes Grave has been Professor of Art History at the Universität Bielefeld since 2012. Before this, he served as deputy director at the Centre allemand d'histoire de l'art and was member of the research project *Iconic Criticism* (eikones) at the University of Basel. His research focuses on Early Renaissance painting, art around 1800, theories of the image and the temporality of image perception. His recent publications include *Giovanni Bellini. The Art of Contemplation* (Prestel, forthcoming). His book *Architekturen des Sehens. Bauten in Bildern des Quattrocento* (Fink, 2015) won an award from the Göttingen Academy of Sciences and Humanities. He is one of the editors of the *Zeitschrift für Kunstgeschichte* and member of the board of directors of the Collaborative Research Centre *Practices of Comparing. Ordering and Changing the World* (CRC 1288).

Christiane Holm is Research Assistant at the Germanistische Institut of the Martin-Luther-Universität Halle-Wittenberg, where she directs a project on *Epistemische Möbel*. Her research focuses on the interaction between literature and material culture, especially in settings like interiors, gardens, archives, and museums. She has curated several exhibitions dealing with objects of everyday culture (Klassik Stiftung Weimar, Museum Angewandte Kunst Frankfurt, Museum für Kommunikation Berlin). Recent publications include articles about furniture and souvenirs in the *Handbuch Literatur und materielle Kultur* (De Gruyter, 2018).

Cindy Kang is Associate Curator at the Barnes Foundation, Philadelphia. She received her Ph.D. from the Institute of Fine Arts, New York University. Her research and publications have focused on the relationship between painting and decorative arts in nineteenth-century France, including 'Faire Tapisserie: Édouard Vuillard's Decoration for Dr. Vaquez,' in *Visualizing the Nineteenth-Century Home: Modern Art and the Decorative Impulse* (Routledge, 2016) and 'Morisot on the Threshold,' in *Berthe Morisot: Woman Impressionist*, exh. cat., Barnes Foundation, Dallas Museum of Art, Musée nationale des beaux-arts du Québec (2018).

Valérie Kobi received her Ph.D. in Art History from the Université de Neuchâtel in 2014 (Prix Nexans de la Recherche). She has held fellowships from the Swiss Institute of Rome, the Swiss Science Foundation and the Getty Research Institute. Since May 2015, she has been a Postdoctoral Researcher at Universität Bielefeld and is associated with the research project *Parergonale Rahmungen. Zur Ästhetik wissenschaftlicher Dinge bei Goethe*. Her most recent book is *Dans l'oeil du connoisseur. Pierre-Jean Mariette (1694–1774) et la construction des savoirs en histoire de l'art* (Presses Universitaires de Rennes, 2017).

Angela Matyssek is Visiting Professor in the Art History Department of Ludwig-Maximilians-Universität München. Her research interests include the history of modern and contemporary art, photography and media arts, theories and practices of conservation and restoration, and art history, as well as exhibitions and museums. Her recent publications include *Kontinuitäten der Kunst. Konservierung-Restaurierung als angewandte Kunstgeschichte* (Edition Metzel, forthcoming 2018) and *Kunstgeschichte als fotografische Praxis. Richard Hamann und Foto Marburg* (Gebr. Mann, 2009).

Peter Schade was made Head of Framing at the National Gallery London in 2005 and has been working in the field of framing old master paintings since 1990. He has been responsible for re-framing about 250 paintings from the National Gallery's permanent collection. Peter Schade contributes annually to the National Gallery's Review of the Year with an essay and a list of paintings reframed that year. He also makes re-framings public on Twitter. He is co-author of *The Sansovino Frame*, a publication which accompanied the Sansovino Frame Exhibition held at the National Gallery in 2015.

Diana Stört is Postdoctoral Research Fellow at the Martin-Luther-Universität Halle-Wittenberg. She works in the project *Parerga and Paratexts—How Things Enter Language. Practices and Forms of Presentation in Goethe's Collections*. Her research interests include collection practices and material cultural history in the 18th- and 19th-centuries. Diana Stört has co-edited several exhibition catalogues and is the author of two monographs *Johann Wilhelm Ludwig Gleim und die gesellige Sammlungspraxis im 18. Jahrhundert* (Verlag Dr. Kovač, 2010) and *Form und Funktion der handschriftlichen Widmung im 18. Jahrhundert* (Akademikerverlag, 2015).

Caroline van Eck has been Professor of Art History in Cambridge since 2016. In 2017 she gave the Slade Lectures in Oxford on Piranesi's colossal candelabra. Research interests include art and rhetoric, the agency of art, and the transformations of the classical tradition, in particular in the *Style Empire*. Recent publications include *Idols and Museum Pieces. The Nature of Sculpture, its Historiography and Exhibition History 1660–1880* (De Gruyter, 2017); with Miguel John Versluys, 'The Hôtel de Beauharnais in Paris: Egypt, Rome, and the Dynamics of Cultural Transformation,' in: K. von Stackelberg and E. Macaulay-Lewis (eds.), *Housing the New Romans* (Oxford University Press, 2017); and 'La scène primitive de l'architecture. Gottfried Semper et Alfred Gell, les origines, le style et les effets de l'art,' *Revue Germanique Internationale* 26 (2018), pp. 207–25.

Elsje van Kessel is Senior Lecturer in Art History at the University of St Andrews. She is the author of *The Lives of Paintings: Presence, Agency and Likeness in Venetian Art of the Sixteenth Century* (De Gruyter, 2017). She has also published various articles and book chapters on the history of display and presentation in the early modern period. The present chapter results from a research project she conducted as visiting researcher at CHAM-Center for the Humanities, Universidade Nova de Lisboa.

Hannah Williams is Leverhulme Early Career Research Fellow at Queen Mary University of London. She is an art historian of early modern France with research interests in religious art, portraiture, material culture, artistic communities, and spaces of the art world. She is the author of *Académie Royale: A History in Portraits* (Routledge, 2015), numerous articles in journals including *French History*, *Art History*, and *Oxford Art Journal*, and producer of the digital resource, www.artistsinparis.org. She is currently writing her second book, *Art & Religion: Inside the Parish Churches of 18th-Century Paris*, and co-authoring with Katie Scott another book on *Artists' Things*. She is a founding co-editor of *Journal18*.

Picture Credits

Cover
Photo: © Wilf Speller

Frontispiece
Photo: © Ivan Gaskell

Ivan Gaskell: Display Displayed
Fig. 1: Eduard Plietzsch, *Vermeer van Delft* (Bruckmann, 1939), Figs. 41–42
Fig. 2: Photo: Ivan Gaskell
Fig. 3: Photo: Ivan Gaskell
Fig. 4: Photo: Ivan Gaskell
Fig. 5: Photo: National Gallery of Art, Washington, DC, © VG Bild-Kunst 2018
Fig. 6: Photo: Ivan Gaskell
Fig. 7: © Maureen Gallace
Fig. 8: © Fairfield Art Publishing
Fig. 9: © Fairfield Art Publishing
Fig. 10: Photo: Ivan Gaskell
Fig. 11: © David Ward

Elsje van Kessel: The Street as Frame: Corpus Christi Processions in Lisbon prior to João V
Fig. 1: Rijksmuseum, Amsterdam. Image in the public domain
Fig. 2: © Victoria and Albert Museum, London
Fig. 3: Tomar, Igreja de São João Batista. Image in the public domain
Fig. 4: Reproduced with kind permission from Santa Casa da Misericórdia de Lisboa / Museu de São Roque
Fig. 5: © Victoria and Albert Museum, London

Hannah Williams: Staging Belief: Immersive Encounters and the Agency of Religious Art in Eighteenth-Century Paris
Fig. 1: Wikimedia Commons – Web Gallery of Art.
Fig. 2: Photo: Hannah Williams
Fig. 3: Photo: Hannah Williams
Fig. 4: Original plan by Mbzt, Wikimedia Commons. Additions and annotations by Hannah Williams
Fig. 5: Photo: Hannah Williams

Mechthild Fend: Order and Affect. The Museum of Dermatological Wax Moulages at the Hôpital Saint-Louis in Paris
Fig. 1: Photo: © F. Marin, P. Simon / Musée des moulages – Hôpital Saint-Louis – AP-HP.
Fig. 2: Photo: © F. Marin, P. Simon / Musée des moulages – Hôpital Saint-Louis – AP-HP
Fig. 3: Photo: © F. Marin, P. Simon / Musée des moulages – Hôpital Saint-Louis – AP-HP
Fig. 4: Photo: © Bibliothèque nationale de France
Fig. 5: Photo: © F. Marin, P. Simon / Musée des moulages – Hôpital Saint-Louis – AP-HP.
Fig. 6: Photo: Mechthild Fend.

Cindy Kang: The Barnes Ensembles, Again
Fig. 1: Photo: © The Barnes Foundation 2018
Fig. 2: Photo: © The Barnes Foundation 2018
Fig. 3: Photo: © The Barnes Foundation 2018
Fig. 4: Photo: © The Barnes Foundation 2018

Dario Gamboni: Ready-made Eye-opener: Models, Functions and Meanings of the Ironwork in Albert C. Barnes's Displays

Fig. 1: Photo: Dario Gamboni
Fig. 2: Photo: © The Barnes Foundation
Fig. 3: Henri René d'Allemagne, *Musée Le Secq des Tournelles. Ferronnerie ancienne*, part I (J. Schémit, 1924), plate CIV
Fig. 4: Albert C. Barnes, *The Art in Painting* (Barnes Foundation Press, 1925), p. 77
Fig. 5: Photo: Dario Gamboni

Peter Schade: The Reframing of Lazarus

Fig. 1: © Victoria and Albert Museum, London
Fig. 2: *The Illustrated London News*, 6 June 1861, p. 547
Fig. 3: © The National Gallery, London
Fig. 4: © The National Gallery, London

Diana Stört: Displaying Knowledge: Goethe's Cabinets as Epistemic Furniture

Fig. 1: K. Knebel and W. Holler (eds.), *The Goethe Residence* (Klassik Stiftung Weimar, 2016), coverpage
Fig. 2: © Klassik Stiftung Weimar 2017, Photo: Katharina Popov-Sellinat
Fig. 3: © Klassik Stiftung Weimar 2017, Photo: Photo: Alexander Burzik
Fig. 4: © Klassik Stiftung Weimar 2017, Photo: Katharina Popov-Sellinat
Fig. 5: © Klassik Stiftung Weimar 2017, Photo: Katharina Popov-Sellinat

Angela Matyssek: Death by/Life by Wall Label

Fig. 1: P. Egan, *Life in London* (Chatto & Windus, 1821), plate 32. Reproduced in D. H. Solkin (ed.), *Art on the Line. The Royal Academy Exhibitions at Somerset House 1780–1836* (Yale University Press, 2001), Fig. 40
Fig. 2: Photo: © Jeffrey Saletnik
Fig. 3: Photo: Angela Matyssek
Fig. 4: Photo: © David von Becker / Ausstellung Harf Zimmermann, C/O Berlin

Imprint

The book series *Parerga und Paratexte* presents the results of a collaborative research project that was carried out by the Klassik Stiftung Weimar and the universities of Bielefeld, Erlangen and Halle from 1 April 2015 to 31 March 2018. The project was realised within the framework of the funding program *The Language of Objects* by the German Federal Ministry of Education and Research.

Editors
Johannes Grave, Christiane Holm, Valérie Kobi, Caroline van Eck

Copy Editing
Rebecca Whiteley

Layout
Norbert du Vinage, Simone Antonia Deutsch, Sandstein Verlag

Typesetting and Reprography
Katharina Stark, Jana Neumann, Sandstein Verlag

Printing and Processing
FINIDR s. r. o., Český Těšín

Cover Illustration
Rose Garrard, *Model's Triptych: Madonna Cascade*, 1982, fresco panel on wood and acrylic paint, 61 × 92 × 122 cm, donated by the artist to the New Hall Art Collection, Murray Edwards College in 2003.

Frontispiece Illustration
Rachel Whiteread, *Cabin*, 2016, concrete and bronze, New York, Governors Island.

The Deutsche Nationalbibliothek holds a record of this publication in the Deutsche Nationalbibliografie; detailed bibliographical data can be found under: http://dnb.dnb.de.

www.sandstein-verlag.de
ISBN 978-3-95498-416-9